TORAH PATTERNS

The Magnificent Unity of Jewish Life and Thought

TORAH

Rabbi Moshe Shlomo Emanuel

PATTERNS

The Magnificent Unity of Jewish Life and Thought

TARGUM/FELDHEIM

First published 1998
Copyright © 1998 by Moshe Shlomo Emanuel
ISBN 1-56871-138-7
All rights reserved

No part of this publication may be translated, reproduced, stored in a retrieval system, or transmitted in any form or by any means, electronic, mechanical, photocopying, recording, or otherwise, without prior permission in writing from both the copyright holder and the publisher.

This book contains holy names of God and also quotations from holy sources. Please treat it with respect.

Published by:
Targum Press, Inc.
22700 W. Eleven Mile Rd.
Southfield, MI 48034

Distributed by:
Feldheim Publishers
200 Airport Executive Park
Nanuet, NY 10954

Distributed in Israel by:
Targum Press Ltd.
POB 43170
Jerusalem 91430

Printed in Israel

Rabbi CHAIM P. SCHEINBERG

Rosh Hayeshiva "TORAH ORE"

and Morah Hora'ah of Kiryat Mattersdorf

הרב חיים פינחס שיינברג

ראש ישיבת "תורה אור"

ומורה הוראה דקרית מטרסדורף

בס"ד, א' דר"ח טבת, נר ששי דחנוכה, תשג"ח

מכתב ברכה

הנה בא לפני הרה"ג ר' משה שלמה עמנואל שליט"א ר"מ דמתיבתא הק' "מנורה" בלונדון, ותלמודו בידו, וכבר איחממחי גברא בספריו הנפלאים, וכבר נתברך מאיתי על ספרו החשוב שכתב מכבר על ד' פרשיות של תפילין, ועל ספרו שכתב בביאור ההגדה של פסח, ועכשיו ביאר באופן נפלא איך שבתורה כולה יש תבנית מיוחדת המקשרת את כל התורה והמצוות לאחד, וכולם מתאחדים יחד ע"פ תבנית זאת וזהו גם בענינים שלפי מבט הראשון (לכאורה) אין שום קשר ביניהם, אמנם תוך הלימוד בספר החשוב שלפנינו ימצא המעיין איך כל הנושאים שבתורה"ק מאוחדים זה עם זה.

והכל עשה בטוב טעם ודעת והביא הרבה מקורות לדבריו. ומתוך הדברים שכתב ניכר רוב עמלו ויגיעו בלימוד התורה הקדושה. ולכן אברך את הרב המחבר שחפץ ה' בידו יצלח ויזכה להרבות תורה ולהאדירה מתוך הרחבת הדעת ומנוחת הנפש.

הכו"ח לכבוד התורה ולומדיה

בס"ד

Nachman Bulman   נחמן בולמן

ישיבת אור שמח ירושלם עיה"ק תו"ו

בע"ה

    Several years ago Rav Moshe Shlomo Emanuel שליט"א, *menahel* of Menorah Grammar School of London authored a striking work on tefillin, which enlarged the focus of our holy tefillin from the particular to the universal interrelation between tefillin and a wide range of Torah ideas and precepts.

    With Hashem's help, he has published this work *Torah Patterns*. The work focuses on the night of the Seder and many other Torah themes. In conception and with diagrams he shows us how the night of the Exodus from Mitzrayim interfaces with and illuminates Torah thought and experience in wide areas that are seemingly unrelated. With Rav Emanuel's penetrating insight, the patterns that emerge become yet another illustration of the principle of our Sages: דברי תורה עניים במקום אחד ועשירים במקום אחר — the entire Torah is an absolute Oneness.

    Many will be grateful for the illumination of our Torah's Divine source.

Nachman Bulman
Nachman Bulman
Yeshivas Ohr Someach

Maalot Dafna 137/21, Jerusalem 97762, Israel ▪ 02-824-321 ▪ ישראל 97762 ירושלים, 137/21 מעלות דפנה

לעילוי נשמת

הרה"ר **נפתלי** בן מוהר"ר **נתן קליין** ז"ל
נפטר ביום כ' אדר א' תשי"ט בפאריז

ואשתו החשובה
מרת **מאדל** בת ר' **פנחס צבי הלוי** ע"ה
נפטרה י"ב אדר תשמ"ח בלאנדאן

In memory of
Theo Klein z"l
and
Marthe Klein z"l
ת.נ.צ.ב.ה.

Acknowledgements

First and foremost I thank the *Ribbono shel olam* for all His kindness, and for giving me the strength to persevere in the publication of this work.

My heartfelt thanks to those who helped make this work possible, and without whose constant patience, encouragement, and help this *sefer* could never have been published.

I would also like to thank the entire Targum staff and, in particular, Rabbi Moshe Dombey, Eli Linas, Surie Brand, Akiva Atwood, and D. Liff, for the excellence they have shown in producing a work of high literary and aesthetic quality.

My deepest appreciation and gratitude to my family in Eretz Yisrael for their open homes and hospitality during this intercontinental project.

I would like to dedicate this *sefer* to the memory of my maternal grandparents, משה שלמה בן אליהו דוב ע״ה ורבקה בת יהודה ע״ה , שטאהל.

Despite many hardships and against all odds they kept Shabbos in a place where its significance was not appreciated. They kept steadfast to their *mesorah* without any compromise. A special glow was seen on my grandfather's face on Shabbos and *Yom Tov*, radiating his love for Torah and mitzvos, after toiling hard during the week to reestablish himself and his family in their new environment where they came, in order to escape Nazi persecution.

I clearly remember my grandmother's striving for and devotion to *shalom bein habriyos*. She was a true example of everything an אם בישראל could be.

Despite the obstacles and hardships they encountered they raised a family of *bnei Torah*. The sacrifices this all entailed are generally not appreciated in this day and age when, *baruch Hashem,* Torah observance has become much easier, more widespread, and often even taken for granted.

They were among the founding members of the Adass Yeshurun Kehillah of Johannesburg, South Africa.

לזכרון עולם

הדפסת הספר הזה נעזרה ע"י קרן ע"ש מרת

אלסע בת ר' מאיר מיינדל ע"ה

ת.נ.צ.ב.ה.

Contents

Preface 1
Introduction 7

The Order of History
The Four Sections of the Seder 15
The Four Stages of History 29

The Matriarchs
The Hidden Factor 39
The Four Matriarchs and the Tetragrammaton. 63
The Patriarchs and Matriarchs 71

Above to Below and Before to Future
The Seder Night: Rising Above Time and Space 77
The Seder from Above to Below 94
From Above to Below: A More Detailed Look 97
The Four Expressions of Redemption 101
Tzitzis from Below to Above. 106
The Ten Plagues 110
Before to Future and Above to Below 113
The Closing of the Circle 116

Related Sets of Four
The *Aleinu* Prayer 127
The *Uva L'Tzion* Prayer 131

The Books of the Torah	134
The Four Sons and the Four Species	151
The Four Mitzvos of the Seder Night	181
The Four Stages of *"Baruch HaMakom"*	194
The First Four Tribes	200
Four Transgressions	204
The Four Elements	217
The Scroll of Esther	223
The Four Rivers	234
Yotzer Ohr	240
The Tetragrammaton	247
The Mishkan	259

Stages One and Three versus Stages Two and Four

Unity versus Multiplicity	273
Giving versus Receiving	281
Dichotomy in the Sons and Species	286
Internal versus External	294

Further Connections

The Special Pattern in Creation	311
God's Day	322
Israel and the Silkworm	325
The Thirteen Principles of Faith	328
Conclusion	337
Appendix I: *Hallel* and Future	339
Appendix II: The Time Line and the Seder Night in the Torah	347
Appendix III: Stages One and Three: A Deeper Look	350

Preface

Torah Patterns is a sequel to *Tefillin: The Inside Story*. Whereas the latter deals more specifically with tefillin, this book gives us a broader appreciation of the magnificent pattern and consistency that are inherent within Torah and Judaism in general. Some of the material that was previously discussed in *Tefillin: The Inside Story* has been repeated here, in order to facilitate the reader's understanding and highlight the parallels between some of the areas they both cover.

Order is the core of all existence, from the composition of the most minuscule cell to that of the largest creature. Without this order nothing can exist. Since this order is Godly, emanating from God, Who is all encompassing, it is also all encompassing and penetrates all dimensions and levels within creation.

Judaism relates to that very order. The Seder night, literally, "the night of order," follows a special order which is related to the pattern of the all-encompassing order within creation.

The Jewish nation became connected to this special order on the night of our freedom. Subsequently each year we celebrate our freedom on the festival of Pesach, beginning with the order of the Seder. It is for this reason that we will begin studying this profound order from the perspective of the Seder night and the Pesach festival. Then we will see how this order manifests itself in many areas of Judaism.

THE ORDER OF HISTORY

One can see how this Divine order is manifest within the time continuum. The study of Jewish time and history is the study of genuine time. History books are the study of the Past, and how the Present and Future may be affected by it. But which history book has touched on the Purpose — the meaning and motivation of history? This is the province of our holy Torah.

Interestingly, when studying the holy Torah, from which we learn our history, we find that there are sections which are not in chronological order. This seems highly unusual, for if the Torah purports to teach history, how can the events recorded not be presented in chronological order?

To understand this, we must realise that from the Torah's perspective, true history embodies a higher dimension — something far Above the time line of history. The Torah shows us that the factor which determines history — its Purpose — is all important. Purpose transcends, yet determines and is contained, within the Past, Present, and Future.

One might ask, How can it be that Purpose is Above and yet it is contained within?

The answer is that Purpose is Godly. It is the *neshamah* of time — the soul of the Past, Present, and Future. Thus, just as the soul is spiritual, something that is Above the body and preceded it, and yet is contained within the body as its life force, so it is with the Purpose of linear time — it is at the core of the Past, Present, and Future. Therefore, while Purpose is Above and Before, it is also enclothed in the body of every facet of time, determining its course. It is therefore no wonder that אין מוקדם ומאוחר בתורה — that many sections of the Torah are not presented in chronological order.[1] Chronology is only the clothing and outer body of the Purpose — the cause and the lessons of history. It is therefore very often sacrificed so as to let the soul — the Purpose — shine forth. The lessons to be learned from this change of order far supersede the mere historical order of events. The portrayal of the Purpose of history and the lessons learned from history are the essence of its study.

Torah is thus not a mere history book; it is the study of the Purpose of creation. Additionally, it cannot be studied on an academic level alone — the dynamic of Purpose demands action on our part, and it is our duty to continuously imbue the "body" of time with the soul of sanctity, which is the Purpose of history. We therefore have daily obligations of sanctification: the mitzvos we practise.

The Seder, which is a microcosm of Jewish history, encapsulates all these aspects of history and relates to the very core of our existence. In the Seder, the *neshamah* — the Purpose of our existence — is revealed in the very first stage of the evening's proceedings: *Kadeish*. This stage imbues the "clothing" — the next three stages of Past, Present, and Future — with *kedushah*, elevating them to a higher dimension.

THE ORDER WITHIN JEWISH LIFE

The life of a Jew is steeped in the concept of סדר, "order." We see this on a daily, weekly, and yearly basis.

Our daily order is reflected in the Hebrew name for our prayer book, the סדור (siddur). "Siddur" means "order," in this instance referring specifically to the order of prayer. Additionally,

---

1. *Pesachim* 6b.

we have what is called a סדר היום (daily order): the day of the Jew revolves around a special order that obligates us to perform specific tasks at specific times each day. Each week, we have the *sidrah* of the week — the *order* of the weekly *parshah*. Yearly we have the Seder, the "Order" on Passover, the festival that celebrates our freedom. Indeed, this order on the night of our freedom is the wellspring from which all the order that is manifest during the rest of the year derives. Thus we see that order and pattern are prevalent in many areas of Judaism.

This emphasis on order and pattern reflects a basic concept in Jewish thought: to be a truly free person means to have a set order in one's life. Contemporary thought would have us believe the exact opposite: that the right to follow a random pattern and choose one's own set of values is what constitutes true freedom. However, this is a fallacious idea. Those who live a random life do not attain true fulfilment and joy. They live only for the Present and do not lead lives that have Purpose. For these people, the Present is divorced from the Past and has no bearing on the Future.

This key to true freedom — compliance with a set order — means, specifically for the Jew, following the pattern established by the Torah and determined by our rabbis. The *Shulchan Aruch* in *Orach Chaim* instructs us in the prescribed order that is necessary for us to follow in our daily, weekly, and yearly lives. The orderly pattern that is implicit within Judaism progresses in a pre-ordained and set sequence. Our every action relates to that special *seder*. This order was initiated before creation and constitutes the blueprint of the universe. It extends through the length of our history and is part and parcel of our daily lives as Jews, permeating every aspect of our existence.

Since this pattern of creation and history is manifest in every area of our lives, it follows that our every action relates to our history, and ultimately to creation, and connects us to it in a tangible way.

Thus, the Jew, guided by Torah and the Jewish way of life, leads an existence that has Purpose. He realises that the Present is continuously connected to the Past and that it all affects his Future.

This order was initiated with the original Seder night — the night of "Order," at the time of the Exodus. From that point onward we have been bound to it with our every thought, word, and deed. Thus it was the original Seder night which bound us to our Purpose and freed us from a random existence.

The purpose of this book is not merely to reveal the existence and configuration of this order in the Seder night, as well as in other areas of Torah and Judaism. Rather, it is to demonstrate how this order permeates the very essence of our lives and is solely responsible for our freedom from a haphazard and aimless existence.

THREE DEFINITIONS OF *SEDER*

Rabbi Dessler, of blessed memory,[1] explains that there are three types of *seder*: (a) order for the sake of order, (b) order for the sake of its results, and (c) order for the sake of unity of function.

Order for the Sake of Order

This is an order that is maintained so that one who beholds it can enjoy the display of an orderly setup. (Human beings derive pleasure from viewing an orderly arrangement because it mirrors man's internal order and harmony.)

Order for the Sake of Its Results

This is an order which is maintained to facilitate results. It is maintained so that the function of each component may be fulfilled correctly and efficiently; for example, the order maintained

---

1. *Michtav MeEliyahu*, vol. 1, p. 92.

so that the one who beholds it will know where to find something, like the orderly arrangement of professional tools so that they should be easily accessible, or books shelved in a specific order.

Order for the Sake of Unity of Function

As its name implies, this is an order that must be adhered to in order for a unit to operate properly. For example, with a motor, a watch, or a cell (or the components of a cell), and the like, each individual part of the unit must fulfil its unique task in the correct place and time, so that there will be collective harmony and function. Both time and place are important because just as the individual parts will not function when they are by themselves, so too, they cannot work in disarray. Therefore they must be specifically arranged and must operate in their correct *seder* — order and sequence — so that the unit may function.

The three types of order mentioned by Rabbi Dessler are not mutually exclusive, and, in fact, all of them come into play on the Seder night. There is a grandeur apparent in the order and ceremony of the Seder. Additionally, each and every part of the Seder must be carried out in its correct place, so that the "machinery" of the Seder can function harmoniously and uniformly. Finally, this special order must also be adhered to in order to create the proper results. The goals we hope to achieve are the freedom engendered by the Seder night itself and a resultant situation wherein the Seder night casts its radiance on the rest of the year, enabling many facets of our existence to receive their energy from it, as will be revealed in *Torah Patterns*.

Introduction

THE PASSOVER SEDER

> Every person must view himself as if he personally went out of Egypt.
>
> (Passover Haggadah)

What is the significance of the Passover Seder? Both religiously observant, as well as the majority of estranged and assimilated Jews, can conjure up fond memories of the Passover night from the Past: a family reunion, the Four Questions, intriguing rituals, matzah, etc. But what does it all mean? Is the Seder merely a series of rites which remind us of our Past? Is it nothing more than a simple account of four sons who react differently to our history, or a series of symbolic foods meant to stir up a recollection of ancient events? Is this all there is to it, or is there perhaps more?

Our rabbis tell us, "One must drink four cups of wine in the proper order, i.e., one cup after each of the four sections of the Seder. If they were drunk one after the other without saying the four sections of the Haggadah in between, the mitzvah of the four cups has not been fulfilled."[1]

---

1. *Shulchan Aruch, Orach Chaim* 472:8, and *Mishnah Berurah*.

Clearly there must be four sections, and they must be in order. Indeed, at the end of the Seder we say, חסל סדור פסח כהלכתו ככל משפטו וחקתו, "The *order* of the Pesach service has been completed in accordance with its laws, its ordinances and statutes."

The reason there is a special order to the proceedings of the Seder, and why one cannot simply drink the four cups one after the other without reciting the concomitant section of the Haggadah is as follows: In reading the Haggadah we are reviewing the history of the Jewish nation from its inception to its climax. The four cups each correspond to a different stage of historical freedom through which we progress at the Seder. There are numerous profound ideas related to this theme that fit into this progression, which we will discuss shortly.

THE SEDER AND TEFILLIN

Concerning tefillin, our sages tell us, "If the four sections of the tefillin are written in the wrong order, the mitzvah is invalidated."[1] The reason why the four scrolls of the tefillin must be in a specific order is because they contain the history of the Jewish nation and various related themes. Therefore if they are in any other order they are invalidated. Thus the number four is representative of four historical stages and spiritual levels both in the Seder and tefillin.

As we have noted previously, the ceremony of Passover night is called "Seder," meaning order.[2] The order referred to is not only the order of the evening's proceedings; it is also the order of the development of Jewish history. Even though the Exodus from Egypt took place over 3,300 years ago in the year 2448, the Seder encompasses all facets of history, from the very Purpose

---

1. *Midrash Tanchuma* and *Mechilta*, end of *parshas Bo*; see also *Shulchan Aruch* 32:1.
2. *Tosafos, Pesachim* 114a; *Seder Rabbeinu Amram; Machzor Vitri.*

of history, through the Past, then to the Present, and finally to the Future.

Purpose necessarily precedes any intentional creation. God determined the Purpose of the Jewish nation. In turn, this Purpose influenced our Past, Present, and Future.

Thus the Seder might be construed as the axis around which the Purpose, Past, Present, and Future of the Jewish nation revolve. At the Seder we first become attached to our Purpose. We then proceed to our Past. From the Past we advance and become linked to the Present, as we say in the Haggadah, "Every person is obliged to consider himself as though he personally went out of Egypt." From the Present we proceed to the Future, in the section of *Hallel*, wherein we praise the Almighty for His Future intervention and salvation. The Seder, therefore, is not a mere retelling of Past events. Rather, it is a blueprint of our very existence, from the first thought in the Almighty's plan to its ultimate fruition in the Future.

Let us concentrate for a moment on the Haggadah that is recited at the Seder. Some of the most priceless Jewish artefacts we have in our possession are rare and ancient Haggados that have survived from centuries gone by. However, the Haggadah is imbued with a significance that far surpasses the sentimental value that might cause us to cherish it as a mere keepsake or admire it as a museum piece. There is a factor embodied in the Haggadah which is active and dynamic in the Present. At the same time, it associates the ideas in the text both with a Past era that long preceded the copying of the oldest Haggadah, while simultaneously binding it to the Future as well. This factor comprises the profound order of the Haggadah, which reveals the transcendence of the Jewish nation Above time and shows that they actually encompass and span all of time. In turn, this shows they possess the key to the very essence of existence — clinging to the timeless God.

The profound order of the Seder parallels the order of the tefillin portions, in that both of them bind the Jew to his Purpose and destiny within the Purpose and destiny of the world.

However, the Seder and the tefillin do not just share the same components; they also complement each other in this respect. The yearly Seder reestablishes our connection with the four historical elements of our existence — Purpose, Past, Present, and Future. The tefillin bind us to these stages on a daily basis. At the climax of each stage of the Seder we drink a cup of wine so that the meaning of each stage may enter our very beings and become part of us. Then each morning we complement this process by tying these four concepts onto our arm opposite the heart, and between our eyes opposite the mind. Thus the daily binding of tefillin constitutes an extension of the Seder night.

WOMEN AND JEWISH HISTORY

The secret foundation of the history and existence of the Jewish people is the Jewish woman. Chazal tell us, "The Jews were redeemed from Egypt in the merit of the righteous women."[1] Thus, the very beginning of the nation was prompted by the women.

Indeed, the very Jewishness and *kedushah* (sanctity) of an infant is determined by the mother, regardless of the status of the father.[2] The first section of the Seder is called "*Kadeish*," and the first portion of tefillin is referred to as "*Kadesh*"; both embody the Purpose and beginning of the Jewish nation. Similarly, it is the women who transmit the sanctity and Jewish status of a person, at conception. The Jewish mother has borne this *kedushah* in the Past, she does so in the Present, and she will be the one to do so in the Future. Therefore, the entire history and development of the

---

1. *Sotah* 11b.
2. *Kiddushin* 68b.

Jewish nation is innately bound, both physically and spiritually, to the Jewish woman.

There is another aspect which women share with tefillin and the Seder. The four Torah portions which comprise the principal component in the tefillin are concealed within leather boxes. Similarly, the four cups of the Seder night must contain wine. Wine, which is called יין in Hebrew, is the inner essence of the grape. The word יין (י [10] + י [10] + ן [50] = 70) has the same numerical value as סוד (ס [60] + ו [6] + ד [4] = 70), which means "secret." Therefore, wine represents the secret hidden within.[1] "Kos," the Hebrew word for "cup," is related to the word "*kissuy*" (covering). In fact, when *kos* is mentioned in the Tanach in connection with prophecy, it alludes to the concealed destiny of history.[2] Thus the four cups of wine of the Seder night hint at the concealed and secret nature of our history.

The Maharal[3] explains that the four cups of the Seder correspond to the four matriarchs: Sarah, Rivkah, Rachel, and Leah. These women, the foremothers of the Jewish people, were the hidden force behind the development of our Purpose, Past, Present, and Future. They were the concealed wine that determined the course of our history. Indeed, it is customary to bless one's daughters with the words, "May God make you like Sarah, Rivkah, Rachel, and Leah," for it is these women who blazed the trail of the four stages of our history.

In truth, every Jewish woman is compared to the hidden wine that directs the course of our nation, as it says, "Your wife is like a *fruitful vine* in the innermost recesses of your home; your children, like olive shoots around your table. This is the blessing bestowed upon the man who fears God."[4] The Jewish woman in

---

1. Maharal in *Divrei Negidim*.
2. See *Bereishis Rabbah* 88:5.
3. *Gevuros Hashem*, ch. 60.
4. Tehillim 128:3–4.

the inner recesses of the home is compared to a fruitful vine. The fruit of the hidden, modest wife are righteous children, who are like the shining light that emanates from the olive (oil), and who will eventually illuminate the world outside. The holy Purpose determined by the Jewish woman has been sustained and upheld by her in the Past, and by being like the vine in the hidden recesses of her home, she inspires her children in the Present, who will continue to fulfil our mission of establishing holiness in the world in the Future.

The relationship between the Jewish woman, the Seder, and tefillin can be illustrated in the following way:

DIAGRAM 1

"Your — WIFE —	is like a fruitful — VINE —	in the — RECESSES —	of your — HOME" —
The matriarchs and women of Israel	Seder wine	within	*kosos*
	Torah portions	within	*batei tefillin*

Let us now embark on a journey through time in order to understand the profound patterns within Judaism. We will begin from the perspective of the Seder night.

The Order
of History

The Four Sections of the Seder

The four cups of the Seder night are drunk at four main points in the Seder, each of which represent one of the four developmental stages of the Jewish nation. In addition to these four main parts, the Seder is comprised of fifteen subsections:

קדש — *Kadeish,* reciting the Kiddush
ורחץ — *Urchatz,* washing hands
כרפס — *Karpas,* dipping a vegetable in salt water and eating it, in order to arouse the child's curiosity
יחץ — *Yachatz,* breaking the middle matzah
מגיד — *Maggid,* reciting the Haggadah
רחצה — *Rochtzah,* washing hands
מוציא — *Motzi,* reciting blessing of *hamotzi* on matzah
מצה — *Matzah,* reciting blessing on the mitzvah of matzah and eating matzah

מרור — *Marror,* reciting blessing on the mitzvah of *marror* and eating *marror*
כורך — *Koreich,* eating the matzah and *marror* combination
שלחן עורך — *Shulchan Oreich,* eating the meal
צפון — *Tzafun,* eating the *afikoman*
ברך — *Bareich,* reciting blessings after the meal
הלל — *Hallel,* praising God
נרצה — *Nirtzah,* completing the Seder, wherein we pray that our Seder be accepted and that the *Mashiach* come soon

These fifteen sections are divided into four parts in the following way:

DIAGRAM 2

KADEISH	Kadeish We drink the **first cup**.
MAGGID	Urchatz Karpas Yachatz Maggid We drink the **second cup**.
MEAL	Rochtzah Motzi Matzah Marror Koreich Shulchan Oreich Tzafun Bareich We drink the **third cup**.
HALLEL	Hallel We drink the **fourth cup**. Nirtzah

Let us now discuss these four stages of the Haggadah and how they relate to the Purpose, Past, Present, and Future of the Jewish nation.

THE FOUR CUPS

TABLE 1

CUP	First	Second	Third	Fourth
SEDER	*Kadeish*	*Maggid*	Meal	*Hallel*
STAGE	Purpose	Past	Present	Future

The First Cup: *Kadeish* and Purpose

In this stage *kedushah* is stressed. In the Kiddush we read:

> ...Who has chosen us from all peoples and raised us above all tongues...and You have given us...this feast of the matzos, the time of our freedom, *a holy convocation,* as a memorial of the departure from Egypt.

The blessing also states, וקדשנו במצותיו, "and made us *holy* through His commandments."

From this we see that the observance of the mitzvos infuses the Jewish nation with sanctity.[1] In fact, the freedom attained on the Seder night was engendered by the *kedushah* of the mitzvos, as we say later in the Haggadah that God saw we were ערום ועריה, "naked and bare," meaning that we were ערום מן המצות, "naked and bare from mitzvos," and therefore we did not yet merit freedom. He then gave us the mitzvos of *korban pesach* and *milah*, and we thereby attained the requisite *kedushah* and were redeemed.[2]

---

1. See also *Tefillin: The Inside Story,* p. 34.
2. *Mechilta* 12, *parshah* 5. This is consistent with the fact that miracles are performed only when *kedushah* is present from the outset. We read in the book

The Purpose of the Exodus from Egypt was so that the Jewish nation should attain *kedushah*.[1] Therefore, the first cup, representing Purpose, is the one of *Kadeish*, sanctity.

It is for this reason we say in the Kiddush that Pesach is מקרא קדש זכר ליציאת מצרים, "a *holy* convocation, as a memorial of the departure from Egypt." This means that the very fact that it is "a holy convocation" is itself a memorial of the departure from Egypt, because the very Purpose and impetus of the Exodus was *kedushah*. *Kedushah* is the Purpose that preceded all and is therefore considered within the realm of Before.

Once we have attached ourselves to this *kedushah*, the next stages can follow, for only when Purpose has been established at the outset can true continuity follow — a Past, a Present, and a Future.

Interestingly, there is a definite connection between the concepts of holiness and first. Indeed, the very fact that the Jewish nation is holy makes it the "first," as we read, "Israel is *kodesh* [קדש] to Hashem, the first [ראשית] fruits of His crops; all who devour him shall be held guilty…"[2] Since *kedushah* is the *reishis*, the first — that is, it preceded everything — it is from that point that the Seder begins.

Kedushah also relates to the concepts of Start and Above. We see this in the text of the Kiddush, the start of the Seder, where we say, אשר בחר בנו מכל עם, "Who has chosen us from all peoples," a choice which constitutes the *start* of the Jewish nation; ורממנו מכל לשון, "and lifted us *above* all tongues," lifting us Above; וקדשנו במצותיו, "and

---

of Yehoshua (3:5), "Yehoshua said to the people, '*Sanctify* yourselves [התקדשו], for tomorrow Hashem will do *wonders* in your midst'" (see *Metzudas David* and *Eliyahu Rabbah* 18). Furthermore, our rabbis tell us that God performed miracles for the earlier generations because "they were prepared to give their lives for the *sanctification* of God's name" (*Berachos* 20a).

1. See *Seforno*, end of *parshas Shemini* 11:45, and *Seforno*, *parshas Kedoshim* 19:2.
2. Yirmeyahu 2:3.

made us *holy* through His commandments," making us *kadosh*.[1]

We may ask, since the first cup of the Seder is the cup of Kiddush, it is apparently just like the Kiddush of every Shabbos and *yom tov*, and therefore is not unique; if so, why is it considered one of the four cups of redemption? The answer is that the Kiddush of the Seder is indeed quite unique. Passover is the point from which the *kedushah* of the Jewish nation began. Therefore, the Kiddush of every Shabbos and *yom tov* stems from *Kadeish* of the Seder night. It is for this reason that when we make Kiddush on Shabbos and *yom tov*, we say that they are "a holy convocation [מקרא קדש], as a memorial of the departure from Egypt": they are a *"mikra kodesh"* because of the *kedushah* attained at the Exodus, which took place on the first Seder night.

Thus, even though the Kiddush of the Seder night appears to share the same basic structure as those of Shabbos and *yom tov*, in fact it has an added dimension — it is the source of all the other *Kiddushim*. Therefore, the Kiddush of the Seder actually performs a dual function. In addition to "merely" serving as the cup of Kiddush, it is also the first cup of freedom of the Seder night, for only *kedushah* causes true freedom.

The Second Cup: *Maggid* and Past

We recite *Maggid*, the telling of the Past history of the Jewish nation, over the second cup. The stage of *Maggid* comes immediately after the declaration of the Purpose of our existence, which was proclaimed in the Kiddush of the previous stage. As we said above, this stage of the Seder includes *Urchatz, Karpas, Yachatz*, and *Maggid*. How do the actions of the first three relate to *Maggid*, the telling of the Exodus of the Past? Let us address each of them separately.

---

1. These concepts of *kedushah*, Start, and Above unite in the *parshah* of *Kadesh* of the tefillin just as they do in *Kadeish* of the Seder. See *Tefillin: The Inside Story*, pp. 155–158.

Urchatz

Since during the rest of the year we usually wash for bread after Kiddush, and now we wash for *Karpas*, a child sitting at the table will notice this difference and ask about it. There is a difference of opinion among the halachic authorities over whether or not it is necessary to wash one's hands before eating something that was dipped in certain liquids while it is still moist. Even those who do not wash their hands in this situation during the rest of the year must nevertheless wash their hands on the Seder night.[1] This is in order that the children will question this deviation from the usual practise.[2]

The inclusion of this seemingly minor procedure as one of the fifteen parts of the Seder accentuates a striking point. *Maggid*, the telling of the Exodus, is not a mere relating of the Past. Rather, it is only properly fulfilled when it is related as an answer to questions that have been posed.[3] In this vein, *Urchatz*, the washing of the hands which precedes *Maggid*, is designed to stimulate a child's curiosity so he will ask questions, which we subsequently answer by relating the story of the Exodus.

Karpas

The function of *Karpas* is similar to that of *Urchatz*, in that it serves as a variation from the usual procedure at mealtime. Thus a child will notice that this night is different, and thereby be aroused to ask questions.[4]

Yachatz

Again, as in *Urchatz* and *Karpas*, one of the reasons for the custom of breaking the matzah and hiding away the larger por-

---

1. Some are accustomed that only the leader of the Seder washes his hands at this point. See *Vayaged Moshe*, ch. 16, and *Mikra'ei Kodesh*, ch. 39.
2. See *Be'er Heiteiv, Orach Chaim* 473:17.
3. See *Pesachim* 116a and *Shulchan Aruch, Orach Chaim* 473:7.
4. *Pesachim* 114b and 116a.

tion before reading the Haggadah is so that a child will take note and ask why we are hiding the matzah before we have even eaten from it.[1]

From all of the above we see that the three actions of *Urchatz*, *Karpas*, and *Yachatz* are to facilitate the mitzvah of *Maggid*. Therefore, they actually form a part of *Maggid*, the second stage of the Haggadah.

Furthermore, both *Karpas* and *Yachatz* actually relate to the Past in their own right. The word *"karpas"* alludes to the fact that the Jews served the Egyptians with *avodas perech* (rigorous work). This is hinted at by the individual letters פרך ס' that make up the word כרפס (*Karpas*): The letter ס' equals sixty and hints at the sixty myriads of Jews who were subjugated in Egypt. פרך means "rigour," alluding to the *avodas perech*, the rigorous work that the sixty myriads were subjected to.[2] The salt water used for *Karpas* is also a reminder of the tears the Jewish people shed during their suffering.[3] Thus we see that both the herb used for *Karpas* and the salt water it is dipped into represent the suffering of the Jewish nation in the Past.

Yachatz (the breaking of the middle matzah) also reminds us of the Past. Our rabbis[4] explain that we perform *Yachatz* because it is called לחם עוני, "bread of poverty," and the way of a poor man is to divide his bread and put part of it aside for future use. Hiding the matzah reminds us of our predicament in the Past in Egypt, when this bread of poverty was our daily lot.

Maggid

It is with *Maggid* that we actually begin to relate the story of

---

1. *Kol Bo, Hilchos Pesach*.
2. *Beis Yosef, Orach Chaim* 473, in the name of the *Roke'ach*; see also *Kol Bo* and *Sefer HaManhig*, os 60, and *Orchos Chaim*, os 25.
3. Heard by the author.
4. *Pesachim* 115b.

our Past. The two chapters of *Hallel* we recite in this section of the Haggadah also deal with the Past Exodus. The first chapter extols the praises of the Almighty:

> *Halleluyah!* Praise, you servants of Hashem; praise the name of Hashem. Blessed be the name of Hashem from this time forth and forevermore. From sunrise to sunset Hashem's name is praised. Hashem is high above all nations, His glory above the heavens. Who is like Hashem our God, Who dwells on high? Who looks far down to behold the things that are in the heavens and on the earth! He raises up the poor from the dust and lifts up the needy from the dunghill. That He may seat him with princes, with the princes of His people. He transforms the barren woman of the house to be a joyful mother of children. *Halleluyah!*
>
> (Tehillim, ch. 113)

The second chapter, specifically the first verse, indicates the point at which we became cognisant of Hashem's grandeur:

> When Israel went out from Egypt, the house of Yaakov from a people of foreign language. Yehudah became His sanctuary, and Israel his dominion. The sea saw it and fled; the Jordan turned back. The mountains skipped like rams, the hills like lambs. What ails you, O sea, that you flee? O Jordan, that you turn back? O mountains, that you skip like rams? And you, O hills, like lambs? Tremble, Earth, before the Master, before the God of Yaakov. Who turned the rock into a pool of water, the flint into a spring of waters.
>
> (Ibid., ch. 114)

Since the above-mentioned passages relate to the Exodus and our Past history, they are included in the second section of the Haggadah.

The climax of the second phase of the *Haggadah*, the Past, is the blessing ברוך אתה ה' גאל ישראל, "Blessed are You, Hashem, Who *has redeemed* Israel." The redemption mentioned here is not in the Present tense (as is the blessing of redemption in the Amidah); it is in the Past tense. This is because this blessing constitutes the conclusion of the section of the *Past* and refers to our redemption from Egypt.

The Third Cup: The Meal and Present

The components of the third stage of the Seder are *Rochtzah, Motzi, Matzah, Marror, Koreich, Shulchan Oreich, Tzafun,* and *Bareich*. In this stage of the Seder, we demonstrate our Present freedom. More than this, we actually draw the Past into the Present and relive it. When we eat the *marror* in the Present, we get a taste of the bitterness that was experienced in Egypt. When we eat the matzah, we experience the taste of the matzah we ate upon leaving Egypt.[1]

---

1. We may ask, Here we have categorised the eating of *pesach*, matzah, and *marror* as being part of the section of the third cup, which deals with the Present. However, the place where they are actually discussed in the Haggadah is in the section of the second cup, where they are mentioned in relation to events that happened in the Past. It says, "The *pesach* offering that our fathers ate...because the Holy One, blessed be He, passed over the houses of our fathers in Egypt." This is clearly an event which took place in the Past. The same is true of matzah and *marror*. If so, how can we say that *pesach*, matzah, and *marror* belong to the section dealing with the Present?

    The answer is simple: when relating to the Past in the second stage of the Haggadah, we mention how *pesach*, matzah, and *marror* are related to the Past Exodus, as that is our obligation at that stage in the Haggadah. However, by actually tasting them in the third stage of the Haggadah, they gain a new dimension, becoming part of our Present.

The Fourth Cup: *Hallel* and Future

The fourth and final stage of the Seder, dealing with the Future, begins as we open the door and recite שפך חמתך, "Pour out Your wrath..." This is a prayer for the Future revenge on the nations. In it we entreat the Almighty to pour out His wrath on the nations who have ravaged the Jewish people. The door is opened in order to signify that it is "a night of guarding" (ליל שמרים), and we need not fear intrusions from the hostile world around us. In the merit of this faith, the *Mashiach* will arrive and pour out his wrath on those who deny the existence and omnipotence of the one true God.[1]

At this stage of the Seder, there is a custom to pour an additional cup, aside from those of the people taking part in the Seder, which is called "the *kos* of Eliyahu HaNavi," the cup of Elijah the prophet. This is done to illustrate our belief that just as God redeemed us from Egypt, so too will He redeem us again in the Future and send Eliyahu the prophet to herald the forthcoming redemption.[2]

We then recite the second part of *Hallel*, in which we praise God for the Future redemption. In this section of *Hallel*, King David, the Psalmist, expresses his thanks to God for delivering him from his trials and tribulations. In fact, he is expressing the sentiments that the entire Jewish nation will express after the coming of the *Mashiach*: their reflections on their Past troubles and their subsequent deliverance from them.[3]

In this fourth section of the Seder we also have הודאה, "thanksgiving." Thanksgiving appears both in this second part of *Hallel* and in the Great *Hallel*, which immediately follows. Thanksgiving pertains especially to the Future, as we will see later on.[4]

---

1. Rema, *Orach Chaim* 480:1.
2. *Mishnah Berurah* 480:10.
3. See Appendix I for an in-depth explanation of this section of *Hallel*.
4. See p. 62.

Both in the latter part of *Hallel* and in the Great *Hallel* we find the words כי לעולם חסדו, "His kindness endures *forever.*" "Forever" refers to both this world and the Future world.[1]

After *Hallel* we say: "All that You have made will praise You, Hashem our God...*from eternity to eternity* You are God." With this we declare that He is eternal, enduring for all time, from the Past to the Future.

After associating ourselves with the Future in this way, we proceed to drink the fourth cup. At this stage in the Haggadah we have passed through all the stages of the order of time and proclaimed God's mastery over our destiny in all these stages. This brings us to the concluding section of the Haggadah, *Nirtzah*, wherein we pray that our performance of the Seder will be found acceptable by God, and that the *Mashiach* will come speedily and redeem us.

THE FOUR CUPS OF PHARAOH

Our rabbis tell us[2] that the four cups of the Seder night correspond to the four cups mentioned in the episode of the dream of Pharaoh's butler and Yosef's interpretation of that dream.

Let us look at this a little closer. We read:

> The chief butler told his dream to Yosef and said to him, "In my dream, behold, there was a vine before me. And on the vine there were three branches, and it was as though it budded and its blossom came forth; its clusters became ripe grapes. And Pharaoh's cup was in my hand, and I took the grapes and pressed them into Pharaoh's cup, and I gave the cup into Pharaoh's hand." And Yosef said to him, "This is the interpretation of it: The three branches are three

---

1. *Roke'ach.*
2. *Bereishis Rabbah* **88**:5.

days. Within three days Pharaoh shall lift up your head and restore you to your place; and you shall give Pharaoh's cup into his hand after the former manner, when you were his butler."

(Bereishis 40:9–13)

There are four stages connected with the four times the word "cup" is mentioned in this dream. The budding, blossoming, and ripening of the grapes are mentioned before the first cup. The grapes are then squeezed into the second cup. The third cup mentioned is placed in Pharaoh's hand. These three cups are included in the butler's account of the dream. A fourth cup is mentioned in Yosef's interpretation. Here also a pattern from Before to the Future may be discerned.

The First Cup: Purpose

Concerning this cup it says: "In my dream, behold, there was a vine before me. And on the vine there were three branches, and it was as though it budded and its blossom came forth; its clusters became ripe grapes. And Pharaoh's *cup* was in my hand."[1] Our rabbis explain that the vine and the three branches mentioned allude to the three forefathers, Yerushalayim, and the Beis HaMikdash.[2] These things all relate to the realm of Purpose and Before.[3]

This first cup is the culmination of the development and maturation of the grapes Before they are transformed into wine. The maturation of the grapes is directed by the hand of God without any human interference, as opposed to the next three stages, relating to the latter three cups.

Our rabbis tell us[4] that these grapes symbolically contained

---

1. Bereishis 40:9–11.
2. *Chullin* 92a.
3. See *Tefillin: The Inside Story*, pp. 106–107, 120–121, and 123.
4. *Zohar, VaYeishev* 192a.

יין המשומר בענביו מששת ימי בראשית, "wine that was guarded within its grapes from the six days of **Bereishis**." This hints at the stage Before Adam's sin. This wine had not yet been squeezed out in the week of creation. Therefore, it was protected from the negative influence effected by the sin on all that was revealed to the outside at the time of the sin.[1] This therefore relates to the first stage of the Haggadah — *Kadeish* — which is the stage of *Bereishis*, embodying Purpose and Before.[2]

The Second Cup: Past

After the grapes matured, the wine was pressed and squeezed from them. The wine thus lost its perfect status of Before. At this stage, the יין המשמור, "the guarded wine," is removed from the protection of the grapes and enters the world of the Past, that is, it becomes exposed to the negativity generated by the first sin. Moreover, the extraction of wine from grapes requires the application of force — *gevurah* — which parallels *din* (judgement). This relates to the second stage of the Haggadah and tefillin, in which the Jewish people were subjected to the "squeezing" oppression of the Egyptians, who in turn were "squeezed" and destroyed. This is alluded to by the verse's telling us that the butler "took the grapes and *pressed* them into Pharaoh's cup."

The Third Cup: Present

We read: "...and I gave the *cup* into Pharaoh's hand."[3] Here the wine is in its third stage, between the Past extraction and the Future drinking — the realm of the Present.

The Fourth Cup: Future

Yosef then interprets the dream and tells what is to transpire:

---

1. Commentaries.
2. See pp. 134–141, and *Tefillin: The Inside Story*, pp. 118–123 and 322.
3. Bereishis 40:11.

"The three branches are three days; within three days Pharaoh shall lift up your head and restore you to your place; and you shall give Pharaoh's *cup* into his hand after the former manner, when you were his butler."[1] The fourth cup is thus mentioned in relation to what will happen in the Future as a Result of the dream.[2]

---

1. Ibid., 12–13.
2. It is interesting to note that the Malbim explains the words כמשפט הראשון, "after the former manner," mentioned in connection with the last cup, to mean, "after the former *judgement*," meaning that the butler was not actually acquitted from the first sentence resulting from the first judgement. This is therefore part of the fourth stage, which is *Malchus*, the sphere of judgement (see *Zohar, parshas Toldos* 137a, and *Tefillin: The Inside Story*, pp. 257–258).

The Four Stages of History

On Seder night we traverse the four stages from the dimension of Before[1] right through to the Future. Let us trace this concept in various sources.

"AN AWAITED NIGHT"

The Seder night was a ליל שמורים, "an awaited night," from Before time right through to the Future, as we see in the following verse:

> It is an awaited night to Hashem to bring them out of the land of Egypt. This is an awaited night to Hashem to all the children of Israel throughout their generations.
>
> (Shemos 12:42)

Before

The first time the term "awaited night" is mentioned in this verse, it is telling us that God waited from the days of Avraham.

---

1. See p. 79.

What was He waiting for? To redeem the Jewish people from Egypt, as He had promised Avraham at the Covenant between the Pieces.[1] This covenant took place exactly 430 years prior to the Exodus, on the fifteenth of Nissan, the night of Pesach.[2] The time of the Exodus was thus a ליל שמרים long Before they ever went into Egyptian exile, from the time of the forefathers, who lived within the historical domain of Before.[3] Additionally, "an awaited night" means that it was a night that Hashem was waiting for from בראשית, the beginning of creation.[4]

The term *"leil shimurim"* is also interpreted as meaning "a night of guarding." It is easy to understand why the fifteenth of Nissan is called "a night of guarding" in reference to the Exodus. However, the first time this expression appears it is a reference to Avraham. What is the "guarding" that is being referred to? The answer is that the fifteenth of Nissan was designated as a night of guarding even Before the Exodus, since it was the night on which God guarded Avraham and saved him from the four kings in his epic battle with them.[5] The Alshich explains that this first mention of ליל שמרים, "a night of guarding," in our verse refers to this episode. Thus, the first ליל שמרים in this verse is referring to the fact that it was a night of guarding even *Before* the Exodus from Egypt.

Furthermore, the Ramban explains that the words "It is an awaited night to *Hashem* to bring them out of the land of Egypt" means that this night is מקודש לשמו, "sanctified to His name," to take them out of Egypt. It thus belongs to the first dimension — Purpose — represented by *Kadeish*.

---

1. *Rashbam*.
2. See *Yalkut Shimoni, parshas Bo* 210, and *Rashi*, Shemos 12:41.
3. See pp. 140–141, where the idea that the forefathers are part of the dimension of Before is discussed.
4. See *piyut* in *ma'ariv* of the second night of Pesach, based on *Rosh HaShanah* 11b.
5. See *Rashi*, Bereishis 14:15.

Past

The verse continues, "to bring them out of the land of Egypt" — in the *Past*.

Present

It then says, "This *is* a guarded night to Hashem..." These words mean that this night is "Divinely protected from the forces of evil and destruction."[1] It is thus a night of guarding in the *Present*.[2]

Future

The verse continues, "This is an awaited night to Hashem to all the children of Israel *throughout their generations*." It is an awaited night to their *Future* generations, for "in Nissan they were redeemed, and in Nissan they are destined to be redeemed once again."[3]

Thus, the freedom of Pesach lies not only in the Past; it also spans the dimension of Before, right through to the Future. Indeed, true freedom encompasses all the facets of time — a freedom that lasts forever, as we say, "He took His people, Israel, out from their midst to *everlasting* freedom."[4] It is a freedom which permeates all the stages of history, bringing Purpose into the Past, and in turn into the Present, and finally into the Future. Consequently, "He took out His people, Israel, from their midst to everlasting freedom" becomes truly fulfilled. Furthermore, true freedom only results if we take the lessons of the Past into

---

1. *Rosh HaShanah* 11b.
2. See also Rema, *Orach Chaim* 480:1.
3. *Seforno; Rosh HaShanah* 11a. See also the liturgy in the Haggadah for the first night of Pesach, in which we say ליל שמרים סימן הוא לעתיד לבוא, "It is an awaited night, a sign for the Future." *Mateh Levi* explains that this is similar to the words of our rabbis (see *Targum Yonasan*, Shemos 12:42), who describe this night as "a night that is protected and awaited *for the Future*."
4. Evening prayer.

the Present and then again into the Future.

FOUR REDEMPTIONS

The parameters of Before, Past, Present, and Future parallel four historic redemptions, which in turn correspond to the four cups.

The first cup — Before — corresponds to God's having chosen Avraham, and Avraham's fathering of the Jewish nation. This was considered the first redemption. With the second cup, we express our gratitude for the redemption from Egypt (Past). The third cup expresses our gratitude to God for protecting us during our current exile and saving us from our adversaries who attempt to uproot our name (Present). The fourth cup corresponds to the Future redemption.[1]

IN TEHILLIM

We have the same phenomenon in Tehillim, where we read:

> You are the Holy One, enthroned on the praises of Israel. In You our fathers trusted; they trusted and You saved them. To You they cried and were saved; in You they trusted and were not ashamed. But I am a worm and not a man; scorned of man and despised by people. All those who see me mock me; they open their lips, they shake their heads. One who casts his burden upon Hashem, He will save him; He will save him, for He favours him.
>
> (Tehillim 22:4–9)

God is mentioned in verse 4 as being *kadosh* — "You are the Holy One" — the One Who was Before. This corresponds to *Kadeish*, the first section of the Seder.

---

1. See *Abarbanel* and *Eliyahu Rabbah* 472:7.

In verses 5 and 6 we read how our fathers trusted in Him and He redeemed them, in the Past. The crying mentioned in verse 6 alludes to the Egyptian exile,[1] of which it is written, "And the Jewish people sighed because of the work, and they *cried*; and their *cry* went up to God from the work,"[2] and as a result God removed them from bondage.[3]

King David then tells of his situation in the Present: "But *I am* a worm and not a man..." This also alludes to the lowly situation of the Jewish nation in the Present exile[4] and therefore corresponds to the third cup.

Finally we read: "One who casts his burden upon Hashem, He *will save* him; He *will save* him, for He favours him."

King David is telling us that God will deliver and save the one who relies on Him. The Jewish nation, who are now as a lowly worm, should rely on God, and thereby they will be saved and exalted in the Future.[5]

IN TEFILLIN

This same pattern emerges with the four sections of the tefillin: *Kadesh, Vehayah Ki Yeviacha, Shema,* and *Vehayah Im Shamoa.* The first *parshah* relates to the Purpose which preceded the Exodus from Egypt, namely, the concept of *kedushah*. The second *parshah, Vehayah Ki Yeviacha,* relates to the Past Exodus from Egypt in more detail.[6] The third *parshah, Shema,* deals with our

---

1. *Midrash Shochar Tov.*
2. Shemos 2:23.
3. *Seforno.*
4. *Redak.*
5. Ibid.
6. In the first tefillin *parshah*, we are told in reference to the Exodus, "*Sanctify* to Me every firstborn... And Moshe said to the people, '*Remember* this day on which you left Egypt from the house of slavery' " (Shemos 13:2-3). This parallels *Kadeish* of the Haggadah, in which we also have the words "a holy [*kodesh*] convocation, as a memorial [*zeicher*] of the departure from Egypt."

Present obligations. The fourth *parshah*, *Vehayah Im Shamoa*, deals with the Future and the Results of our actions.

Thus the four sections of the Seder parallel the four *parshiyos* of the tefillin:

TABLE 2

TEFILLIN	Kadesh	Vehayah Ki	Shema	Vehayah Im
SEDER	Kadeish	Maggid	Meal	Hallel
STAGE	Purpose	Past	Present	Future

The Seder joins us to these four stages on the anniversary of our freedom, and the tefillin bind us to them every weekday of the year.[1]

SIX THOUSAND YEARS

The Talmud[2] relates that the history of this world consists of six thousand years, in three stages. The first stage was a two-thousand year period of confusion. This was followed by two thousand years of Torah. Finally, there is a two-thousand-year period characterised as the Messianic era. Thus, there are three sets of two thousand years after creation. However, there is also a set of two thousand years that came Before creation.[3]

The words *"kodesh"* and *"zeicher"* are stressed here. This parallels the verses in the *parshah* of *Kadesh*, which stress the remembrance of the Exodus in conjunction with **kedushah**, the Purpose of the Exodus.

In the second *parshah* we read, "And it came to pass, when Pharaoh was stubborn and would not let us go, that Hashem killed all the firstborn in the land of Egypt, from the firstborn of the people to the firstborn of the animals" (ibid., 15). Here the history of the Exodus is enumerated in some detail, paralleling *Maggid* of the Seder.

1. For a more detailed study of the four *parshiyos* see *Tefillin: The Inside Story*.
2. *Avodah Zarah* 9a.
3. This stage of Before is not discussed in the above-mentioned *gemara*. It is mentioned in *Bereishis Rabbah* 8:2, and in *Rashi* on *Shabbos* 88b. There we

This sequence is in accordance with the pattern of the Seder and the tefillin *parshiyos*. The first stage of the Seder and the first *parshah* of tefillin corresponds to the time Before the period of six thousand years begins.

The stage after creation is that of שני אלפים תוהו, "the two thousand years of confusion." Rashi calls this *"tohu b'lo Torah —* confusion without Torah." It was during this time that evil had the upper hand in the world. The Flood occurred during this time, and the wicked perished, along with the debacle of the Tower of Babel and the subsequent dispersion of mankind. This corresponds to the second stage of the Seder and the second *parshah* of tefillin, which deals with the fall and destruction of the wicked Egyptians.

The next stage is the two thousand years of Torah. This corresponds to the third stage of the Seder and the third *parshah* of tefillin, which includes the concept of a never-ending acceptance of the Torah.[1]

The fourth stage is that of the two thousand years of the Messianic era. This corresponds to the fourth stage of the Seder and the fourth *parshah* of tefillin — the stage of the Future.

---

are told that God wrote the Torah two thousand years before the world was created.

1. See *Tefillin: The Inside Story*, p. 65, where it is mentioned that both the first and third stages deal with Torah, the first stage being the Torah of Before and the third stage being the Torah of the continuous Present.

The Matriarchs

The Hidden Factor

We enjoy many products of the grapevine: grapes, raisins, jelly, and even grape leaves, used for cooking. However, the crowning glory of the grape is considered to be wine. In fact, there is so much significance ascribed to wine that we do not make a *shehakol* over it, as we do with other drinks. Similarly, we do not make a *borei pri ha'etz* over it, as we do with some other products derived from fruits, for example, olive oil.[1] Instead, wine has its own special blessing: *borei pri hagafen*. Although when eating the actual grape we recite *borei pri ha'etz*, nevertheless, on wine, the innermost, concealed part of the grape, we recite a special *berachah*. This indicates that the quintessential product of the vine is wine.

The matriarchs, who are compared to the four cups, are thus compared to wine, the hidden, innermost part and essence of the grape, concealed from the eye. This association is consistent with the comparison seen above,[2] where the modesty of the Jewish woman is likened to a hidden vine and to the *sod* (secret) of *yayin*, the wine concealed inside the grape, and to the relationship be-

---

1. See *Shulchan Aruch, Orach Chaim* 202:4.
2. Page 11.

tween *kissuy* (covering) and *kos* (cup).

There is a concept in Judaism of the Jewish woman's place being באהל, "inside the tent."[1] However, this does not only mean that the Jewish woman's role is within the home. It also means that just as the nucleus and secret behind a thing are concealed and not readily visible, and just as the foundations of a building are hidden in the ground, so too is the Jewish woman the nucleus, the secret, and the foundation upon which the Jewish nation depends.

It is interesting to note that the Hebrew word for "foundation" is יסוד, which contains the word סוד (secret). Thus foundation and secret are intimately related. Presumably this is so because the foundation is the hidden part of a building. Thus, the women, who are the hidden factor *(sod)* of the Jewish people, are the foundation *(yesod)* that supports our people.

It is also interesting to note that Yosef, who mastered the domain of secrets and who Pharaoh therefore called צפנת פענח, "the one to whom all secrets are revealed,"[2] excelled in the realm of *Yesod*.[3] He was Yosef HaTzaddik (Yosef the Righteous), and it says, "...But the righteous is the foundation *[yesod]* of the world."[4] He therefore had within him the *sod* of *yesod*.

THE SECRET OF REDEMPTION

The Jewish woman was the *yesod* and the *sod* in the foremost salvations of the Jewish nation. Concerning the redemption from Egypt our rabbis say, "The Jews were redeemed from Egypt in the merit of the righteous women."[5] The question arises: if

---

1. See Bereishis 18:9.
2. Ibid. 41:45.
3. See p. 68, n. 1, where the ten realms are listed and Yosef is shown to represent *Yesod*.
4. Mishlei 10:25.
5. *Sotah* 11b.

this is so, why does the Torah make no clear mention of the central role the women played in bringing about the Exodus, whereas the men — Moshe and Aharon — are certainly mentioned in conjunction with the role they played in taking Israel out of Egypt?[1]

The reason for this is that the righteous women in Israel are the *hidden* cause behind the external achievements and deeds of the men. This may also be seen with the patriarchs, who performed certain actions because their wives were acting behind the scenes (as we will see later in this chapter).

Similarly, in the battle against the army of Sisra, the commander-in-chief of Yavin, the king of Canaan,[2] a woman was the hidden, secret cause of our salvation. We are told that Barak was chosen to lead the forces of Israel into war against the army of Sisra. Sisra, however, did not fall into the hands of Barak, but into the hands of a woman, Yael, who killed him. On hearing of his death, Sisra's huge army fled in panic. In "The Song of Devorah" we are told, "Blessed more than other women shall be Yael, the wife of Chever the Keini; more than women in the tent shall she be blessed."[3]

Yael is mentioned here in her capacity as one of the women who are באהל — a modest woman of Israel in the tent. This is stressed because the very fact that she was in the tent, behind the scenes, is what caused the salvation of Israel and not the external actions of Barak. Thus we see here also the salvation that was wrought on the surface by men was actually due to the actions of a woman in the the hidden, innermost recesses of the home.

Likewise in the salvation of the Purim story, it was a man, Mordechai, who was made the celebrity. He was led publicly

---

1. Shemos 6:26.
2. Shoftim, ch. 4 and 5.
3. Ibid. 5:24.

through the streets clothed in royal robes,[1] and a great ado was made over him. The Scroll of Esther ends with the following words:

> For Mordechai the Jew was viceroy to King Achashveirosh and a great man among the Jews and approved of by a multitude of his brethren; he sought the good of his people and was concerned for the welfare of all his descendants.
>
> (Esther 10:3)

No mention is made of Esther's greatness, even though it was she who played the central role in that salvation. This is because Esther was the *secret* behind the Purim story, acting within the confines of the palace, whereas Mordechai acted from without.

Indeed, the very name אסתר is associated with the word סתר, "hidden,"[2] and this is exactly what she was — the hidden hand behind the salvation. In fact, we are told that the whole reason she was chosen to bring about this salvation was because she was modest and hid herself[3] and because she was discreet and "hid her words" (מסתרת דבריה).[4]

It is illuminating to note that the hidden salvation she wrought was achieved on Pesach[5] and that she caused Haman's downfall through a feast of wine.[6] Thus the "hidden wine" of Pesach brought about salvation through a woman who was the secret behind the scenes and thus paralleled the hidden aspect of wine. In this way her behaviour was commensurate with that of the matriarchs, who are analogous to the secret of the Pesach wine.

---

1. Esther 8:15.
2. *Chullin* 139b.
3. *Yalkut Shimoni* 1053.
4. *Megillah* 13a.
5. *Esther Rabbah* 8:7.
6. Esther, ch. 7.

Later in history, when the Jews were oppressed by the Greeks, it was yet again a woman who brought about our salvation from behind the scenes. Her name was Yehudis, and she killed the Greek commander Holofernes. This caused the Greek army to retreat.[1] Yehudis acted in secret and killed Holofernes where no one could see her act. No mention is made of it in our prayers or in any of the Chanukah ceremonies. In contrast, the role played by the men in the Chanukah story receives prominent mention in the Chanukah prayers, in the blessings after meals during Chanukah, and in the menorah-lighting ceremony. The reason for this as well is because Yehudis was the secret behind the salvation, acting in the background and hidden from the eye. Thus her role remains in the background. On the other hand, the battle of the men was visible to all and is therefore at the forefront of our prayers and blessings.

THE MATRIARCHS AND THE FOUR CUPS

Let us now examine the correspondence between each of the four cups and its respective matriarch.

TABLE 3

MATRIARCH	Sarah	Rivkah	Rachel	Leah
CUP	First	Second	Third	Fourth
STAGE	Purpose	Past	Present	Future
SEDER	*Kadeish*	*Maggid*	Meal	*Hallel*

The fourfold theme of Purpose, Past, Present, and Future is evident in the lives of the four matriarchs. From their hidden places, these women directed and steered events.

---

1. See *Otzar Midrashim*, p. 192; Rema, *Shulchan Aruch, Orach Chaim* 670:2; *Mishnah Berurah* 670:10.

The First Cup and Sarah

The cup of *Kadeish* corresponds to Sarah Imeinu. It was she who infused the Jewish nation with *kedushah*, bearing the first child ever to attain sanctity in the womb. This is reflected in one of the blessings we say at a bris milah — אשר קדש ידיד מבטן, "Who sanctified the beloved one from the womb..." — which is a reference to Yitzchak.[1] Thus it was Sarah's womb which initiated the sanctity of Israel.

Furthermore, Yitzchak, the recipient of this sanctity, was born on the first day of Pesach.[2] Thus, the sanctity which the first cup of the Seder represents relates to the first day of Pesach.

Additionally, we see Sarah's close relationship to *Kadeish* reflected in the Torah's reference to her as Yiskah.[3] The reason for this, Rashi tells us, was שסכתה ברוח הקדש, "because she could gaze with holy inspiration."[4] Sarah employed her *ruach hakodesh* to nurture the *kedushah* which Yitzchak received from the womb, as we see in the following episode:

> Sarah saw the son of Hagar the Egyptian, whom she had born to Avraham, mocking. And *she said* to Avraham, "*Cast out this maidservant and her son*, for the son of this maidservant shall not possess with my son, with Yitzchak." The thing was very evil in the eyes of Avraham because of his son. God said to Avraham, "Let it not be evil in your eyes because of the lad and because of your maidservant; all that Sarah says to you, *listen to her voice*; for in Yitzchak shall your seed be called..." Avraham woke up early in the morning and took bread and a waterskin and

---

1. *Rashi, Shabbos* 137b; see also *Rashi*, Bereishis 17:19.
2. See *Rosh HaShanah* 11a; *Rashi*, Bereishis 18:10.
3. See Bereishis 11:29.
4. Sarah was the only matriarch who prophesied with *ruach hakodesh* (see *Megillah* 14a). She thus corresponds to *Kadeish*.

gave it to Hagar, putting it on her shoulder and the child, and sent her away; and she went and wandered in the wilderness of Be'er Sheva.

(Bereishis 21:9–14)

Yitzchak was merely an infant, yet Sarah was terribly concerned about the negative influence Yishmael might have on him, for Yishmael was involved in practises foreign to the Jewish way of life and diametrically opposed to *kedushah*. She therefore wanted to have him sent away.[1] Avraham was reluctant to do so, until God said to him, "...all that Sarah says to you, listen to her voice," which our rabbis explain as meaning that Avraham should listen to her *ruach hakodesh*.[2] Thus, her *holy* inspiration preserved the *holiness* she instilled in Yitzchak while he was in the womb. This ensured that he would remain *kadosh* for the rest of his life.

Accordingly, even though it was Avraham who outwardly performed the physical act of turning Yishmael out, it was Sarah who was responsible for the episode from behind the scenes, advising her husband to send the boy away in the first place. In doing so, she acted in the capacity of the hidden wine of the first cup. Thus, while Avraham and Sarah complemented each other in the domain of *Kadeish*, it is Sarah who was the secret driving force behind it all.

Sarah was "the fruitful vine in the inner recesses of the home," sustaining the holy light of her children. She was the one who began the preservation of our holiness. She was the one who was first concerned with shielding her household from foreign influences that would counter the holiness she was instilling in her child. Her descendants are therefore compared to olive shoots, for just as olive shoots do not tolerate grafting, so too, the

---

1. See *Rashi*, Bereishis 21:9.
2. *Rashi*.

children of the modest Jewish woman do not become attached to the other nations.[1]

Sarah is thus seen as the guardian of *kedushah* for her progeny, and she therefore parallels the cup of *Kadeish*.

The Second Cup and Rivkah

The cup of Rivkah, our second matriarch, is the cup over which *Maggid*, the recounting of our Past history, is recited.

Our rabbis tell us:

> When the first night of Pesach arrived, Yitzchak called Eisav, his oldest son, and told him, "*Hallel* is recited on this night, and the stores of dew are opened. Prepare tasty food for me so that I may bless you whilst I am still able." Eisav then went out into the field to hunt for his father, but he was delayed. Rivkah said to Yaakov, "My son, your descendants are destined to be redeemed from servitude on this night and to sing songs of praise to God. Make tasty food for your father so that he will bless you while he is still able." He went and brought two kid goats. Was this the size of Yitzchak's meal [i.e., so much]? [No, it was much smaller.] One of the goats was to be the Passover sacrifice, and one was for the tasty food, as the Passover sacrifice must be eaten after a meal.
>
> (*Pirkei D'Rabbi Eliezer*, ch. 33)

We see that our mother Rivkah in a way initiated the redemption from Egypt. She commanded that Yaakov prepare the *pesach* offering for his father so that Yaakov could receive the blessings on the night of Pesach, and as a result his children would be redeemed on this same night.

Further on in the Torah we read:

---

1. *Yalkut Shimoni* 881.

> Rivkah said to Yitzchak, "My life is harassed because of the daughters of Cheis. If Yaakov takes a wife of the daughters of Cheis, like these of the daughters of the land, what is life to me?" Yitzchak called Yaakov, and blessed him, and commanded him, and said to him, "You shall not take a wife of the daughters of Canaan. Arise, go to Padan Aram, to the house of Besuel, your mother's father, and take for yourself a wife from there, of the daughters of Lavan, your mother's brother..." And Yitzchak sent away Yaakov, and he went to Padan Aram, to Lavan, son of Besuel the Aramean...
>
> (Bereishis 27:46–28:5)

Though Yitzchak is the one who actively sent Yaakov away, it was Rivkah who was the motivating force behind the scenes, advising this course of action to be taken so that Yaakov would not marry the daughters of Canaan. She also advised that Yaakov depart from Eretz Yisrael in order to save him from the murderous intentions of his brother Eisav.[1] Again, it is the mother behind the scenes who caused her child to be as olive shoots so that he could live and eventually sit "around her table."[2]

Rivkah saved Yaakov from the forces of the Past — the forces of destruction which aim to reduce *kedushah* to the Past. She therefore corresponds to the second cup, that of *Maggid,* which relates to the Past history of the Jewish nation. This was the stage in which those who wished to destroy the Jewish people, thereby relegating them to the Past, were themselves reduced to historical memory.

Furthermore, the narrative of *Maggid* begins with the words "*Arami oveid avi,*" in which we are told that Lavan desired to de-

---

1. Bereishis 27:42–45.
2. See Tehillim 128:3–4; see also above, pp. 11–12.

stroy Yaakov and that Yaakov went down to Egypt. Who initiated Yaakov's descent to Egypt? It all started when Rivkah demanded that Yaakov go to Lavan. She convinced Yitzchak that this was the best course of action to take. In turn, Lavan was responsible for Yaakov's descent to Egypt. Since he caused Yaakov to marry Leah before Rachel, Rachel's son Yosef did not become the firstborn. This bred friction between the brothers, which ultimately caused Yaakov and his family to descend to Egypt, due to the brothers' sale of Yosef.[1]

Thus, "*Arami oveid avi* — An Aramean sought to destroy my father" (meaning Lavan intended to destroy Yaakov) began with Rivkah telling Yaakov to go to Lavan. She was the initial cause of "*vayeired Mitzraymah* — And he [Yaakov] went down to Egypt." To top it all, Rivkah's actions took place on the first day of Pesach.[2]

In short, Rivkah initiated *Maggid* of the Seder night by making Yaakov prepare the *pesach* offering for his father. She also caused Yaakov's going to Lavan on the first day of Pesach, which eventually affected the section of *Maggid* of "*Arami oveid avi*," Lavan's desire to destroy Yaakov, and "*vayeired Mitzraymah*," Yaakov's eventual descent to Egypt. She was thus an integral catalyst of the section of *Maggid*. Therefore, Rivkah corresponds to the second cup, the cup of *Maggid*, which is the relating of the Jewish nation's Past history.

The Third Cup and Rachel

We mentioned earlier[3] that the third cup is used to express our gratitude to God for protecting us in this long exile and for saving us from adversaries who attempt to uproot our name. It

---

1. *Mahari Bei Rav.*
2. She urged Yitzchak to send Yaakov away immediately after he received the blessings, on the first night of Pesach, so that Eisav would not kill him.
3. Page 32.

thus represents our predicament in exile in the Present.

Rachel is the matriarch who is concerned about her children in the Present. She cries for her children in exile, as we read, "A voice is heard on high, lamentation and bitter weeping. Rachel weeping for her children; she refuses to be comforted for her children, because they are not."[1]

Rachel was buried on the way to Beis Lechem in order to enable her children to come and pray at her grave, which they do to this very day. It therefore says, "Yaakov set up a pillar upon her burial place; that is the pillar of Rachel's burial place *to this day*,"[2] i.e., till the *Present* day, unlike other graves which are only intensely remembered for a relatively brief span of time.[3] Consequently, Rachel is the matriarch of the Present.

Rachel's praying is hidden and not visibly seen. She is thus also connected to the secret wine of history, which is veiled in the *kissuy*, the covering of the *kos*.

Furthermore, Rachel corresponds to the Present exile that we are in. She was buried *outside* the settled part of the Land of Israel,[4] so that she could cry and pray for her children who are exiled *outside* the Land of Israel.[5]

Likewise, Rachel's son Yosef was exiled to Egypt *outside* the Land of Israel and saved the Jewish nation from starvation. A father blesses his children that they may be like Efrayim and Menasheh, the sons of Yosef, for they were the first Jews born *in exile* who remained loyal to Torah despite the adverse foreign environment. They were therefore chosen as models for us to follow.[6] Similarly, Rachel's descendants Mordechai and Esther,[7] who ef-

---

1. Yirmeyahu 31:14.
2. Bereishis 35:20.
3. *Malbim*.
4. See *Rashi* and *Mizrachi*, Bereishis 48:7.
5. *Rashi*, loc. cit.
6. See Bereishis 48:20 and *Oznayim LaTorah* there.
7. See Esther 2:5 and *Megillah* 13b.

fected the salvation of the Jewish people, did so *outside* the Land of Israel.[1]

Furthermore, Rachel is the matriarch whose cup we drink after the following phases of the meal: *Motzi, Matzah, Marror, Koreich, Shulchan Oreich, Tzafun, Bareich*. These phases are closely associated with Rachel and her descendants. Let us see how this is true.

Motzi

The blessing of *hamotzi* parallels Rachel's son Yosef. This is because it is a blessing to God for being the One "Who brings forth bread from the earth." Yosef was the one who (acting as a messenger of God) sustained the Jewish nation, along with the rest of the world, with bread.[2]

Matzah

Matzah, which represents the negation of the desire for immorality,[3] is associated with Yosef, who excelled in controlling his desires.[4]

Marror

Marror is particularly relevant to Rachel, as we are told that she cries בכי תמרורים, "a bitter cry."

Marror is also connected to Yosef, Mordechai, and Esther, the descendants of Rachel. Yosef experienced *marror* (bitterness), as

---

1. Although we endure the Present exile both in the Land of Israel and outside of it, Rachel and her descendants are exemplified as being associated with the exile outside the land, where the exile is magnified. It is worthy to note that the tefillin *parshah* of *Shema*, which represents this stage, is the only *parshah* that has no mention of the Land of Israel in it. The allegiance to Torah and the giving of the Torah is not restricted only to the Holy Land; it is universal. For this reason the giving of the Torah, which the *Shema* represents, transpired outside the Land of Israel.
2. Bereishis 47:12.
3. *Tzidkas HaTzaddik* 194.
4. Bereishis, ch. 39.

we are told, **וימררוהו ורובו**, "And they *embittered* him and became his adversaries..."[1] Rashi tells us, "His brothers dealt bitterly with him, and Potifar and his wife dealt bitterly with him, putting him in prison." Rashi explains that the word "*vayemararuhu*" is similar to the word "*vayemararu*"[2] mentioned in reference to our enslavement in Egypt. Thus the bitterness of Yosef's life is reflected in the bitterness of *marror* of the Seder night.

With Mordechai, we find that before the eventual salvation of the Purim story, he experienced *marror*. It says, **ומרה גדולה זעקה ויזעק**, "And he cried with a loud and *bitter* cry."[3] Furthermore, both Mordechai and Esther are associated with *marror*. Mordechai is said to be associated with the spice **מר דרור**, "pure myrrh."[4] This hints at the fact that at first the situation was *mar* (bitter) for the Jews, but it was later transformed into *deror* (freedom) through the actions of Mordechai.

Esther was also called "Hadassah,"[5] which means "myrtle." Just as a myrtle has a sweet smell and a *bitter* taste, so was Esther sweet to Mordechai and *bitter* to Haman.[6] Thus, both Mordechai and Esther are associated with bitterness.

Koreich

Koreich is a combination of matzah, which represents true good, and *marror*, which symbolises bitterness. It therefore represents all of the above-mentioned situations, in which the bitterness contained an element of good which was not initially apparent. We therefore combine matzah and *marror*, to symbolise that all that looks bad and bitter is in fact bound up with the good.

---

1. Ibid. 49:23.
2. Shemos 1:14.
3. Esther 4:1.
4. Shemos 30:23; see also *Chullin* 139b.
5. See Esther 2:7.
6. *Esther Rabbah* 6:5.

Shulchan Oreich

Through the salvation they effected, Yosef, Mordechai, and Esther are all associated with the concept of *Shulchan Oreich*. Yosef saved the Jewish nation when there was a famine, as he himself says, "For God sent me before you to sustain you."[1] Of him it says, "From there he became the feeder of the stone of Israel,"[2] i.e., he fed the Jewish nation, and they were saved from extinction due to his provisions.

Yosef is compared to an ox, as it says, בכור שורו הדר לו, "The firstling of his bullock will have glory."[3] This indicates that he is the one who provided food, as it says, ורב תבואות בכח שור, "An abundance of produce comes by the strength of an ox."[4]

The salvation prompted by Mordechai and Esther also came about through a meal.[5] Indeed, it is for this reason that we partake of a festive meal on Purim.[6] The Jews were destined to be annihilated by the evil Haman, but were saved through the *shulchan oreich* (laying of the table) of Esther, which caused the downfall of that wicked man. His undoing transpired on the night of Pesach, for the king became jealous that Esther had invited both him and Haman to the feast she had prepared. Also, God caused the king's sleep to be disturbed that night, which resulted in Haman's downfall and the salvation of the Jews. We therefore say in the Haggadah, "You aroused Your triumph over him [Haman] when You disturbed the sleep of [the king Achashveirosh] at night."[7] Thus we see that *Shulchan Oreich* corresponds to Rachel and her descendants.

---

1. Bereishis 45:5.
2. Ibid. 49:24.
3. Devarim 33:17.
4. Mishlei 14:4.
5. See Esther, ch. 7.
6. *Shulchan Aruch, Orach Chaim* 695.
7. In the section ויהי בחצי הלילה.

Tzafun

Tzafun means "hidden." This corresponds to Rachel and her progeny, who excelled at keeping secrets. Rachel did not divulge Lavan's trickery on the night of Leah's marriage to Yaakov.[1] She therefore merited descendants such as Shaul and Esther, who could keep secrets.[2]

Similarly, Yosef was מפענח צפונות, "the one who uncovered the hidden secrets," through his skill in interpreting dreams. He was therefore called צפנת פענח, "the one who knew and revealed the hidden secrets."[3] Consequently, Yosef corresponds to *Tzafun*.[4] Moreover, this stage is not called *Tzafun* because we hide the *afikoman* — this was done in an earlier section of the Seder. Rather, it refers to the fact that we are now revealing the *afikoman* that was previously hidden. This parallels Yosef, who revealed the hidden things.

Tzafun and Bareich

There is another connection between *Tzafun* and Yosef. To understand this we will discuss the word *"tzafun"* (hidden) as it relates to another, very similar word, *"tzafon,"* the Hebrew word for "north."

Why does the north have the connotation of being hidden? Due to the short spells of light in the northern part of the world, the sun sometimes appears to be hidden from it.[5] But there is a deeper meaning behind the similarity of the two words.

The north seems to be characterised by a duel nature. The prophet says, מצפון תפתח הרעה, "From the north *evil* will break forth."[6] In Yoel we read, "And the northern one [*Tzefoni*] I shall

---

1. *Megillah* 13b; see also *Rashash* there.
2. Ibid.
3. Bereishis 41:45.
4. See also p. 40.
5. See *Ramban*, Shemos 26:17.
6. Yirmeyahu 1:14.

distance from you."[1] This refers to the *evil* forces that come from the north.[2] Our rabbis explain that this means, "I will remove the *evil* inclination [*yetzer hara*], which is *hidden* within the heart of man, from you."[3] Similarly, when the Jewish people left Egypt, God destroyed all of the Egyptian idols except for one, which was left in the desert. God commanded that the Jewish people turn back and camp by this idol, and the Egyptians trapped them there. This idol was called Ba'al Tzefon, "the idol of the *north*." From these sources it appears that the north is associated with darkness and evil.

On the other hand, we find that the north is the direction in which the most holy sacrifices (the *kodshei kodashim*) were slaughtered. Furthermore, the Table with the twelve showbreads, which represented the sustenance of the Jewish people, was on the northern side of the Temple. All this would seem to imply that the north is associated with *kedushah* (holiness) and good.

We find this same duality with regard to צפן, "hidden things." On the one hand they appear bad, as above with the *Tzefoni* — the *yetzer hara* that is hidden within.[4] On the other hand, the hidden also seems to be good, as it says, וצפונך תמלא בטנם, "You fill their bellies with Your *hidden* treasure."[5]

This apparent contradiction can be explained in the following manner: It is true that evil comes from the north and is hidden. However, this evil can be subdued through the power of *kedushah*. It is for this reason that the Table was on the northern side of the Temple, and why the slaughtering of the most holy sacrifices took place there: in order to subdue the evil of *tzafon*.[6]

---

1. Yoel 2:20.
2. *Rashi*.
3. *Sukkah* 52a.
4. See also *Ramban*, Shemos 26:17, and *Ramban*, Bamidbar 2:2.
5. Tehillim 17:14.
6. The evil of the north is also subdued because of the Jewish people. The evil mentioned in the verse "From the north evil will break forth upon all the

Let us now return to the Egyptian idol, Ba'al Tzefon. Interestingly, it was the last of the Egyptian idols to remain and therefore appeared to be the mightiest. However, it was this supposition that brought the Egyptian downfall. As Rashi points out,[1] the reason the Almighty didn't destroy it was in order to mislead the Egyptians into thinking that they still had a powerful god on whom they could rely. As a result, the Egyptians felt confident enough to pursue the Jewish people, an act which led to their demise at the Sea of Reeds.

Thus Ba'al Tzefon in the north looked bad, but on account of the Jewish nation fulfilling God's command and traveling toward that very evil, it was ultimately transformed into good. Therefore it says in the Torah:

> Speak to the children of Israel that they should turn and camp before Pi HaChiros, between Migdal and the sea, before Ba'al Tzefon; over against it you shall camp by the sea. And Pharaoh will say of the children of Israel, "They are closed in the land; the desert has shut them in." And I will allow Pharaoh's heart to be hardened, and he will pursue them [seeming bad], and I will be honoured through Pharaoh and through all his forces, and Egypt will know that I am Hashem [bad transformed to good].
>
> (Shemos 14:2–4)

A sanctification of God's name transpired through the seeming bad. This, of course, is similar to the Table in the Temple and the most holy sacrifices being situated on the northern side of

---

inhabitants of the land" (Yirmeyahu 1:14) will not reach the Jewish nation, as it says there, " 'They shall fight against you, but they shall not prevail over you, for I am with you,' says Hashem, 'to save you' " (ibid., 19). They will not be able to overcome you, for the *tzafon* is subdued on behalf of the Jewish nation.

1. On Shemos 14:2.

the Temple in order to transform bad to good. Thus we see that yet again *tzafon*, which is generally construed as bad, is transformed into something good.

Let us study the episode of Ba'al Tzefon in more depth. Moshe Rabbeinu is told:

> Speak to the children of Israel that they turn and camp before Pi HaChiros, between Migdal and the sea, before Ba'al Tzefon.
>
> (Ibid., 2)

Later in the *parshah* we read:

> And the Egyptians overtook them, encamping by the sea...beside Pi HaChiros, before Ba'al Tzefon.
>
> (Ibid., 9)

The Jews were told to encamp at a place called Pi HaChiros (פי החירות), which means "the opening of freedom." However, the location of this "opening of freedom" was situated before Ba'al Tzefon, which symbolised the strength of Egypt. The idea here is that although the Jews were in a place of evil and were facing the evil force of *tzafon*, nevertheless, by listening to the command of God, the situation was transformed to one of good and became the "opening of *cheirus*," freedom.[1]

Our rabbis tell us[2] that the encampment before Ba'al Tzefon brought about the fulfilment of the promise "And afterwards they shall go out with great wealth,"[3] which God had made to Avraham. This was because all the silver and gold that Yosef had

---

1. Similarly, Pi HaChiros was originally called Pitom, "The Blocked Opening." It became Pi HaChiros, "The Opening of Freedom," because it was from there that the *cheirus* of the Jewish nation began (*Rashi*, Shemos 14:2). This change was the result of the Jews listening to the command of the Almighty.
2. *Yalkut Shimoni* 229.
3. Bereishis 15:14.

amassed during his regency over Egypt was hidden in the idol of Ba'al Tzefon, and when the Jewish people reached there, they took it. The name "Ba'al Tzefon" has the connotation of "the one who oversees the *hidden* things." This, of course, is reflected in the fact that the idol contained *hidden* riches — the silver and gold that Yosef had gathered.

Similarly, Yosef was the one known as Tzafnas Panei'ach — the one in charge of the *hidden* things and the one who knew and revealed the hidden things. Thus, in the episode of Ba'al Tzefon, the Jewish people revealed the *hidden* things of Yosef, in the idol which "oversees" the *hidden* things.

We have seen so far that the return of the Jewish people to Ba'al Tzefon was actually for the good, for the following reasons: (a) because of the impact of the salvation that took place there and (b) because a great treasure that had been hidden was uncovered there. This is a reflection of the idea of transforming *Tzafun* into *Bareich* — hidden things or evil into blessing. This is exemplified by Yosef, for Yosef did not only control *tzafun*, the hidden dimension, and reveal it, but he was actually party to the transformation of the evil Ba'al Tzefon, the idol of the north, into good. We see from this that not only does Yosef embody the concepts of *Tzafun* and *Bareich* separately (as we shall see below), he actually combines both, transforming *Tzafun* into *Bareich*, to become *Tzafun Bareich* (צפון ברך), i.e., the blessing of the hidden and of the north. This concept is reflected in the Seder, where *Tzafun*, the eating of the *afikoman*, occurs immediately before *Bareich*, the blessings after the meal. Thus the Seder also teaches us that *Tzafun* may ultimately be *Bareich*. Indeed, every Jew carries within him the potential to transform *Tzafun* into *Bareich*, just as Yosef did.

The *afikoman* is the last food we eat before the blessings after the meal, so as to keep the *afikoman* closely connected to *Bareich*. Indeed, we are told that blessing (ברכה) comes to a person as a result of reciting the blessings after the meal.[1] Thus, by eating the *afikoman* just prior to the blessings after the meal, the blessings rest upon the *tzafun*.

Yosef's association with *Tzafun Bareich*, the *blessing* of the *hidden*, fits in beautifully with the halachah that one may not eat anything after the *afikoman*, which is *tzafun*, that which is hidden. This is in order that the *Bareich*, the blessing of the hidden, remains with us.

Indeed, the verse וצפונך תמלא בטנם, "You fill their bellies with Your *tzafun* [hidden treasure],"[2] parallels the concept of *Tzafun* of the Seder. God's *Tzafun*, that which He hides for the righteous to receive in the World to Come, is a good *tzafun*, and on the Seder night His *tzafun* — the *afikoman* that was hidden — is *Tzafun Bareich*, "a blessed *tzafun*," which fills our bellies.

Bareich

As with *Tzafun*, *Bareich* also corresponds to Rachel's descendants Yosef, Mordechai, and Esther. We find that Yosef incorporates the concept of blessing more than any of the other tribes, as it says in Yaakov's blessing to Yosef on his deathbed: "The blessings of your father have prevailed above the blessings of my progenitors, even to the boundaries of the everlasting hills; they shall be on the head of Yosef, and on the crown of he who was separated from his brothers."[3] Yaakov thus informs us that all of the great blessings which he himself received from Yitzchak shall transfer to Yosef. Therefore, we see that Yosef has a greater blessing than his brothers.

We also read that Yosef's portion of Eretz Yisrael is blessed more than that of any other tribe: "Blessed of Hashem be his land,"[4] on which Rashi comments that no other tribe had land

---

1. *Sanhedrin* 92a; *Shulchan Aruch, Orach Chaim* 180:2; *Kitzur Shulchan Aruch* 44:3.
2. Tehillim 17:14.
3. Bereishis 49:26.
4. Devarim 33:13.

which was as blessed as that of Yosef. We also find that Yaakov said to Yosef, "In you shall Israel bless."[1] This means that when the Jewish people wish to bless their sons, they will do so by using the descendants of Yosef as examples, saying, "May you be like them."[2] We see from all of the above that Yosef has more of a connection to blessing than any of the other tribes.

Mordechai and Esther are also strongly associated with blessing. Each year on Purim we say, "Blessed be Mordechai" and "Blessed be Esther," for their roles in the salvation of Israel that occurred at that time. Thus, *Bareich* corresponds to Rachel's children more than it does to anyone else.

The stage of the third cup, which embodies all the factors we have just discussed, thereby corresponds to Rachel and her descendants. They affect our existence in the Present. Rachel prays for her descendants to have relief within the period of the Present exile. Her descendants Mordechai and Esther brought about a salvation of the Jewish nation which occurred long before the final redemption, also within the period of the Present exile. Furthermore, we are told[3] that prior to the final redemption in the Future, which will be brought about by the *Mashiach*, who descends from David, there will arise a *Mashiach* descending from Yosef.[4] Thus we see again that Rachel's descendants function as saviours in the Present, the stage before the Future, just as the third cup, which corresponds to Rachel and the Present, precedes the fourth cup, which corresponds to Leah and the Future.

---

1. Bereishis 48:20.
2. See *Rashi*, loc. cit.
3. See *Sukkah* 52a and *Maharsha* there.
4. This *Mashiach* will be a mighty warrior, and he is destined to die in battle (see *Sukkah* 52a and *Maharsha* there).

The Fourth Cup and Leah

The fourth and final cup, that of the future, corresponds to Leah. We have already touched on how the second part of *Hallel*, which is recited in this section of the Haggadah, refers to the Future redemption.[1] We have also noted that the *Mashiach*, who will bring about the Future redemption, descends from Leah.

In addition, another intrinsic part of this section, thanksgiving, corresponds to Leah. We are told in the Talmud:[2] "From the day God created the world, there was no one who thanked God till Leah came and thanked Him, as it says, 'This time I will thank Hashem.' "[3]

Leah became the first to thank God, upon the birth of her fourth son, Yehudah. Let us examine this episode more closely.

The Torah tells us, "She conceived and bore a son, and she said, 'This time I will thank Hashem.' Therefore she called his name Yehudah. She then stopped having children."[4] Thus we see that Leah thanked God on this occasion, and as a result she called her fourth son יהודה, related to the Hebrew word for thanksgiving, הודאה.

Interestingly, Yehudah's name contains the Tetragrammaton, the four-letter name of God. The remaining letter, the *dalet*, has the numerical value of four. Our rabbis explain: Leah thanked God at the birth of her fourth son, because now that he was born, the name of God was complete, as is reflected in Yehudah's very name. The situation before his birth resembled the Jewish people in exile, when the holy name of God is not complete. When Yehudah was born it said, ותעמוד מלדת. Although we translated this according to the simple meaning of the verse as "She then stopped having children," the literal translation is

---

1. See also Appendix I.
2. *Berachos* 7b.
3. *Bereishis* 29:35.
4. Ibid.

"She then *stood* as a result of giving birth." This hints at the idea that the throne of God will *stand* firmly on its legs, i.e., that the four letters of God's name will be complete.[1]

Leah is thus saying that this fourth son, Yehudah, is the one who will prompt the completion of the name of God when the *Mashiach*, his descendant, will bring the final redemption. For this reason the whole Tetragrammaton is contained in Yehudah's name. This, together with the letter *dalet*, which has the numerical value of four, alludes to the fact that the completion of the Tetragrammaton will take place at the end of days, when the *fourth* stage — the Future — ensues. Of that era it says, "On that day *Y-h-v-h* will be One, and His name One."[2]

Consequently, Yehudah the fourth son of Leah, will herald the fourth stage of history, corresponding to the fourth cup. Leah, who saw the Future redemption stemming from her offspring, thanked God for it and in this way parallels the Future.

Leah's experience in life is analogous to the situation of the Jewish nation in the world. As the Midrash explains,[3] Leah experienced intense dejection for the first several years of her life. This was due to her thinking that her younger sister would marry the righteous Yaakov, while she, the older sister, was doomed to marry Eisav, his wicked older brother. However, her sadness did not dissipate with her marriage to Yaakov, for she felt she played second fiddle to Rachel. Only with the birth of Yehudah, who represents the Future, were her negative feelings ameliorated, causing her to thank God. The tribulations of Leah's life symbolise the hardships and suffering of the Jewish nation, along with their ultimate deliverance.

Leah also becomes part of the Future by dint of her introducing the concept of thanksgiving to the world. Our rabbis tell us

---

1. *Zohar, parshas VaYeitzei* 154b and 155a.
2. Zechariah 14:9.
3. *Bereishis Rabbah* 70:16.

that the act of הודאה pertains to the Future: "All the sacrifices are destined to disappear in the Future, except for the thanksgiving offering."[1] They further say: "All the prayers are destined to disappear in the Future, except for thanksgiving."[2]

The fourth part of the Seder is replete with thanksgiving. It even mentions the thanksgiving offering,[3] the only offering that will not disappear in Future times. Therefore we see that the fourth part of the Seder parallels this aspect of the Future.

Having reviewed the relationship between the four matriarchs and the four sections of the Seder, we are now in a position to answer a question raised by the Mordechai:[4] Why did our rabbis institute four cups of wine to commemorate the Exodus rather than four matzos? Based on all of the above, we now understand that cups of wine are indeed most appropriate for this observance, for they allude to the secret of the matriarchs, this behind-the-scenes approach to life.

Let us end this section by noting that the three principal foods which we eat on the Seder night, corresponding to our three forefathers,[5] are clearly mentioned in the Torah. However, the four cups, which correspond to the four matriarchs, are not explicitly mentioned. On a simple level, we might say that this parallels the modesty of the Jewish woman and the fact that she represents the internal, whereas the Jewish man represents the external manifestation of the internal. On a deeper level, we can add that the four cups are thus concealed because they represent the matriarchs, the hidden secret of our existence — the "secret of the wine" — directing the four-staged course of Jewish history.

---

1. *Vayikra Rabbah* 9:7.
2. Ibid.
3. In *Hallel*, from Tehillim 116:17.
4. *Perek Arvei Pesachim*.
5. See *Mechilta* 12:13; *Shemos Rabbah* 15:12; *Gevuros Hashem*, ch. 60.

The Four Matriarchs and the Tetragrammaton

We have seen in the previous section that Leah plays a role in completing the Tetragrammaton, the four-letter name of God. In fact, all of the four matriarchs are connected to the Tetragrammaton. In this section, we shall delve into this relationship. First, however, let us examine the Tetragrammaton itself.

This name of God consists of the letters *yud, key, vav,* and *key,*[1] which correspond to the stages of Purpose, Past, Present, and Future.

The *yud* represents Start, Beginning, and Purpose. Interestingly, each letter of the Hebrew alphabet begins with the shape of the letter *yud*.[2] *Yud* is the smallest letter and therefore resembles the starting point of everything. Indeed, all the other letters are made up of *yud*s, since the *yud* resembles a dot or point, and everything can be viewed as being made up of small dots. Since all of

---

1. It is customary to write *key* in lieu of the actual letter *hey* of the Tetragrammaton, in order to avoid pronouncing the name of God (see *Tosafos* in *Avodah Zarah* 18a).
2. *Bnei Yissaschar, Ma'amar Chodesh Elul.*

creation came about through the agency of the Hebrew alphabet, everything can ultimately trace itself back to the *yud*. Thus, the *yud* symbolises the foundation and beginning of everything, and, as the first letter of the Tetragrammaton, it hints that God is the first cause and Start of the universe.

This *yud* at the beginning of Hashem's name also symbolises the World to Come, which was created with the letter *yud*[1] and is the Purpose of creation. Consequently, the *yud* represents both the starting point and the ending point. This is in accord with the idea that the goal is in existence before any part of an object has yet come into being, the concept of "the last to be created, yet the first in thought," i.e., the thought that preceded creation. Thus Purpose is the potential, and the Future is the actualisation of that potential.

Hey, the second letter of the Tetragrammaton, hints at Olam HaZeh (this world), which was created with the letter *hey*.[2] Since this world is transient and temporary, it symbolises the Past.

The Talmud[3] explains further that Olam HaZeh was created with a *hey* to teach us a valuable lesson. The *hey* has an opening both on the bottom and on its side:

DIAGRAM 3

The opening at the bottom indicates that if a person sins, he "drops out." Thus one who remains a sinner will be destroyed and left in the dimension of the Past. However, if the sinner wishes, he may return and repent, but he can do so only if Divinely assisted, with God raising him up and helping him through the side aperture of the *hey*.[4] Therefore, the *hey* illus-

---

1. *Menachos* 29b.
2. Ibid.
3. Ibid.
4. The penitent's return is principally the dimension of the second *hey* of the Tetragrammaton, as we shall see.

trates that this world is the world of choice. If one wishes, he may choose to sin and "drop out." However, he still retains the capacity to choose, and if he subsequently wishes to return and repent, it is within his power to do so.

The third letter of the Tetragrammaton is the *vav*. This letter is used to join other grammatical parts of speech (*vav* conjunctive). In fact, the very word *"vav"* means "hook," which is an object that joins things. Interestingly, the letter itself is shaped like a hook.

Grammatically, adding a *vav* to a word can also be used to change the Past tense into the Future tense or vice versa (*vav* conversive). *Vav* Links the Past and the Future and is analogous to the Present, which is the Link between Past and Future.

Additionally, the *vav* contains a line from Above to Below, representing the joining of heaven and earth. In fact, the *vav* is an elongated *yud*. The *yud* represents God in creation but not His connection with the world. By elongating the *yud* and lowering it, it becomes the *vav hachibur*, "the linking *vav*," representing God's connection to this world and the Link between Upper and Lower. Thus the *vav*, the Link between Past and Present and between Above and Below, demonstrates that God is in control at Present and that He is not divorced from this lower earth.

The final letter of the Tetragrammaton is *hey*. This is a repeated letter, but not a repeated concept. The first *hey* represents Olam HaZeh in its imperfect state, a passing world, whereas the final *hey* represents its perfection in the Future, the World to Come.

God created man in a state of perfection. But with the first sin and the expulsion from the Garden of Eden, man fell from this perfect state. However, in the Future, man will return to his previous exalted position. In keeping with this, we might say that the second *hey* is the perfection of the first *hey*, representing the Future return of the world to its state of perfection. Similarly, the first *hey* represents the sinner before his repentance, and the second *hey* represents the penitent returning through the side of the *hey*, thereby gaining existence in the Future.

We have mentioned previously that the birth of Yehudah made it possible for God's four-letter name to be completed in the Future. However, until we reach that stage, God's name will be incomplete in the world. Indeed, there is an event recorded in the Torah,[1] which explicitly bears this idea out. Shortly after the Exodus from Egypt, the nation of Amalek attacked Israel in the wilderness. In that narrative, God's name is spelled in an unusual way, as *yud-key*, instead of *yud-key-vav-key*.[2] Why were the *vav* and *hey*, which depict the Present and Future, removed?

Seeing the Jews leave Egypt through Divine intervention profoundly disturbed Amalek, for this clearly demonstrated that God was in control of the world. Amalek wanted to erase this impression and show instead that they themselves were *reishis* — the primary power in the world,[3] and that they, and not God, were in control of the Present. And this was not all. Amalek could also not accept God as being the Future King of the world, nor would they admit to a Future time of reward for the righteous and punishment for the wicked.

Thus, by attacking Israel, Amalek aspired to cast doubt on God's control in the Present and, by extension, on His authority in the Future. This is why the Torah writes the name of God here without the *vav* and *hey*. Amalek succeeded in temporarily covering the revealed appearance of God in the Present (symbolised by the *vav*) and thereby dampened the belief in God's intervention in the Future (hinted at by the second *hey*). When will the *vav* and *hey* be returned? In the Future, when the hand of God will be seen with a permanent clarity once again.

---

1. See Shemos 17:8–16.
2. Ibid., 16.
3. See *Rashi*, Bamidbar 24:20.

THE TETRAGRAMMATON AND THE MATRIARCHS

Let us now discuss the relationship between the four matriarchs and the four letters of the Tetragrammaton.

TABLE 4

MATRIARCH	Sarah	Rivkah	Rachel	Leah
LETTER	Yud	Hey	Vav	Hey
SEDER	Kadeish	Maggid	Meal	Hallel
STAGE	Purpose	Past	Present	Future

We have seen previously how the matriarchs correspond to the four stages of history: Sarah corresponds to the "Before" of the Jewish nation, while it was still "in the womb" — the stage of the feotus before coming into this world, which is Before its Past, Present, and Future. This is the realm of *kedushah*, the point of inception, the Purpose which preceded the existence of everything else. This, of course, fits in nicely with the concept of the *yud* which we noted above. The tiny *yud*, the smallest letter in the Hebrew alphabet, represents the starting point of everything. Conversely, it also represents the goal of creation, the World to Come, which was created with the *yud*. Thus *yud* is the Purpose of creation, which both precedes it and is its ultimate goal, and Sarah, who preceded the Jewish nation, corresponds to this letter.

Rivkah, who has a connection with *Maggid* and the Past of the Jewish nation, corresponds to the first *hey* of the Tetragrammaton, which represents the creation of Olam HaZeh in the Past.

The letter *hey* can be broken up into a *dalet* and a *yud*, which spell the word די (enough), symbolising limitation. This relates to דין (judgement), which also contains the letters of די: in the realm of judgement there is limitation.[1] *Maggid*, the realm of Rivkah,

---

1. As opposed to its opposite, mercy, which in Hebrew is *rachamim* (רחמים),

also relates to these aspects of the letter *hey*, wherein the idolatry of our ancestors, the evil of Lavan, the slavery of the Jews, and the wickedness of Egypt have a limited time span and eventually vanish to the Past. *Maggid* further relates to the letter *hey* because it is broken up into two letters; in the realm of *Maggid* there are two aspects: the destruction of Egypt, on the one hand, and the emergence of the triumphant Jewish nation on the other.

We now come to the third stage, that of Rachel, who corresponds to the Meal and the Present, and thus to the letter *vav* of the Tetragrammaton. As we discussed above, Rachel is the one who looks out for her children in the Present. From a Kabbalistic point of view, the letter *vav* is also associated with Rachel's son Yosef, as the *vav* represents *Tiferes,* which culminates with *Yesod,* the *sefirah* of Yosef.[1]

---

having the same root letters as *rechem* (רחם), meaning "womb," symbolising creativity, the opposite of limitation.

1. God is above human comprehension, and therefore man has no conception of His essence. We can only achieve some perception of God's ways through His connection to the lower worlds. God controls the lower worlds through ten spiritual levels called *sefiros*, or emanations. These ten levels are *Keser* (Crown), *Chochmah* (Wisdom), *Binah* (Understanding), *Chesed* (Kindness), *Gevurah* (Strength), *Tiferes* (Glory), *Netzach* (Victory), *Hod* (Splendour), *Yesod* (Foundation), and *Malchus* (Kingship). They, too, correspond to the four letters of the Tetragrammaton. *Keser* corresponds to the apex of the *yud*. *Chochmah* corresponds to the *yud* itself. *Binah*, to the first *hey*. The six *sefiros* from *Chesed* through *Yesod* correspond to the *vav*. (These six *sefiros* are also known as *Tiferes*.) Finally, there is *Malchus,* which corresponds to the second *hey* of the Tetragrammaton (see *Sefer HaKlalim* in *Klalei Ma'amar HaChochmah* and *Sha'arei Kedushah* 3:1). Additionally, Avraham, Yitzchak, Yaakov, Moshe, Aharon, Yosef, and David, who perfected themselves in the traits represented by the last seven *sefiros*, symbolise these last seven *sefiros* respectively (see *Zohar Chadash* 26c, 26d). See diagram 4 on the next page.

Furthermore, *Yesod* is the sixth *sefirah* of those that represent the *vav* (see note below), and therefore Yosef corresponds to the letter *vav*, which has the numerical value of six.

Finally, there is Leah, who symbolises *Hallel* and the Future. She is the one from whom the *Mashiach* will come, who will bring the Future salvation and perfection of the world. Accordingly, Leah corresponds to the final *hey* of the Tetragrammaton, which represents Olam HaZeh in its Future state of perfection, when all bad will be transformed into good. The letters *dalet* and *yud* contained within this *hey* also hint at the limitation of bad which will take place in the Future when Hashem will say די, "Enough!" to all our suffering. This letter also represents the establishment of God's Kingship (*Malchus*),[1] which will be truly established only in the Future, as it says, "And Hashem shall be King over the whole world; on that day Hashem will be One, and His name will be One."[2]

On a final note, let us add that the relationship between the matriarchs and the four-letter name of God parallels the fact that the four cups of the Seder (associated with the matriarchs) correspond to the four letters of the Tetragrammaton in and of themselves. As Rabbeinu Bachya tells us:[3]

DIAGRAM 4

The Ten Levels	The Tetragrammaton	Patriarch
Keser (Crown)	Apex of the y*ud*	
Chochmah (Wisdom)	*Yud*	
Binah (Understanding)	First *hey*	
Chesed (Kindness)		Avraham
Gevurah (Strength)		Yitzchak
Tiferes (Glory)	*Vav*	Yaakov
Netzach (Victory)		Moshe
Hod (Splendor)		Aharon
Yesod (Foundation)		Yosef
Malchus (Kingship)	Second *hey*	David

1. See n. 1 on previous page.
2. Zechariah 14:9.
3. On Shemos 12:23.

Furthermore, the four cups of Pesach correspond to the four letters of the Tetragrammaton. The first cup of Kiddush corresponds to the *yud*, which represents the realm of *kedushah*. The second cup, over which the Haggadah — the narrating of the miracles — is recited, corresponds to the *hey*, from which the miracles and the plagues stem [with which God metes out *din* (judgement) to those who rebel against Him].[1] The third cup, that of Birkas HaMazon, corresponds to the letter *vav*...and from there comes sustenance...as it says, "Behold, I will rain bread from heaven for you"[2] [and *vav* represents the joining of heaven to earth].[3] The fourth cup, on which one says "*Shefoch Chamascha*," corresponds to the final *hey* of the Tetragrammaton, which is the trait of judgement.[4]

---

1. See pp. 67–68.
2. Shemos 16:4.
3. See p. 65.
4. See also *Shlah HaKadosh* in *Shnei Luchos HaBris, Pesachim* 9a, in *Matzah Shemurah*. This last idea is yet another indication of the fact that the four stages of the Seder parallel the four tefillin *parshiyos*, which also correspond to the four letters of the Tetragrammaton in sequence (*Zohar, Bamidbar* 258a; *Tikkunei Zohar, tikkun* 22; *Seder HaYom* 7a).

The Patriarchs and Matriarchs

We have seen[1] that the Seder and tefillin parallel and complement each other. Through the forefathers and the matriarchs, even more similarities come to light. We mentioned[2] that the three chief foods and the four cups of the Seder night correspond to the three patriarchs and the four matriarchs respectively. Similarly, the three- and four-armed *shin* of the head tefillin correspond to the three patriarchs and the four matriarchs.[3]

Furthermore, the four-armed *shin* on the head tefillin represents the letters of the two tablets of the covenant, which were engraved by the Almighty all the way through the stones, as it says, "...engraved in the tablets."[4] Those letters were legible only because of the outline which was defined by the stone that re-

---

1. In the Introduction, pp. 8–10.
2. Page 62.
3. *Eliyahu Rabbah* 32:65; *Sefer Matamim* in the section dealing with tefillin, *os zayin*; *Keser Shem Tov*, p. 7, in the name of the *Sefer Matamim*.
4. Shemos 32:16.

mained around the engraving. These letters are represented by the four-armed *shin* of the tefillin since the negative space on the tablets (that which was left when the letter was carved out of the stone) of the three-armed *shin* is actually a four-armed *shin*. Thus the four-headed *shin* of the tefillin represents the Godly writing of the tablets and is not used by us in writing.

DIAGRAM 5

On the other hand, the Torah was written by Moshe Rabbeinu with ink on parchment. It is represented by the three-headed *shin* of the tefillin, which is the common *shin* we use.[1]

The four-armed *shin* belongs to the hidden dimension and corresponds to the matriarchs, who are the hidden foundation of the Jewish nation. The three-armed *shin*, used by us, corresponds to the patriarchs. Again we see that the revealed *kedushah* corresponds to the forefathers, and the hidden *kedushah* to the matriarchs.

Moreover, the four *parshiyos* hidden in the *batim* of the tefillin correspond to the four matriarchs, whereas the three letters of *Shaddai* (ש-ד-י), formed on the outside of the head tefiliin and by its knots, which are manifest externally, hint at the forefa-

---

1. *Hagahos Smag*, brought down in *Beis Yosef* 32.

thers.[1] Again, the matriarchs correspond to the hidden *kedushah*, and the patriarchs to the revelation of that *kedushah*.

---

1. We read the following in *Binyamin Zev*, ch. 190: "The *shin* formed by the creases of the head tefillin hints at the merit of Yaakov. This is so because the last letter of Yaakov's name is *beis*, and it is exchanged for a *shin* in the numerical system known as *At Bash*..." (This system is a code frequently used by the sages. In it the first letter of the *alef-beis* is exchanged for the last letter [*alef/tav*], the second letter of the *alef-beis* for the second-to-last letter [*beis/shin*], and so on. Hence its name *At* [א״ת] *Bash* [ב״ש].)

 "Next is Yitzchak, whose name ends with a *kuf*. The *kuf* in the *At Bash* code is exchanged for a *dalet*. This is the *dalet* worn on the nape of the neck.

 "The last letter of Avraham's name is a *mem*. In the *At Bash* code, the *mem* is transformed into a *yud*. This completes the letters of *Shaddai* — *shin, dalet,* and *yud*. The name *Shaddai* thus appears on the tefillin in the merit of our forefathers."

Above to Below
and
Before to Future

The Seder Night: Rising Above Time and Space

A brief overview of the Torah reveals that God is referred to by many different names. We are taught that each name emphasises a different Divine attribute.[1] Let us look at the Tetragrammaton, which emphasises the aspect of God's eternal, infinite nature. The *Shulchan Aruch*[2] writes that this name denotes that God was, is, and will be. The combination of all these together denotes a fourth dimension — one that precedes and is Above time, for God is not bound by time.

Since this name denotes the four dimensions of the time line, it therefore parallels the components of the four stages of the Haggadah:

1. *Kadeish* — the dimension that preceded time (Before)
2. *Maggid* — was (Past)
3. Meal — is (Present)
4. *Hallel* — will be (Future)

---

1. *Tanchuma, Shemos* 20.
2. *Orach Chaim* 5.

The Tetragrammaton, which consists of the letters *yud, key, vav*, and *key*, is the name God employed to take us out of Egypt, as we see from the verse "Therefore tell the children of Israel that I am *Y-h-v-h* and that I will bring you out from under the burdens of Egypt."[1] This means, "Because I am God, to Whom all the demarcations of time are really one, I can manipulate nature when and how I wish. Therefore trust me that I can and will deliver you."

The name *Y-h-v-h* is also used to cause renewal.[2] Thus, this name indicates both the eternity of God and the fact that He is the Source of renewal. The four sections of the Seder, which parallel this Divine name, thus indicate the renewal generated at the Exodus.

Let us delve into this concept a little further. We have seen that the first section of the Seder encompasses the concept of *kedushah*, which corresponds to the concept of Purpose — the beginning of all. This is alluded to by the letter *yud*, the first letter of the Tetragrammaton, which represents the realm of *kedushah* and Start. This is the realm Above time, whence Past, Present, and Future all emanate and wherein they are all unified. The *yud*, from which the separate demarcations of Past, Present, and Future spread out, is the smallest letter in the Hebrew alphabet. This corresponds to the first part of the Seder — *Kadeish*. It is the shortest of all the Seder's stages, and yet it actually encompasses the other three concepts of time within itself.

Rabbi Eliyahu of Vilna explains, "The beginning of any matter already contains everything that is to follow. The beginning is therefore considered like and is equivalent to the whole."[3] In *Kadeish* we become bound to the level of timelessness and are ele-

---

1. Shemos 6:6.
2. *Ramban* and *Malbim*, Shemos 6:2.
3. *Avnei Eliyahu*, in explanation to the prayer of the three pilgrimage festivals. See also *Tiferes Yisrael*, ch. 37.

vated to the dimension which unifies all the demarcations of time. This parallels our experience at the Exodus, when the Jewish nation was transported into supernatural time.¹

Thus *Kadeish* is our entry into the dimension Above time. And although the four sections of the Seder parallel four different stages of time — *Kadeish* representing the realm Before time, *Maggid* representing the Past, the Meal equalling the Present, and *Hallel* the Future — the concepts they embody are all included and compacted within the realm of *Kadeish*, wherein all time is unified and enveloped in *kedushah*. Based on the above, we can construct the following diagram:

DIAGRAM 6

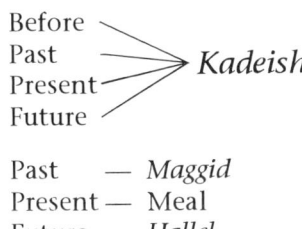

Past   —   *Maggid*
Present —   Meal
Future   —   *Hallel*

On the night of the anniversary of our freedom from Egypt we relive the moment of freedom, becoming attached to our Purpose, Past, Present, and Future. Thus we are freed from the shackles of our everyday Egypt — the *meitzarim*, the confines and restrictions of this world² — gaining a new beginning. In stark contrast to the freedom engendered by the Exodus, the Jewish people in Egypt were trapped within the physical dimensions of time and space. Indeed, all their time was subservient to Pharaoh, as it says: "Let the service be hard upon the men, that they may la-

---

1. See *Targum Yonasan*, Shemos 19:14.
2. "Mitzrayim," the Hebrew word for Egypt, is related to the word "*meitzarim*" (restrictions). Egypt was the place where the Jews were subjected to restriction and limitation (*Michtav MeEliyahu*, vol. 2, p. 17).

bour therein, and let them not speak vain words."[1] Pharaoh said further: "You are idle, you are idle; therefore you say, 'Let us go and sacrifice to our God.' "[2] Thereafter Pharaoh did not even give the Jews any time to think.[3]

In addition to having all their time enslaved by Pharaoh, the Jews were trapped within the confines of space — a country from which no slave had ever escaped.[4]

Their only deliverance from these all-encompassing *meitzarim* lay in the realm of the miraculous. They had to attach themselves to the dimension which is Above that which is physical. Even though time is invisible and intangible, it is still a physical creation.[5] Their escape and extrication from the physical restriction of time, the most intangible facet of physicality, could be achieved only by uniting themselves with the realm of matzah, which is not within the constraints of time. This is the meaning of what we say in the Haggadah, "This matzah that we eat — for what reason? Because the dough of our fathers *did not have time to rise* before the King of kings, the Holy One, blessed be He, revealed Himself to them and redeemed them." Matzah represents the idea of rising to the dimension Above the forces of the physical world — the forces which cause dough to become *chametz* — in order to achieve true freedom.

We also had to attach ourselves to the *korban pesach*, which represents God rising Above *place*, as we say, "The *pesach* offering that our fathers ate at the time the Holy Temple stood — for what reason? Because the Holy One, blessed be He, passed over the houses of our fathers in Egypt": He rose Above the restrictions of place, i.e., He sought out the Egyptian houses with unsurpassed precision and passed over our houses, leaving us unharmed.

---

1. Shemos 5:9.
2. Ibid., 17.
3. See *Mesilas Yesharim*, ch. 2.
4. See *Rashi*, Shemos 18:9, and *Siach Yitzchak* on "*Emes V'Yatziv*."
5. *Seforno*, Bereishis 1:1.

The Seder Night: Rising Above Time and Space

We thus attached ourselves to the realms Above time and place in order to rise Above these two dimensions and ensure our freedom.

Let us look into this matter a little further. We are told: "The children of Israel journeyed from Raamses to Sukkos, about six hundred thousand on foot, adult males, besides little ones. A mixed multitude also went up with them and flocks and herds, even very much cattle."[1] Rashi explains that from Raamses to Sukkos there was a distance of 120 *mil*, and yet they reached there *in one moment*, as it says, "...and I carried you on eagles' wings."[2] Rashi further tells us that it was not just a small band of people who managed to span this vast distance in such miraculous time. There were hundreds of thousands of men (six hundred thousand men above the age of twenty alone), a similar number of women, and all of their children, together with the mixed multitude and many sheep and cattle, all of whom rose Above *place* in *no time*.

Concerning the night of the Exodus we are told: "You have seen that which I have done to Egypt, and I carried you on eagles' wings and brought you to Me."[3] *Targum Yonasan* explains, "You have seen what I did to the Egyptians and how I carried you on clouds as though on eagles' wings from Raamses and brought you to the place of the Holy Temple to sacrifice the Passover offering *and on that same night I returned you to Raamses*, and from there I brought you near to the learning of My Torah." Thus we are told how on that very night God took us Above *time* and thereby Above the constraints of *place* in a most miraculous way.

The above-mentioned verse states: ואבא אתכם אלי, "And I brought you to Me." The Baal HaTurim explains that the word ואבא has the numerical value of ten. This is quite significant, for

---

1. Shemos 12:37–38.
2. Ibid. 19:4.
3. Ibid.

the numerical equivalent of the letter *yud* is also ten. Additionally, the *yud* of the Tetragrammaton does not extend downwards as much as the other letters do. It therefore represents the dimension of Above. This indicates that the Jewish people became connected to this dimension Above time and place at the Exodus from Egypt when God brought them out.

Every year at the Seder we reattach ourselves to this dimension, when we unify the stages of Past, Present, and Future, and thus become attached to the realm Above time. In turn, we are provided with the opportunity to attach ourselves to the realm Above the confinement of place and the material world. Thus it is that *Kadeish* unifies the subsequent stages of Past, Present, and Future and thereby "renews" the Exodus.

ON THE WINGS OF EAGLES

Let us look a little further into the "eagles' wings" representing the dimension of Above. The prophet Yechezkel describes a prophetic vision in which he saw four angelic beings with facial features that resembled those of four creatures on this earth. We are told, "The forms of their faces were the face of a man, the face of a lion...the face of an ox...and the face of an eagle..."[1] The Abarbanel[2] says:

> These forms that Yechezkel ascribes to the angels reflect their functions in their service to the Creator when He sends them to carry out His will in the lower world.
>
> Sometimes He sends an angel to inspire the prophets and place His word in their mouths, or to impart the spirit of wisdom and discernment in the wise ones. This role is represented by the face of a

---

1. Yechezkel 1:10.
2. On Yechezkel 1:9, *BaDerech HaSheini*.

human, for humans have the ability to understand and prophesy more than any other creature.

Sometimes He sends His angels to perform mighty acts and judgements against His enemies, like the angels who went to overturn Sedom, and the angel of God who went out and smote the camp of the king of Assyria — 185,000 men — in one night. Coinciding with this function, Yechezkel saw the face of a lion, which is the greatest ravager among the flocks of sheep — and who can tell him [the lion] what to do?

Sometimes God sends His angels to perform good and to grant success and to bless His servants in all that they set their hands to do...and this role was alluded to by the face of an ox, for the ox brings blessing to the house and causes success with the harvest.

Sometimes God sends His angels to save His servants from distress and to lead them upon the way so that they will not stumble...and to hint at this function Yechezkel saw among them [an angel with] the face of an eagle, who [through the command of his Creator] is, "As an eagle stirs its nest, over its young it hovers; it spreads its wings, takes them, bears them on its pinions."[1]

The Eagle

We have seen that the eagle has an association with the letter *yud* and that it is associated with rising Above. In fact, the eagle flies Above all other birds, as Rashi explains on the verse, "You have seen that which I have done to Egypt, and I carried you *on*

---

1. Devarim 32:11.

eagles' wings and brought you to Me."[1] Hence, the eagle alludes to the dimension that is Above the influence of the angels, stars, and constellations,[2] and thus to *Kadeish* of the Seder and the first *parshah* of tefillin, which deal with the realm Above and are directly associated with Hashem.[3]

Furthermore, the eagle hints at renewal and a fresh Start, as the verse says, "Your youth will be renewed like the eagle."[4] Rashi explains, "This means you will be as the eagle, who annually renews its feathers."[5] This also parallels the first *parshah* of the tefillin, in which the word "*chodesh*" — referring to the renewal of the month and the situation of the Jewish people — is stressed.

The Lion

We have seen from the Abarbanel that the lion reflects the role of an angel performing mighty acts and judgements against the Almighty's enemies. This corresponds to the second stage of the Haggadah and to the second *parshah* of the tefillin, in which we are told that God punished the wicked Egyptians.

The Man

Man is the one who fuses heaven and earth, by elevating the physical into something spiritual through his Torah observance. The heavenly image of man thus hints at the third stage of the Seder — the Meal — wherein we Link Above with Below, uniting our physical food and the act of eating with the spiritual. It also parallels *Shema*, the third *parshah* of the tefillin, which emphasises our maintaining a daily Link between heaven and earth

---

1. Shemos 19:4; see also *Rashi*, Devarim 32:11.
2. *Rabbeinu Bachya*, Devarim 32:11.
3. See Rabbi S. R. Hirsch's commentary on *parshas Terumah*, p. 488, where he mentions that the eagle represents the Godly, the dimension Above the level of *adam* of the *Merkavah*.
4. Tehillim 103:5.
5. See also Yeshayahu 40:31.

through the mitzvos mentioned therein. Man being representative of the Link between heaven and earth is shown by Yaakov Avinu, our third forefather, whose facial image is etched on God's Throne of Glory.[1] It is for this reason that he saw in his epic vision[2] a ladder that stretched from earth heavenward, showing that Torah and mitzvos are the ladder whereby man Links earth with heaven. This is why סלם, the Hebrew word for "ladder," adds up to the same numerical equivalence as סיני,[3] because the acceptance of Torah on Mount Sinai established that ladder for the Jewish nation, whereby they could climb and Link themselves to Above.

The Ox

The Abarbanel said that the ox "brings blessing to the house and causes success with the harvest." This hints at the fourth *parshah* of tefillin, which deals with success in the material world and with the harvest. The fourth stage of the Seder represents the Future perfection of this Lowest world wherein only prosperity and success will reign even in the material realm.

RISING ABOVE TIME AND SPACE: THE SEDER AND TEFILLIN

In the first *parshah* of tefillin, *Kadesh*, it says, "And Moshe said to the people [*ha'am*], 'Remember this day you left Egypt...' " We are told[4] that whenever the term "*ha'am*" is used to describe the community being addressed, it refers to the masses, including those on a lower spiritual level. The employment of the term here indicates that even the lowliest of the people can become attached to the highest degree of *kedushah* through the mitzvos mentioned

---

1. *Bereishis Rabbah* 68:12; *Rabbeinu Bachya*, Bereishis 28:13.
2. See Bereishis 28:12–15.
3. *Bereishis Rabbah* 68:12.
4. *Sifri* and *Rashi*, Bamidbar 11:1.

in *Kadesh*. Whoever performs them can become attached to the level of Above, no matter what level he was on previously. Even they can wear tefillin, which contain this concept of Above, and become attached to the highest level of spirituality (provided he has the correct intentions).[1]

The *parshah* continues with the mitzvah of not eating *chametz*. The difference between *chametz* and matzah is a difference of time. *Chametz* is allowed to ferment and rise as long as desired. It is thus within the dimension of time. Matzah, however, may not be left to rise; it may not be allowed to become subject to the effects of time, and therefore it is Above time.

Consequently we understand why matzah takes the place of *chametz* only on Pesach. We rose Above the time zone on Pesach because of the miracles we experienced. Therefore, every Pesach, on the anniversary of our rising Above time, we refrain from that which is within the constraints of time. Thus we have matzah, which puts us on the plane Above time.

The next verse in the *parshah* is "Today you are coming out in the spring month of Aviv." Rashi explains that God timed the Exodus to take place in the month of Aviv, for that month is neither too hot, too cold, nor too wet. God's Divine providence from Above regulated the situation so that it would be just right for us.

God's providence is reflected in the very name of the month, "Aviv," which is related to the word "*av*" (father). Just as a father watches over his son, God watched over us and took us out of Egypt with miracles Above the normal course of nature. We thus rose Above the zodiac sign that is operative during the month of Aviv — Aries — the representative of the Egyptian god, the sheep.

---

1. See *Tefillin: The Inside Story*, p. 32, n. 1.

Therefore the next verse says, "When God brings you into the land of the Canaanites, Hittites, Emorites, Chivites, and Yevusites...a land flowing with milk and honey, you shall perform this service in this month." One explanation is that "this service" refers to the *pesach* offering, the slaughter of the paschal lamb. We are told to do "this service" in the land of the five nations, which flows "with milk and honey," in order to free ourselves from the negative aspect of milk and honey — desires and pleasures for their own sake. We rise Above that danger by doing "this service" every year on the anniversary of our freedom.

The next verses tell us, "Seven days you shall eat matzos, and on the seventh day there shall be a festival to Hashem...and no *chametz* belonging to you shall be seen, nor shall leaven belonging to you be seen in all your borders." We must eat matzos and refrain from seeing *chametz* so that we can become attached to the dimension of true freedom, which is Above the time zone (as matzos are). In this way we bind ourselves to the level of the miracles of the Exodus.

During the rest of the year we maintain our connection to this dimension by wearing tefillin, which also contain the commandment, "On the seventh day there shall be a festival to Hashem." The seventh day of Passover is the day God split the Sea of Reeds to save the Jews from Pharaoh's army. This is another example of Divine guidance that is Above the normal course of nature. We attach ourselves to this on a daily basis by donning the tefillin, which contain these words.

The *parshah* continues, "And you shall tell your son on that day, saying, 'It is because of this that God did for me when I left Egypt.' " In the Haggadah we read:

> "And you shall tell your son on that day..." — one might think that this obligation [of telling one's son] begins from the first of the month... It [the verse]

therefore comes to teach "because of this," meaning that the obligation [of telling one's son] is only when the Passover sacrifice, matzah, and *marror* are lying before you.[1]

We read further in the Haggadah:

Rabban Gamliel says, "Anyone who has not said these three things on Passover night has not fulfilled his duty. They are *pesach,* matzah, and *marror."*

Commenting on these three principal foods of the Seder night, the Shlah explains that they hint at the dimensions of was, is, and will be. Says the Shlah:

Pesach [the Passover sacrifice] alludes to the Past, in that God preceded everything, and all other gods are as nothing before Him. The Passover sacrifice alludes to the downfall of the god and archangel of Egypt, which was considered the highest of all the archangels of the nations... It follows, therefore, that all the gods of the other nations were also subdued, and it then became known that there is a Cause of all causes, Who preceded all, Who is without measure, and Who brought all into existence. This is the concept of *was.*

Matzah alludes to the Present, hinting at the Almighty's ever-present Providence... Matzah is simple bread which contains nothing but flour and water. So is God's watching over His people plain... The seeming changes are only according to the perception of those who receive it, but from His side it is unchanging and perfect unity... This is the secret of

---

1. See *Shibolei HaLeket* and *Rashi* on the verse, which explain that "because of this" encompasses all three foods of the Seder night and not only matzah and *marror.*

the flour and water, which are plain elements and allude to simplicity and unity.

Marror alludes to the Future. The Tola'as Yaakov writes that the [preferred type of] *marror* is called *chassah*.[1] The word חסה literally means "compassion." Therefore, *chassah* represents the fusion of bitterness and compassion. This is an allusion to the Future, when bitterness will be shown to have been part and parcel of God's compassion.

(Shnei Luchos HaBris, masseches Pesachim, derush shishi)

As the Shlah comments, the Passover sacrifice represents the Past. However, according to his explanation, it is not simply the Past; it is the dimension of Before. As he said, the Passover sacrifice shows that God *preceded* everything and that He is the primary Cause. Therefore this is the dimension that existed Before the Past of physical time. It also shows that God is Above all the other forces, all the gods and archangels. Following the Passover sacrifice is matzah, which represents God's connection to us in the Present, and then *marror*, which hints at the Future.

We have still not seen which factor in the Seder represents the Past, which exists within the physical dimension. This is because until now we have only discussed the mitzvos of the Seder which relate to food. In truth, the Seder has one more mitzvah: the mitzvah of *sippur*, the telling of our Past — that which befell the Jewish nation in times gone by. Thus the mitzvah of *sippur* represents the Past that is within the physical dimension of time. Accordingly, we see that the four dimensions of time are alluded to in the four mitzvos of the Seder night.

When the Torah says והגדת לבנך, "And you shall tell your son," referring to the mitzvah of *haggadah* (הגדה) — the relating of the Past — it says that we should do so only "when the Passover sacrifice, matzah, and *marror* are lying before you," i.e., only

---

1. *Pesachim* 39a.

when those things which represent Before, Present, and Future are in front of you. By doing so, we are telling the son that because of the unification of all these dimensions of time into the level of timelessness, God took us out of Egypt.

The next verse in the *parshah* tells us, "And it shall be for you as a sign on your arm and for a remembrance between your eyes, so that God's Torah shall be in your mouth, because with a strong hand God brought you out of Egypt." What does "it shall be" refer to? It refers to the concept of being Above time. This lesson of being Above "shall be a sign." For what purpose? So that the Torah shall always be on your lips. The tefillin are able to lift us Above and to put the Torah, which is Above, into us. "Above" means *kedushah*, and Torah has the greatest *kedushah* of anything in existence, as we see in the *Zohar*: "We have learned that the sanctity of Torah rises Above all other *kedushos*."[1]

In *Nefesh HaChaim* it is written:[2]

> The holiness of the Torah is Above that of the other mitzvos. It elevates the one who learns it, as the Mishnah tells us, "Rabbi Meir said, 'Whoever learns Torah for its own sake merits many things... It moves him away from sin, draws him near to merit...makes him great, *and elevates him Above all things.*' "[3]

The *Nefesh HaChaim* explains that this is so because the heavenly source of Torah rises Above all the other spiritual worlds, and therefore anyone adhering to Torah will rise Above all else. This is why the verse "in order that Hashem's Torah shall be in your mouth" appears in the *parshah* of Above — *Kadesh*.

Thus we are told to tell the son: "And it shall be for you as a sign on your arm and for a remembrance between your eyes, so

---

1. *Kedoshim* 81a.
2. 4:30, 31, 32.
3. *Avos* 6:1–2.

that God's Torah shall be in your mouth, because with a strong hand God brought you out of Egypt." The message we must convey is, "Wear tefillin and learn Torah, and you will become elevated."

Another allusion to tefillin raising one Above time is in the verse, "And all the nations of the earth shall see that God's name [Y-k-v-k] is called upon you, and they will be afraid of you."[1] Comments the Gemara, "Rabbi Eliezer the Elder said, 'This refers to the head tefillin.' "[2]

The above-mentioned verse means that since you are attached to the dimension Above earthliness (ארציות), all the people of the *earth* (עמי הארץ) — those attached to the lowly earth — will see that the name Y-k-v-k is upon you, and they will fear you. They will fear you because the name of Y-k-v-k — which means the unity of was, is, and will be (היה הוה ויהיה), and is therefore Above physicality — is upon you. The tefillin thus assist us to rise Above the earthliness of Egypt.

AVRAHAM RISING ABOVE TIME AND PLACE ON SEDER NIGHT

We have seen previously that through the letter *yud* the name Y-k-v-k combines Past, Present, and Future into a unified point Above time. We have also seen[3] that the letter *yud* has the numerical value of ten, which represents the dimension which is Above place and time, and that the power to rise Above time and space that is invested in the *yud* manifests itself on Pesach. In truth, however, the potential to rise Above on this night existed even before the Exodus actually took place. We see this in the story of Avraham's battle with the four kings who vanquished

---

1. Devarim 28:10.
2. *Megillah* 16b.
3. Page 82.

the five kings.[1]

The four kings captured Avraham's nephew Lot. Avraham subsequently went out to battle against them to rescue him. We are told, "When Avram heard that his nephew was taken captive, he armed his trained servants, born in his own house, 318, and pursued them [the captors] to Dan."[2] This happened on the night of the fifteenth Nissan (Seder night).[3] We are then told: "And the night was divided for them, he and his servants, and he smote them, and pursued them to Chovah, which is on the left of Damascus."[4] This was a miraculous battle that was won at midnight.[5]

In his commentary on this episode, the Ramban quotes the words of Chazal, who note that it is well known that there is a distance of many days between Eilonei Mamrei, where Avraham lived, and Damascus, which is outside the Land of Israel. Therefore, it is obvious that only a great miracle enabled Avraham to cover such a great distance in half a night.[6] Thus Avraham managed to break the barriers of time and space on the night of Pesach, as his descendants would many years later in Egypt.

In fact, Avraham's victory poses even more significance for us. Avraham miraculously conquered four mighty kings who had conquered five kings, to become the victorious tenth king.[7] He thereby showed that God is the *Supreme* King. Avraham's being the *tenth* king hints at his association with the domain *Above*

---

1. See Bereishis 14:14–24.
2. Ibid., 14.
3. See Rashi and other *midrashim*.
4. Bereishis 14:15.
5. *Bereishis Rabbah* 43:3 and commentaries of *Rashi* and *Yedei Moshe* there.
6. See also *Yalkut Shimoni* 448 on Yeshayahu, ch. 41, concerning this feat achieved in miraculous time. In addition, we refer to Avraham's miraculous victory at the end of the Passover Haggadah, in the liturgy ויהי בחצי הלילה (It came to pass at midnight), in which we say, "To the righteous convert [Avraham] You gave victory when the night was divided for him."
7. See *Rashi*, Bereishis 14:17.

time and space and his attachment to God, Who leads His world from Above. This is exactly what occurred many generations later on the same night, when the number ten (the tenth plague, in which the firstborns were slain) proved to the Egyptians that God is King (and not Pharaoh) over the physical dimensions of time and space.

There is yet another connection between Avraham and the number ten. After Avraham's victory, he gave a tenth of his possessions to Malki Tzedek the priest.[1] The king of Sedom then offered Avraham the spoils of the conquest, but Avraham refused and said, "I will take nothing from you so that you will not say, 'I made Avraham wealthy.' "[2] Avraham knew that the secret to wealth (עושר) is *ma'aser* (מעשר), giving a tenth of one's wealth as tithes.[3] This also happened on the first day of Pesach.

Some time later, Avraham was told that he would beget a child, even though he was ninety-nine years old and time was against him. He was given this remarkable news on Pesach,[4] the festival that attaches one to the dimension Above time. He was told that next year at this same time Sarah would bear a child.[5] Thus the news and the birth were both on Pesach. Once again, Avraham was associated with the level Above the dimension of time on Pesach, the festival that attaches us to this realm.

---

1. See Bereishis 14:20.
2. Ibid., 23.
3. As our rabbis tell us (*Ta'anis* 9a), if someone wants to become wealthy he should give away a tenth of his earnings to tithes, as the verse says, עשר תעשר את כל תבואת זרעך (Devarim 14:22) — עשר, "take tithes," בשביל שתתעשר, "in order to become rich." Thus wealth starts by clinging to the realm of ten, the dimension of the *yud*.
4. *Rashi*, Bereishis 18:10.
5. Ibid.

The Seder from Above to Below

There are four levels from Above to Below that can be traced in the Seder: Above, Higher, Link, and Lowest. We have already discussed the level of Above. This is the level represented by *Kadeish*. Higher (a level that is lower than Above) shows Divine providence, in which God saves His people and destroys their enemies. This is the level represented by *Maggid*. The next level is Link, in which *kedushah* is brought down into the physical realm. This is represented by the Meal and the blessing. In this stage, Above and Below become Linked. We consume food in the service of God and make blessings after eating it, thus Linking the material world — the food — to a higher dimension.

Birkas HaMazon, the blessings after the meal, cause a blessing to enter the food we have on the table at the time.[1] Our rabbis therefore say that one should have some bread on the table at the time of reciting the blessings after the meal, so that the blessing

---

1. As mentioned previously, p. 57.

can enter the bread, for a blessing cannot enter an empty vessel.[1] That is, a blessing is spiritual energy that is released from the Source of blessings Himself and must enter some substance that serves to hold it. Just like a soul cannot exist on this earth without a body, a blessing cannot settle unless it has a "body" that it can enter.

A blessing is the fusion of the *two* dimensions of *upper* and *lower*. Therefore, the Hebrew root letters of the word "blessing" are ברך — letters whose numerical value are all based on the number two: ב = 2, ר = 200, ך = 20.[2]

We can now understand in a deeper sense the verse in *Toldos* where Eisav exclaims: "For he has outwitted me these two times; he took my birthright, and behold now he has taken my blessing."[3] He exclaims that Yaakov outwitted him twice by taking בכרתי, "my birthright," and also ברכתי, "my blessing." Both words contain the root letters representing the number two, in hundreds, tens, and units.

The reason for this equivalency is that both "birthright" and "blessing" embody the concept of double, for they both have the characteristic of fusing the *upper* and the *lower*. Yaakov and Eisav made a pact that Eisav would take this world as his portion, and Yaakov would take the World to Come as his.[4] However, Eisav lost this world to Yaakov, for a person who lives in this world for the sake of this world alone loses it to the person who lives for the sake of the World to Come. This is because the latter gets the gifts of this world in order to facilitate his endeavours to gain the World to Come. Therefore Yaakov ultimately gained the material

---

1. *Zohar, Lech Lecha* 88a.
2. See *Ba'al HaTurim* (on Devarim 21:17) on the word בכר (firstborn), where he explains that since the letters בכר symbolise the number two, in units, tens, and hundreds (2, 20, 200), it is an allusion to the fact that the firstborn receives a double portion for his birthright.
3. Bereishis 27:36.
4. *Yalkut Shimoni* 111.

blessing[1] that was seemingly destined for Eisav.

The blessings after the meal, which are referred to in the Seder as *Bareich*, the letters of which are based on the number two in the *alef-beis*, also cause the fusion of the upper and the lower, as they cause a blessing to descend from Above to Below.[2]

Finally, there is the level of Lowest, in which the evil that is incorporated in this Lowest world is changed into good. This level is represented by *Hallel*, wherein it talks of how the Jews will be delivered from their Past troubles and from the exile, wherein "the stone that the builders rejected [and brought low] has become the cornerstone."[3]

---

1. See Bereishis 27:28–29.
2. This corresponds to what we have seen (p. 70) that the *vav* represents the raining down of "bread from heaven," i.e., the connection between the *upper* and the *lower* — the Link. The *vav* of the Tetragrammaton thus corresponds to this stage, which is the fusion of the upper and the lower.
3. Tehillim 118:22.

From Above to Below: A More Detailed Look

The four sections of the Haggadah also extend from Above to Below in relation to *chomer* (physicality), as do the four sections of tefillin.[1]

THE FIRST SECTION

Kadeish

Kedushah, which is a spiritual concept, is Above physicality.

THE SECOND SECTION

Urchatz

The second section of the Haggadah begins with washing, cleansing one of the impurities of *chomer*.[2]

---

1. See *Tefillin: The Inside Story*, p. 152.
2. It would seem that the logical order of the Seder would be to first remove negativity through washing, and only then rise to *kedushah*, as it says,

Karpas

Karpas, the letters of which can be transposed to read פרך ס', is dipped into salt water to remind us of the ס' — the 600,000 who experienced עבודת פרך, "back-breaking work,"[1] which broke the *chomer* (the bodies) of the Jewish nation.

Yachatz

We break the matzah, also synonymous with breaking the physical *chomer*.

Maggid

In this stage, we tell of our servitude and of the downfall of Egypt — the breaking of their *chomer* and the resultant departure of the Jewish nation from Egypt.

All this parallels the second *parshah* of the tefillin, wherein the Egyptians are crushed and the Jewish people go free.

THE THIRD SECTION

At this level we are no longer concerned with the breaking of negative *chomer*. Rather, we turn toward its utilisation for *kedushah*, in other words, with taking physicality and uniting it with the spiritual, thus making it subservient to God.[2] The stages

---

"Turn from evil," and then "Do good" (Tehillim 34:15). Why, then, does *Kadeish* precede *Urchatz*? The answer is that the Seder night does not necessarily follow the logical order, as God lowered Himself to us from Above at the Exodus, which transpired on this night, even though we were still on a very low level. Thus, the imperative of this night is the attainment of *kedushah* from Above even though we have not yet prepared ourselves fully from Below (see p. 195). Consequently, we first rise Above the *chomer* with *Kadeish*, and only then do we approach the *chomer* and cleanse it with *Urchatz* — a lower level.

1. *Mishnah Berurah* 473:19.
2. This parallels the *parshah* of *Shema* (see *Tefillin: The Inside Story*, p. 149).

of *Rochtzah, Motzi, Matzah, Marror, Koreich, Shulchan Oreich, Tzafun,* and *Bareich* all relate to this theme.

Rochtzah

This is the second washing of the Seder. The first washing, preparatory to *Karpas*, was the cleansing of the negativity of *chomer*. The second washing, however, causes the *kiddush* (sanctification) of the *chomer*, Linking it with Above. In accordance with this, the blessing we say prior to this second washing includes the words, "Who has made us *holy* by His commandments," because through this washing we sanctify ourselves.

Motzi, Matzah

At this stage we say the blessings on the matzah, elevating it and utilising the *chomer* for a mitzvah.

Marror, Koreich

Whereas matzah is the semblance of the good inclination and pure good, *marror* symbolises the bitterness resulting from evil. We sandwich these two opposites and thereby Link them. This parallels the *parshah* of *Shema*, wherein we see the Link of negativity with good.[1]

Shulchan Oreich

The table, as we have seen, is the place where, through our eating, the spirituality of Above and the physicality of Below fuse and Link. The soul from Above and the body from Below thereby maintain their Link with one another.[2]

Rabbi Chaim of Volozhin teaches[3] that someone who eats

---

1. See *Tefillin: The Inside Story*, pp. 217–218.
2. See also p. 266 and *Tefillin: The Inside Story*, p. 415, concerning the Shulchan in the Mishkan being a Link between the upper and the Lower.
3. *Ruach Chaim* 3:3.

with the proper intent, i.e., to sustain his body and soul for the service of Hashem, and who says the correct *berachah* and learns Torah while he eats, is actually identical to one who brings a sacrifice. This is because just as the *korbanos* are the food of the universe, Linking Above and Below, so does food generate and maintain the Link between body and soul and between Above and Below. For this reason our rabbis say[1] that whereas in the past the altar atoned for a person, now it is his table that atones for him. Thus, the meal in the third section of the Seder generates the Link between Above and Below.

Tzafun

The *afikoman* we eat is called *Tzafun* (צפון) and parallels the showbreads of the Table in the Mishkan, which represent the dimension of Link and which were on the north side (צפון) of the Beis HaMikdash.[2] Again, we see the Link of physical bread (*chomer*) to the service of Hashem.

Bareich

As mentioned, blessings, and especially the blessings after the meal, are the fusion and Linkage of both the spiritual and the physical.[3]

THE FOURTH SECTION

Hallel, Nirtzah

Hallel and *Nirtzah* symbolise the Future, when the *chomer* of the Lowest world will be cleansed and transformed to good universally, and bad will exist no more.

---

1. *Berachos* 55a.
2. See pp. 53–54.
3. See also pp. 57, 95–96.

The Four Expressions of Redemption

There are four expressions of redemption mentioned in connection with the Exodus from Egypt. These four expressions follow the order from Below to Above.[1] God says to Moshe Rabbeinu:

> Therefore say to the children of Israel, "I am Hashem, and *I will bring you* out from under the burdens of Egypt, and *I will deliver you* from their service, and *I will redeem you* with an outstretched arm and with great judgements. And *I will take you* to Me for a people, and I will be to you as a God, and You shall

---

1. The order of the four levels are sometimes portrayed as from Above to Below, and at other times as from Below to Above. This all depends on the perspective from which we are looking. From God's viewpoint, the sequence is always from Above to Below, for He showers His influence from Above to us down Below. However, when we are elevated or we strive to climb upwards and reach the Almighty, we do so from Below to Above; hence the reverse direction. When God redeemed us from Egypt, we were elevated from the Lowest to the Highest level.

know that I am Hashem your God, Who brings you out from under the burdens of Egypt."

(Shemos 6:6–7)

Our rabbis tell us[1] that the four cups of the Seder night correspond to these four expressions of redemption. The levels of these four expressions also coincide with the four *parshiyos* of the tefillin.

Let us see how the four expressions follow the order from Below to Above.

THE FIRST EXPRESSION

The first expression is "I will bring you out *from under* the burdens of Egypt." This is the *Lowest* level of redemption — from under the physical burdens of Egypt. It corresponds to the last *parshah* of the tefillin — *Vehayah Im Shamoa* — which deals with our involvement in this Lowest world.

THE SECOND EXPRESSION

The next level of redemption is "And I will deliver you from their service." This is the next stage up and corresponds to the third *parshah* of the tefillin — *Shema*. It does not say here "from under," as this stage is a higher level. However, it is still a salvation from the negative aspect of "their service," similar to the previous level, where it mentions "the burdens of Egypt." Hence, these two lower stages are merely a release from the negative. In contrast, the next two stages are the positive and higher aspects of redemption.

---

1. *Bereishis Rabbah* 88:5.

THE THIRD EXPRESSION

The third expression is "And I will redeem you with an outstretched arm and with great judgements." This expression has a twofold message. The words "with an outstretched arm" refer to taking the Jewish people out of Egypt, whereas "and with great judgements" refers to the destruction of the Egyptians.[1] This parallels the second *parshah* of the tefillin — Vehayah Ki Yeviacha — which deals with the destruction of the Egyptian empire, on the one hand, and with the emergence of the Jewish nation in their stead on the other.

THE FOURTH EXPRESSION

We now come to the fourth and Highest level of redemption: "And I will take you *to Me* for a people..."

This is the only time in these four levels of redemption in which לי, "to Me" — that is, reaching God — is mentioned.

This parallels the first *parshah* of the tefillin — Kadesh — which hints at the level of Above, where the word לי, "to Me," is also stressed: "Sanctify *to Me* every firstborn...both of man and of beast, it is *Mine*."[2]

These four levels also parallel the four levels of the Tetragrammaton.[3] It is for this reason that the four expressions of redemption are prefaced in the Torah with the words "Therefore say to the children of Israel, I am *Y-k-v-k*."[4] God is in effect saying that with this four-lettered name, which represents the four above-mentioned levels, He will prompt the four stages of redemption.

---

1. *Malbim*.
2. Shemos 13:2.
3. See pp. 65 and 82 and *Tefillin: The Inside Story*, pp. 214–225.
4. Shemos 6:6.

THE FOUR EXPRESSIONS AND THE FOUR STAGES OF THE SEDER

The final expression of redemption — ולקחתי, "And I will take" — is the *highest* level of redemption and therefore corresponds to the highest of the four stages of the Seder — *Kadeish*.

The next level down is וגאלתי, "And I will redeem," in which it says: "And I will redeem you with an outstretched arm and with great judgements." This deals with both the destruction of the Egyptians and the salvation of the Jewish nation. This corresponds to *Maggid*, which also deals with the destruction of the Egyptians and the salvation of the Jewish nation.

The next level down is והצלתי, "And I will deliver you from their service" — from the negative aspect of physicality. This corresponds to the Meal, where we utilise the physical in the service of God.

Finally, there is the Lowest level of redemption — והוצאתי, "and I will bring you out *from under* the burdens of Egypt." This corresponds to the fourth stage of the Seder, where the Lowest are elevated. Thus it says in *Hallel*, "The stone which the builders rejected has become the cornerstone" — the Lowest is elevated and becomes the Highest.

We therefore have the following:

DIAGRAM 7

Two Upper Levels — Positive Aspects of Redemption
"And I will take" (ולקחתי)   Above   First cup   *Kadeish*
"And I will redeem" (וגאלתי)   Higher   Second cup   *Maggid*

Two Lower Levels — Release from Negative
"And I will deliver" (והצלתי)   Link   Third cup   Meal
"And I will bring out" (והוצאתי)   Below   Fourth cup   *Hallel*

One may ask, Why do the levels of the Seder commence with the cup of *Kadeish* — the level of Above — and then descend downwards; shouldn't they follow the order of the expressions of redemption as mentioned in the Torah, ascending from Below upwards? Don't the expressions of redemption progress from והוצאתי, "and I will bring out," the Lowest; to והצלתי, "and I will deliver," the Link; and then to וגאלתי, "and I will redeem," the next level up, Higher; and finally to ולקחתי, "and I will take," the level Above. Why does the Seder advance in reverse — from the Highest level to the Lowest level? Furthermore, how can we logically commence from the highest level without first climbing step by step through the lower levels in order to reach it?

The answer is that the Seder night is an exception, for on it we experience what is called אתערותא דלעילא, "an arousal from Above." This means that God gives us a special *kedushah* from Above, which in turn raises us Above, without us having to first go through the Lower levels.[1]

---

1. See *Pri Eitz Chaim*, "*Chag HaMatzos*," ch. 1 and 2; see also *Chesed L'Avraham, Ma'ayan Sheini, Nahar* 56; *Sefas Emes* in *likutim* of *parshas Tzav, Chodesh Nissan*; *Haggadas Chodesh HaAviv*, p. 53.

Tzitzis from Below to Above

The four-tiered progression from Below to Above is apparent with the mitzvah of *tzitzis* as well: We are told:

> And it shall be for you as *tzitzis*, and you shall see and remember all the commandments of Hashem and perform them, and do not venture after your heart and after your eyes after which you go astray. So that you remember and perform all My commandments, and you shall be holy to your God.
>
> (Bamidbar 15:39–40)

The levels advance in ascending order from Below to Above:

DIAGRAM 8

    4. "...and you shall be holy to your God."
   3. "So that you remember and perform all My commandments..."
  2. "...and after your eyes, after which you go astray."
 1. "Do not venture after your heart..."

As with the four expressions of redemption, *tzitzis* also have two upper positive levels and two lower levels which negate the negative.

DIAGRAM 9

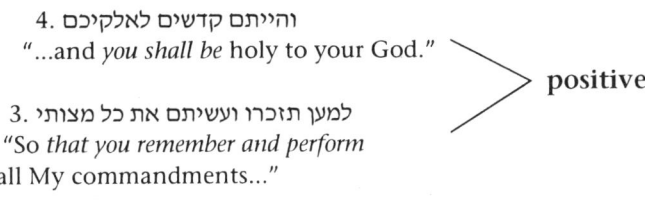

4. והייתם קדשים לאלקיכם
"...and *you shall be* holy to your God."

3. למען תזכרו ועשיתם את כל מצותי
"*So that you remember and perform* all My commandments..."

positive

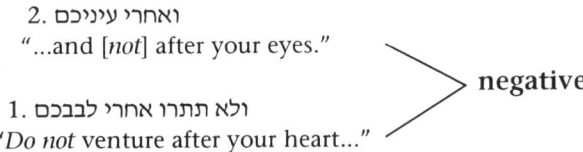

2. ואחרי עיניכם
"...and [*not*] after your eyes."

1. ולא תתרו אחרי לבבכם
"*Do not* venture after your heart..."

negative

We see that the first and second level are the distancing and detachment of oneself from the negative — the departure and separation from evil. The next two upper levels then initiate positivity.[1]

In fact, there is a direct connection between the four expressions of redemption and the mitzvah of *tzitzis*. Our rabbis tell us:

> The *tzitzis* are to be placed על כנפי בגדיהם, "on the corners [literally, 'wings'] of their garments," alluding to [God having delivered them from Egypt, as it states] ואשא אתכם על כנפי נשרים, "And I carried you on eagles' wings."[2] [Furthermore,] the *tzitzis* are to be placed on a garment having four corners...*alluding to the four different expressions of redemption* which are said concerning the going out from Egypt...
>
> (Rashi, Bamidbar 15:41)

---

1. Here also the most elevated level is *kedushah* as it says, "...and you shall be *holy* to your God." This parallels the most elevated level of the Seder and the tefillin.
2. Shemos 19:4.

Consequently, the *tzitzis* on the four corners are directly connected to the four expressions of redemption. Therefore, it is not surprising that the *tzitzis* have such a profound effect on an individual. Indeed, the *tzitzis* function to take the one who wears them out of his own personal Mitzrayim — the *meitzarim* of temptation and desire.[1]

We are therefore told at the end of the *parshah* of *tzitzis*: "I am Hashem your God, Who took you out from the land of Egypt..."[2] Rashi asks, "Why is the Exodus from Egypt mentioned in connection with the *tzitzis*?" — in other words, what does the Exodus have to do with the mitzvah of *tzitzis*? According to what we have seen above, we can say that the *tzitzis* represent an extension of the Exodus. God therefore tells us here, "*I am Hashem your God*, Who took you out from the land of Egypt, to be for you as a God; *I am Hashem your God*."[3] The double expression of "I am Hashem your God" is telling us, "I am Hashem your God, Who took you out fom the land of Egypt," in the Past, and I am also "Hashem your God" now. I will take you out of your personal Egypt — the restrictions and constraints of life in the Present — the same as I did in the Past.

Thus the four levels of redemption, alluded to by the four corners of the *tzitzis*, correspond to the four levels of spiritual ascent mentioned in the *parshah* of *tzitzis*.[4]

In addition, we may add the following:

Besides the fact that *tzitzis* on a four-cornered garment alludes to the four expressions of redemption, the four corners of the garment also symbolise the four-dimensional material world. This shows that through the agency of the *tzitzis* one can rise above the physical world and reach the elevated level of *ke-*

---

1. See *Menachos* 44a.
2. Bamidbar 15:41.
3. Ibid.
4. As shown above in diagram 8.

dushah, which is Above the realm of the physical. Thus, the four *tzitzis*, which parallel the four expressions of redemption, enable us to rise through the four levels of redemption every day of the year. This is equivalent to what the four cups — which correspond to these selfsame expressions — help us to accomplish on the Seder night.[1]

---

1. It is interesting to note that the tefillin and *tzitzis*, with their four levels, are both worn during the morning prayers, which also comprise these same four levels (see *Tefillin: The Inside Story*, pp. 361–364). This coincides with what the Ramchal says (*Derech Hashem*, pt. 4, ch. 6:6, 9): "And behold after a man is adorned with *tzitzis* and crowned with the tefillin, [he recites] the order of the prayers [which] was instituted for him to rectify that which is necessary... The morning prayers are divided into four sections." One approaches the four levels of the morning prayers only after he is attached to the four levels of the *tzitzis* and tefillin, which were given in order to instil *kedushah* into the Jewish people (ibid.). It is for this reason that the Torah mentions *kedushah* in relation to the highest of the four levels of *tzitzis* and tefillin.

The Ten Plagues

As punishment for not granting the Jews their freedom, Egypt was visited with ten plagues. The plagues occurred in the following order: blood, frogs, lice, wild beasts, pestilence, boils, hail, locusts, darkness, and the slaying of the firstborn. These ten plagues are divided into four levels, which progress in ascending order. The first level includes blood, frogs, and lice (דצ"ך), arising from the water and the ground, and it is the lowest level.

The next group comprises beasts, pestilence, and boils (עד"ש). This is a level up, occurring directly on man and animals, who stand on top of the ground.

The next level is hail, locusts, and darkness (באח"ב). This is an even higher level, as these plagues descended from the sky.

The highest level is that of the slaying of the firstborn (בכורות). This plague is in a class of its own.[1] It is on the fourth level, the level of Above and *kedushah*, paralleling the firstborn of Israel receiving their own special *kedushah* at this time.[2]

The tenth plague is also "Above" because it came about di-

---

1. See *Seforno*, Shemos 8:12.
2. See Bamidbar 3:13.

rectly from God, without the use of intermediaries. Concerning this plague we read, "I will pass through the land of Egypt on that night, and I will smite every firstborn in the land of Egypt from man to beast..."[1] We are given the following interpretation of these words: " 'I will pass through the land of Egypt' — I and no angel; 'I will smite every firstborn in the land of Egypt' — I and no *saraf* [burning angel]."[2] Thus the tenth plague was through God Himself, using no external agency. This is in contrast to all the other plagues, which were brought about by the utilisation of physical means, e.g., blood, frogs, lice. The tenth plague therefore corresponds to the stage of *Kadeish*, which is associated with the level of Above (and the three lower levels of plagues correspond to the three lower levels of the Seder).

The Egyptians had debased the four levels of sanctity and had denied the four levels of Divine connection to this world. God demonstrated to them through the ten plagues that He is involved in this world and that He intervenes on all levels. God's *kedushah* was reestablished in this world at the very moment the fourth and highest level — that of the smiting of the firstborn — was executed, as it says, "Because all the firstborn are Mine, for on the day I smote all the firstborn in the land of Egypt I sanctified to Myself all the firstborn of Israel..."

As with the four expressions of redemption and *tzitzis*, the plagues incorporate two upper and two lower levels. The first two groups are the lower levels, being associated either with water and ground or with creatures of the water and ground. The second two groups are higher up, coming from the air and from God Himself.[3] We thus have the following picture:

---

1. Shemos 12:12.
2. Passover Haggadah; see also *Mechilta* and *Yerushalmi, Sanhedrin* 2:1.
3. See also *Tefillin: The Inside Story*, pp. 421–422, 440–443, and 455, for other examples of sets of two upper and two lower levels.

DIAGRAM 10

PLAGUES	LEVELS	
בכורות (v)	Above	⎫ Two higher levels
בא״ח (B'acha)	Higher	⎭
עד״ש (Adash)	Link	⎫ Two lower levels
דצ״ך (D'tzach)	Lowest	⎭

Before to Future and Above to Below

Thus far we have seen two themes in the order of the Seder. The first is the order of time, ranging from Purpose through Past, Present, and Future. We then saw four stages of direction, from Above to Below. Upon close examination, it becomes apparent that the stages in these two themes correspond to each other, with Before corresponding to Above, Past corresponding to Higher, Present to Link, and Future to Lowest. Let us study this in depth.

KADEISH: BEFORE AND ABOVE

The stage of Purpose precedes Past, Present, and Future. It is therefore outside and Above the time zone. Without having Purpose beforehand, the time zone is meaningless. It is therefore the first stage in both the Pesach Seder and tefillin.

MAGGID: PAST AND HIGHER

Whereas *Kadeish* encompasses that which is Before time, *Maggid* relates to that which is lower down in our physical time zone. *Maggid* illustrates that if the physical is misdirected and opposed to Purpose it is destroyed and reduced to the Past. It is for this reason that the destruction of Egypt is stressed in this section.

THE MEAL: PRESENT AND LINK

The Meal represents the Present, which is the Link between the Past and the Future. At the same time, it serves as the Link between Above and Below by fusing the spiritual and the physical, thus reminding us of our obligation to use this world to serve God.

HALLEL: FUTURE AND LOWEST

We have seen that *Hallel* represents Future and Result. In it we are told of the Future perfection of the material world — the world Below.

MERGING CIRCLES

The time line and the line of direction might be viewed as two merging circles.

The circle of time will close in the Future, when the Purpose becomes fulfilled. As the verse says, "And it shall be that he who survives in Zion and he who is left in Jerusalem, '*holy*' shall be said of him."[1] The *kedushah* of the Future is the fulfilment of the Purpose (*Kadeish*).

The circle of the time line is a horizontal ellipse.

---

1. Yeshayahu 4:3.

DIAGRAM 11

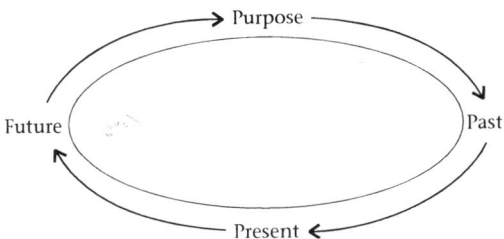

The line of direction is a vertical ellipse, with Above at the highest point and Lowest at the bottom.

DIAGRAM 12

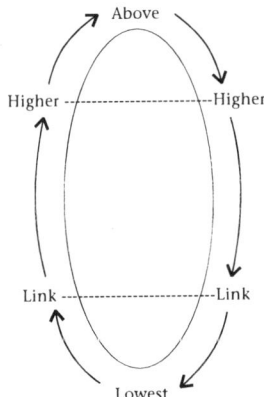

The circles of the two themes merge as follows:

DIAGRAM 13

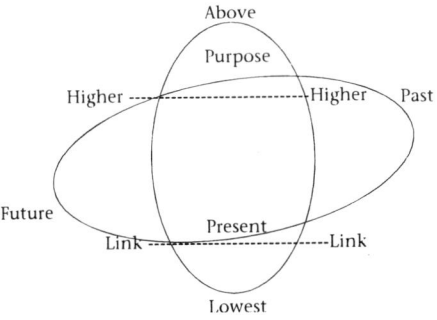

The Closing of the Circle

IN *KADEISH*

Kadeish and *Kadesh*, the first stages of both the Seder and the tefillin, direct the other stages of history. Since *kedushah* is the Start and Purpose of creation, of the Exodus, and of God's whole historical plan for the Jewish people, we see *kedushah* emerging again and again through the various stages of the Haggadah. We say in *Kadeish*: "And You have given us...this feast of the matzos, the time of our freedom, a holy convocation [מקרא קדש], as a memorial of the departure from Egypt." Thus Pesach is a holy convocation whose function is to aid us in recalling the Exodus. We are to remember the Exodus through holiness, since holiness was the Purpose of the Exodus — the concept of *Kadeish*.

IN *MAGGID*

We now come to *Maggid*, the second stage, in which the wicked — the forces of the Past — tried to extinguish the light of *kedushah* of the Jewish nation. However, God, the *Holy* One, saw to it that this would not happen.

The Closing of the Circle

We say in the Haggadah:

> Blessed be He Who keeps His assurance to Israel, blessed be He, for the *Holy* One, blessed be He [הקדוש ברוך הוא], calculated the end... And it is this that has stood by our fathers and us, for not only one has risen against us to destroy us, but in all ages they rise up against us to destroy us, and the *Holy* One, blessed be He, delivers us from their hands.

This passage emphasises that the *kedushah* and the assurance of the *Holy* One, blessed be He, stands continuously through the generations to save us and thus directs all events.

Lest one think that the term "the Holy One, blessed be He," is used arbitrarily, the *Nefesh HaChaim*[1] tells us:

> God is referred to as "the Holy One, blessed be He," in the words of our sages. This title implies two distinct facets, which are really one and the same: God is *holy* in and of Himself, meaning that He is separate and exalted. However, from the level of our perception...He is called "*baruch,*" the Source of all *blessings*. He is thus called "the *Holy* One, *blessed* be He" — He Himself is *kadosh*, but from our point of view He is also called *baruch*, the Source of blessing. The two concepts of *kadosh* and *baruch* are really *one and the same*.

We see that the term "the Holy One, blessed Be He," relates to God letting His influence of *kedushah* flow down from *Kadeish* — the highest level.

We continue in *Maggid*: " 'And Hashem took us out from Egypt' — not through an angel, not through a *saraf*, and not through a messenger, but the *Holy* One, blessed be He, He Himself in His glory..."

---

1. 3:5.

Yet again *Kadeish*, the first stage, breaks through, destroying the forces opposed to it and releasing us from the shackles of the powers of the Past.

Concerning the ten plagues we say: "These are the ten plagues which the *Holy* One, blessed be He, brought upon the Egyptians in Egypt." Again, we see that it is *kedushah* that directed the salvation. This passage stresses ten plagues which were brought upon the Egyptians by "the Holy One." Ten is the number of *kedushah*[1] and therefore plays a role when *HaKadosh*, "the Holy One," is saving the Jewish nation and destroying the forces of evil of the Past.

We then recite the section: "For how many favours are we indebted to the Master of place?" saying at its climax, "And He built for us the Chosen House." This is the Beis HaMikdash (Holy Temple). The destructive forces failed to quell *kedushah*, and with its survival, the house of *kedushah* was ultimately built. In fact, this was the Purpose of the Exodus from Egypt, as the Jews expressed in their song after the splitting of the Sea of Reeds: "This is my God, and I will build Him a *holy* sanctuary...[2] The people whom You have redeemed, You have led them in Your Might to Your *holy* sanctuary... You shall bring them and plant them on the mountain of Your inheritance...the *holy* sanctuary, O Lord, which Your hands have established."[3] Thus, the whole Purpose the Jews had in mind when exiting Egypt was primarily to build a house of *kedushah*.

We further say in *Maggid*, "The *pesach* offering that our fathers ate at the time the Holy Temple stood — for what reason? Because the *Holy* One, blessed be He, passed over the houses of our fathers in Egypt." The Haggadah continues: "This matzah that we eat — for what reason? Because the dough of our fathers

---

1. See p. 247.
2. See *Targum Onkelos*.
3. Shemos 15:2, 13, 17.

did not have time to rise before the King of kings, the *Holy* One, blessed be He, revealed Himself to them and redeemed them." Thus, the glory of *HaKadosh*, "the Holy One," radiated from the level of *Kadeish* in order to deliver His people.

IN THE MEAL

Kedushah surfaces again in the third stage of the Seder, that of the Present. We say "...Who has *sanctified* us through His commandments and has commanded us to eat matzah...to eat *marror.*"

Similarly, in the blessings after the meal, the *kedushah* of God, Yerushalayim, and the Temple are stressed. Thus *Kadeish* permeates the third stage of the Seder.

IN THE FINAL STAGE

Kedushah again surfaces in the fourth stage of the Haggadah, where we say, "Show the strength of Your hand, and may Your right hand be exalted as on the night the festival of Pesach was *sanctified.*" This means that just as at the Exodus You, God, showed Your strength when *kedushah* prevailed, do the same when You bring the Future redemption.

Further, in *"Chad Gadya"* we say, "Then came the *Holy* One, blessed be He, and slew the Angel of Death." This refers to the Future perfection of the world, when HaKadosh Baruch Hu will extend His *kedushah* over everything, and evil will cease with the termination of the Angel of Death, who is synonymous with the evil inclination.[1] Hence the Purpose in the first stage of *Kadeish* will come to full fruition in the fourth and final stage, when the Most *Holy* will reign supreme.

Finally, we are told that the Future redemption will come

---

1. *Bava Basra* 16a.

through "the *Holy* One of Israel," as it says, "For your Master is your Maker...and your Redeemer the *Holy* One of Israel..."[1] Thus in the Future, the Purpose will be accomplished and the circle closed.

FROM *KADEISH* TO *HALLEL*

We have seen that the first cup relates to *Kadeish* and the last cup, to *Hallel*.

DIAGRAM 14

קדש — **Kadeish** ⟶ first cup
ורחץ — Urchatz
כרפס — Karpas
יחץ — Yachatz
מגיד — Maggid
רחצה — Rochtzah
מוציא — Motzi
מצה — Matzah
מרור — Marror
כורך — Koreich
שלחן עורך — Shulchan Oreich
צפון — Tzafun
ברך — Bareich
הלל — **Hallel** ⟶ fourth cup

This relationship of *Kadeish* and *Hallel* being the first and last respectively is most interesting in the light of what we read concerning the mitzvah of *orlah*: "When you shall come into the land and plant any tree for food, then you shall regard the fruit thereof as uncircumcised. Three years shall it be uncircumcised; it shall not be eaten of."[2] Thus, in the first three years of the tree's growth, the fruits are *orlah*, barred, and one may not derive any

---

1. Yeshayahu 54:5.
2. Vayikra 19:23.

benefit from them.

Our rabbis tell us[1] that the prohibition of *orlah* was a result of Adam's having eaten from the fruit of the tree of knowledge before he was permitted to do so. Therefore God made us wait to eat the fruits of our trees. If Adam would have waited till the night of *Shabbos kodesh*, the *holy* Shabbos, he would have made Kiddush on the wine that came from the fruit of the tree of knowledge.[2]

The Purpose of creation was for the tree of knowledge to be sanctified, and the prohibition of *orlah* in the first three years of a fruit tree's growth only came about because this did not occur. Adam failed in this respect, and only in the Future will this *kedushah* finally be realised.

So far we have seen that *orlah* represents the missed opportunity of fulfilling the Purpose at the outset of creation, i.e., being *mekadeish* the wine when the first Shabbos came in. However, in the next verse we are told: "But in the fourth year, all the fruit thereof shall be *holy* in praise of Hashem."[3] This means that if we are patient and regard the fruits of the first three years as *orlah*, then the fruits of the fourth year can be brought to a level of *kedushah*. Indeed, that the *kedushah* of the fruits comes to fruition in the fourth year is not surprising, for the fourth stage is that of the Future. Thus the mitzvah of *orlah* hints at the idea that after the extended period of creation's *orlah* — the first three stages of history, when *kedushah* fought to surface in its absolute form — *kedushah* will finally prevail.

This fourth stage is referred to in the mitzvah of *orlah* as *kodesh hillulim*, "holy in praise," indicating that in the Future the *kedushah* will be *hillulim* — a praise — and recognised as the only truly worthy feat.

---

1. See *Or HaChaim*, Vayikra 19:26.
2. See *Zohar* 1:192a, where it says that Adam sinned by partaking of wine squeezed from grapes.
3. Vayikra 19:24.

The Haggadah also follows the pattern of *kodesh hillulim*, as the Seder begins with *Kadeish* and ends with *Hallel* — praise of God for His intervention in Future events whereby the whole world will recognise the *kedushah* of God and praise Him. We therefore begin the *Hallel* of the fourth stage with the words "Not to us, O Hashem, not to us, but to Your name give glory, for the sake of Your kindness and for your truth."[1] This is said in reference to the Future battle of Gog and Magog.[2] We ask that God intervene in this battle to give honour to His name — to make a **kiddush** Hashem (sanctification of God's name). In this way, the Purpose of *Kadeish* at the beginning will result in *kodesh hillulim* — the unifying of *Kadeish* and *Hallel* at the finishing line in the Future.

DIAGRAM 15

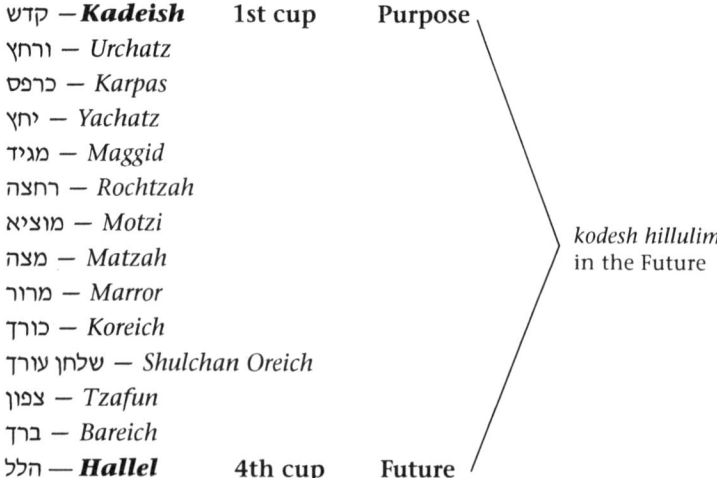

In the final stage, the *orlah* — the bad of the tree of knowledge itself — will be transformed into *Kadeish* and *Hallel*. The result will be total unity. This is the meaning of what is said con-

---

1. *Tehillim* 115:1.
2. *Pesachim* 118a.

The Closing of the Circle

cerning the Future: "On that day Hashem will be *One*, and His name will be *One*." All will be one — even that which appears to be bad now will fit into the Purpose of *Kadeish* and be part of *Hallel*, the praise of God. This parallels what we say in the *Hallel*, "I thank You, for You have answered me, and You have become my deliverance. The stone which the builders rejected has become the cornerstone. This is Hashem's doing; it is wondrous in our eyes."[1] Not only do we thank God for the final salvation, we thank Him for the rejection and hardships we went through from the outset, realising that it was all to facilitate the final *praise* at the end, when rejection will be transformed to good.

Let us look further into the final stage of the Haggadah. The last two liturgical poems we say at the end of the Haggadah, are "Who Knows One?" and "One Kid Goat." A close examination of these poems reveals that they both contain thirteen elements. This is quite illuminating, for thirteen is the numerical value of the word אחד (א [1] + ח [8] + ד [4] = 13), which means "one." Indeed, both of these poems relate to the theme of God being One, which will be truly recognised only in the Future, as it says, "On that day Hashem will be *One* and His name *One*."

"Who Knows One?" begins with "Who knows one?... One is our God Who is in the heaven and the earth." We thus state that God is One. It ends with "Who knows thirteen?" and we mention the Thirteen Attributes of Mercy. God said these Thirteen Attributes of Mercy following the sin of the golden calf. Their purpose was to help effect a reconciliation for the Jewish people after they had caused a rift between themselves and God — the opposite of unity. When God expressed His will to reunite with them again, He said the Thirteen Attributes of Mercy, which represent His being once again *echad* — the numerical value of thirteen — with them.

We then say, "One Kid Goat." This poem is an allusion to

---

1. Tehillim 118:21–23.

thirteen historical stages.[1] The thirteen stages are as follows:[2]

DIAGRAM 16

Then came the Holy One, blessed be He, and slew the Angel of Death, who killed the slaughterer, who slaughtered the ox, which drank the water, which quenched the fire, which burnt the stick, which beat the dog, which bit the cat, which devoured the kid, which my father bought for two *zuzim*, one kid goat, one kid goat.

(numbered 13, 12, 11, 10, 9, 8, 7, 6, 5, 4, 3, 2, 1 respectively)

The final stage is: "Then came the Holy One, blessed be He, and slew the Angel of Death." God is seen as the *thirteenth* personality and kills the the Angel of Death (the twelfth one). As we mentioned, the Angel of Death is synonymous with the evil inclination. Therefore, when God slays him, duality and evil will cease to exist. God will then be left as the only force — "*Hashem echad.*" Thus we see the number thirteen once again hinting at *echad*, unity.

In summary, the Seder progresses from *Kadeish* to *Hallel*. *Kadeish* represents the first stage of history. This was the time Before Adam sinned and diversity entered the world, the time when the unity of God was revealed. *Hallel* represents the return to this state in the Future, the time when "Hashem will be *One* and His name *One.*"

---

1. See *Ma'aseh Nissim*.
2. In this section of the liturgy, the thirteen stages are mentioned from the thirteenth to the first, as illustrated in diagram 16 above.

Related Sets of Four

The *Aleinu* Prayer

The *Aleinu* prayer contains the same four stages as the Passover Haggadah and the tefillin. This prayer, which is said at the conclusion of the morning, afternoon, and evening prayer services, is powerful indeed. It was composed by Yehoshua when he conquered Yericho. Tradition tells us that he recited it forwards and backwards, and in this manner broke down the walls of Yericho.[1]

Let us analyse the *Aleinu* prayer in detail.

PURPOSE

The prayer starts out by saying the following:

> It is our duty to praise the Master of all, to ascribe greatness to the Creator of *Bereishis*.

"The Creator of *Bereishis*" refers to the One who created everything for the sake of *reishis*. Israel is called *"reishis"* (beginning)[2] i.e., the Purpose of creation. Thus, in the first part of *Al-*

---

1. *Seder HaYom*, p. 12.
2. *Rashi*, Bereishis 1:1.

einu we praise God for creating the world for the sake of Israel.

PAST

Aleinu continues:

> That He did not make us like the nations of the lands and has not placed us like the families of the earth; that He has not placed our portion like theirs, nor our lot like all their multitudes.

This is saying that in the Past God did not make us like the other nations of the world. We were created to fit in with the higher Purpose of stage one. Thus, in this stage, our Purpose is carried over into the Past (stage two).

PRESENT

The prayer continues:

> (For they bow to vanity and nothingness and pray to a god that does not deliver them.) But we bend our knees, bow, and give thanks before the King of kings, the Holy One, blessed be He. For He spreads out the heavens and founds the earth, and the seat of His glory is in the heavens above; and the presence of His strength is in the loftiest heights. He is our God; there is no other. True is our King; there is none besides Him, as it is written in His Torah: "And you shall know this day, and you shall settle it in your heart that Hashem is *the God* in the heavens above and on the earth below; there is no other."[1]

We mention the difference between ourselves and the other nations in the Present, and we also acknowledge our service to

---

1. Devarim 4:39.

the Almighty in the Present. We proclaim that God continuously maintains all that exists, demonstrating that creation was not just something of the Past. Thus we have a vivid portrayal that the Almighty has not left the world. He "spreads out the heavens and founds the earth" at every moment of the Present. We then state that there is no other force besides Him, thereby fulfilling our obligation of "And you shall know *this day,*" in the Present, that "there is no other."

FUTURE

Aleinu concludes with the following paragraph:

> We therefore put our hope in You, Hashem our God, to soon see the glory of Your might, to remove idols from the world, and the false gods shall be totally cut off, to perfect the world with the kingdom of *Shaddai*, and all humanity will call upon Your name, to turn all the wicked of the world toward You. All the inhabitants of the world shall recognise and know that to You every knee shall bend; every tongue shall swear. Before You, Hashem our God, they will bend their knees and fall, and to the glory of Your Name they will give honour; and they will all accept the yoke of Your Kingship, and You will reign over them soon and forever. For the kingdom is Yours, and You will reign forever in glory, as it is written in Your Torah, "Hashem shall reign forever,"[1] and it says, "And Hashem shall be King over the whole world; on that day Hashem will be One, and His name will be One."[2]

---

1. Shemos 15:18.
2. Zechariah 14:9.

This stage clearly deals with the Future. In it we express our hope that God will bring creation to its perfection. Fundamental concepts relating to the eventual outcome of this world are revealed in this section, including the return to the perfection of the first stage, with the world fulfilling its Purpose and the wicked doing *teshuvah* (repentance). Consequently, we come around full circle, with stage four being the accomplishment of *Bereishis* mentioned in stage one. Thus the *Aleinu* prayer also comprises the circular pattern of the four stages of our history. God being recognised as One (אחד) in the last stage of *Aleinu* parallels the fourth stage of the Haggadah, where we see the number thirteen — the numerical equivalent of אחד — representing the final stage where God will be *echad* in the Future.

The *Uva L'Tzion* Prayer

In *Uva Le Tzion*, another part of the daily order of prayers, we see a similar phenomenon. Part of this prayer reads: "Blessed is our God, Who created us for His glory, separated us from those who stray, gave us the Torah of truth, and implanted eternal life within us." In this passage we find the four stages of time.

PURPOSE

"Blessed is our God, Who created us for His glory" is the Purpose of the Jewish nation. We are created for the glory of the Creator, as it says: "Everyone who is called by My name I have created, formed, and made for My glory."[1] This revelation of the Almighty's glory mentioned in Yeshayahu is called *kiddush Hashem* — sanctification of the name of the Almighty.[2] Therefore, even though we have said that *kedushah* is the Purpose of creation, when it states here that we were created in order to reveal the glory of Hashem — to make a *kiddush Hashem* — it is in effect saying the same thing.

---

1. Yeshayahu 43:7.
2. See *Michtav MeEliyahu*, vol. 1, p. 22.

PAST

"[He] separated us from those who stray," the second stage of the prayer, parallels the second stage of the Passover Haggadah, where we read, "At first our ancestors worshipped idols... But then I took Avraham your father..." The inception of our nation occurred when Avraham isolated himself from his contemporaries, who were all idolaters. As a result of this outstanding behaviour, God separated him and his descendants from the rest of the world. This is the Past history of the Jews, when God separated us from the nations who strayed.

PRESENT

"[He] gave us a Torah of truth": The Taz[1] says that the giving of the Torah is a constantly occurring event. The Torah is always being bestowed upon us in the Present. This is reflected in the fact that the Torah makes no mention of a specific date for when the greatest event in our history — the giving of the Torah — took place. Similarly, Shavuos — the day we celebrate receiving the Torah — is unique among the three pilgrimage festivals. While there is no mitzvah of matzah before or after Pesach, and there is no mitzvah to dwell in a sukkah before or after Sukkos, there is a mitzvah to learn the Torah that was given on Shavuos every day and at every available moment of the Present. Additionally, Pesach and Sukkos have fixed dates. However, Shavuos has no fixed calendar date mentioned in the Torah.[2] Furthermore, on Pesach and Sukkos we perform specific mitzvos that pertain to these festivals alone. However, Shavuos has no specific mitzvah that is performed only on that day and not on the other

---

1. *Orach Chaim* 47:5.
2. Before the Hebrew calendar was instituted, Shavuos, being seven weeks after Pesach, could fall on the fifth, sixth, or seventh of Sivan, depending on how many days the lunar months of Nissan and Iyar had. Today Shavuos always falls on the sixth of Sivan.

festivals. That there is no fixed date and no special mitzvah to commemorate the giving of the Torah on Shavuos teaches that the giving of the Torah is timeless, and that it is continuously occurring in the Present.

One may ask, We have noted that the verse "So that God's Torah shall be in your mouth"[1] belongs to the first *parshah* of tefillin, which represents Purpose. If so, how can we now say that the Torah represents the Present?

It is true that Torah was the Purpose of creation; "that God's Torah shall be in your mouth" was the intended Purpose of the Jewish nation even before the Torah was given. (Indeed, this verse was actually said on the day the Jews left Egypt, before they received the Torah.) However, once the Torah was given, it became a continuous giving in the Present. Therefore the *giving* of the Torah corresponds to the Present.

FUTURE

"[He] implanted eternal life within us": This refers to the eternal life of the Future. In keeping with this, the prayer continues with a request for a positive Future and says, "He *shall* open our hearts in His Torah, and He *shall* fill our heart with love and awe of Him, that we *may do* His will and serve Him with a whole heart, so that we *will not* toil for nothing nor bring forth needlessly." Thus we stress here our hopes for the Future and our yearning for positive results.

We carry on our request and say: "May it be Your will...that we observe Your statutes in this world, and merit, and live, and see, and inherit good and blessing in the years of the time of the *Mashiach* and for the life of the World to Come, so that my soul may sing to You and not be silent" — a prayer with a view to the Future!

---

1. Shemos 13:9.

The Books of the Torah

The Torah consists of five books — Bereishis, Shemos, Vayikra, Bamidbar, and Devarim. The last book, Devarim, is actually a summation of the previous four. For this reason, it is also known as *Mishneh Torah*, the reiteration of the Torah.[1]

The *parshiyos* of the tefillin correspond to the books of the Torah: the four separate *parshiyos* in the head tefillin correspond to the first four books of the Torah. The arm tefillin, which has the same four *parshiyos* written on one parchment, matches the fifth book of the Torah, Devarim, which we noted is a repetition of the first four books.[2] Let us examine how the four *parshiyos* relate to the initial four books and how this has a bearing on the four sections of the Seder.

TABLE 5

BOOK	Bereishis	Shemos	Vayikra	Bamidbar
TEFILLIN	Kadesh	Vehayah Ki	Shema	Vehayah Im
SEDER	Kadeish	Maggid	Meal	Hallel
STAGE	Purpose	Past	Present	Future

---

1. *Megillah* 31b.
2. *Sefas Emes, parshas Bo.*

PURPOSE

How does the first book of the Torah parallel the Purpose of the first *parshah* of tefillin and the first stage of the Seder? Rashi tells us that the word *"bereishis"* means "because of that which is called *reishis* [first]." The world was created on account of those things that are considered *reishis*, the beginning (we shall discuss this concept in depth below).

The first *parshah* of the tefillin starts out by saying, "Sanctify to Me every firstborn…" Commenting on this mitzvah, the *Sefer HaChinuch*[1] explains that God gives the owner of the newborn cattle the opportunity to do a mitzvah "with the *first* of his cattle's offspring" so that he should know that everything belongs to the Almighty. As the *Chinuch* says, "He therefore gives the **reishis**, the first of his cattle, which is the most cherished by him, to the Almighty." Thus, *kadesh* (sanctification) of the firstborn, and the book of Bereishis both deal with firsts. Furthermore, the word בראשית has the numerical value of the words בראש קדוש, which means that the *Holy* One is at the *beginning*.[2]

There is another connection between the *parshah* of *Kadesh* and Bereishis. The *parshah* of *Kadesh* contains the verse "Matzos shall be eaten during the seven days"[3] to hint that anyone who eats matzos is considered a partner with the Almighty in creation.[4] This means that *"the* seven days," with the definite article, refers to the seven days of creation. By eating matzah on Pesach one becomes connected to the commencement of creation. The one who eats matzah connects the first days of the world with the first days of the emergence of the Jewish nation and thereby becomes a partner in creation. This is because matzah, made from plain dough and arrested at the Start of its production, Be-

---

1. Mitzvah 18.
2. Rabbeinu Efrayim, *Ba'alei HaTosafos*.
3. Shemos 13:7.
4. *Roke'ach*, ch. 291.

fore the fermentation process, binds us to בראשית, the beginning — the initial Start and holy Purpose of creation.

In the same verse it says, "And no *chametz* belonging to you shall be seen, nor shall leaven belonging to you be seen in all your borders." The numerical value of the phrase ולא יראה לך חמץ, "And no *chametz* belonging to you shall be seen," is 441. This is identical to the numerical value of the word אמת (truth). The verse continues, ולא יראה לך שאר בכל גבלך, "...nor shall leaven belonging to you be seen in all your borders." This phrase has the numerical value of 911, the same as the word ראשית. Thus we are told that only by avoiding *chametz*, which symbolises falsehood,[1] can we be connected to God, the First cause, and hence justify our own Beginning. Only by eating matzah, which exists in the realm of *reishis* and is the symbol of *emes*,[2] are we able to have a correct Start.

We have just seen the juxtaposition of truth and Start in the above verse from *parshas Kadesh*, which forbids the sight of *chametz* and *se'or* on Pesach. This corresponds to another manifestation of the connection between truth and Beginning, as shown in the account of creation. Creation starts off with the word בראשית, "because of *reishis*," i.e., because of Torah and Israel, the Purpose and Start of all. Thus *reishis* is mentioned in the very first word of creation. Looking at the initials of the last three letters of the following three words of creation — ברא אלקים את — we see that they spell out the word for truth, אמת. Consequently, Start and truth are closely connected at creation just as they are in matzah and the prohibition against *chametz* and *se'or*. This indicates that one who detaches himself from *chametz* and *se'or* and attaches himself to matzah is a partner to Hashem in the Beginning and the truth of creation. Thus, *parshas Kadesh* corresponds to the first word of the first book — "*bereishis*" — and to the last

---

1. See p. 187 and n. 1 there.
2. See p. 186.

three letters of the next three words of creation.

Bereishis is also the book of Purpose, as it indicates the Purpose of creation — *kedushah*. As Rashi explains, "The word '*bereishis*' indicates that the world was created for the sake of Torah, which is called '*reishis*'[1] and for the sake of Israel, who are also called '*reishis*.' "[2] Both Torah and Israel, for whom the world was created, are manifestations of *kedushah*. Torah is the highest form of *kedushah* in this world.[3] Indeed, the Talmud says that it is forbidden to sell a *sefer Torah* and buy something else with the proceeds — even something holy — because of its great *kedushah*.[4] The lofty *kedushah* of Israel is related by the prophet: "Israel is *kodesh* to Hashem, the first fruits of His crops; all who devour him shall be held guilty..."[5]

There is yet another connection between Bereishis and *kedushah*. The word "*bereishis*" alludes to the first Holy Temple in Jerusalem, which stood for 410 years. בראשית can be broken up into the letter 'ב, which is spelled out as בית, "house" (i.e., the Temple); ראש, which means "first"; and the letters ית, which have the numerical value of 410. Thus the word "*bereishis*" hints that the First Temple stood for 410 years.[6]

DIAGRAM 17

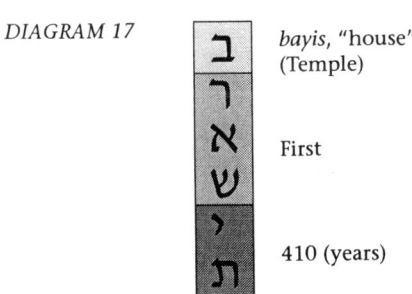

ב — bayis, "house" (Temple)

ראש — First

ית — 410 (years)

---

1. See Mishlei 8:22.
2. See Yirmeyahu 2:3.
3. *Zohar, Kedoshim* 81a.
4. *Megillah* 27a.
5. Yirmeyahu 2:3.
6. *Rabbeinu Bachya,* Bereishis 1:2.

The fact that the Temple is hinted at in the opening word of creation, even before the creation of heaven and earth, alludes to what our rabbis say: "The Temple — the center of *kedushah* in the world — was [conceptually] established even before the heavens and the earth."[1] The next verse, "The earth was without form and empty," also refers to the Temple, specifically to its eventual destruction and the departure of the Divine Presence. Indeed, the Midrash[2] tells us explicitly that *"Bereishis"* (verse 1) is the Temple, "formless and chaotic" (verse 2) is its destruction, and "let there be light" (verse 3) is the rebuilding of the Temple in the Future. Thus, from *Rabbeinu Bachya* and the Midrash we see yet again that the Purpose of creation — holiness — is alluded to in the word *"bereishis,"* since the Temple, which is called Beis Ha-Mikdash, "the house of *kedushah*," is alluded to therein.

Along the same lines, we see that the opening verses of the Torah contain a preview of history. The second verse states, "The earth was *without form* and *empty*, and *darkness* was on the face of the *deep*." These four negative factors allude to the four exiles of the Jewish nation, which were initiated by Babylon, Persia, Greece, and Rome.[3] These four nations represent the forces which want to destroy the sanctity embodied in the word *"bereishis."* They tried — and are still trying — to achieve this by attempting to destroy the holy nation, Israel, which is called *"reishis."* However, the Torah reveals to us that ultimately they will not succeed and that the light of *kedushah* will prevail and reign supreme. Therefore in verse 3 it says, "God said there shall be light, and there was light," which refers to the future (third) Temple.[4] Again we see סוף מעשה במחשבה תחלה — the end is hinted at in the beginning. The aim of creation is that it should be a vessel

---

1. *Pesachim* 54a.
2. *Bereishis Rabbah* 2:5.
3. Ibid., 4.
4. Ibid., 5.

for holiness, and in the end it will be so, even though the odds seem to dictate otherwise.

The Torah continues, "God saw that the light was good, and God divided between the light and the darkness."[1] This shows that in the future God will separate the darkness of the nations from the light of *kedushah,* and darkness will no longer prevail.

We read in the next verse, "And God named the light 'day,' and the darkness He named 'night.' And there was evening, and there was morning, one day." Rashi asks, Since the later verses refer to each subsequent new day as "second day," "third day," "fourth day," etc., should this verse not have said "first day"? Why, then, does it say "one day"? Rashi answers that by using the expression יום אחד, "one day," it is showing that on the first day there was no other besides God. It was the day of the "One" — the One and only God. We see, therefore, that in addition to this verse referring to the outset of creation, it also bespeaks of that great day in the Future when there will be only light, and He will be seen by all as One. On that day, God will again be One forever, and the entire world will see it and know it, as we read, "On that day God will be one, and His name will be One."[2] At that time, the realisation of "there was evening and there was morning, one day" will finally be fulfilled. Thus, both the Purpose of creation and its eventual fulfilment appear in the first chapter of Bereishis. Once again, we see that the beginning contains the end.

We see the connection between Bereishis and *kedushah* in yet another way. By permutation of the letters, the word בראשית can be read as ירא שבת, "respect the Shabbos." Therefore, the sanctity of Shabbos is embodied by Bereishis. The question arises: how can Shabbos be synonymous with Bereishis if Bereishis is the very beginning and Shabbos came about at the end? (it was the last thing to be created). By now the answer should be quite

---

1. Bereishis 1:4.
2. Zechariah 14:9.

obvious: Shabbos is סוף מעשה במחשבה תחלה, the finale of the *act* of creation, yet the First in the *plan* of creation. The holiness of Shabbos was simultaneously the Purpose and the end goal of creation. Indeed, in the Shabbos evening prayer, we read, "You sanctified the seventh day for Your name. It is the *Purpose* of the creation of heaven and earth." It is therefore hinted at in the first word of creation, בראשית, as ירא שבת.

Furthermore, we know that the Shabbos day is a remembrance of creation, as we say in the Shabbos evening Kiddush, "...and He gave us His holy Shabbos with love and favour as a remembrance of the act of creation." However, in addition to being a remembrance of the beginning, it also alludes to the Future Shabbos — the World to Come — as we say in our Shabbos prayers: "A song for the Shabbos day, a song for the Future, for the day which will be entirely Shabbos and rest, for everlasting life." Consequently, Shabbos is once again shown to be both the beginning and the Future at the same time.

The book of Bereishis continues from the account of creation to cite the early history of mankind and then discusses the lives of the patriarchs. The early history of mankind functions as a prologue to the story of the patriarchs, as we see from *Pirkei Avos*:[1] "There were ten generations from Adam to No'ach... There were ten generations from No'ach to Avraham — to show His [God's] patience, for all those generations continuously angered Him, until Avraham our father came and received the reward of them all."

The forefathers are called קדושים, "holy."[2] Similarly, the verse, "This is my God, and I will glorify Him; my *father's* God, and I will exalt Him,"[3] exclaimed by the Jews at the time of the splitting of the Sea of Reeds, points to the holiness of the forefa-

---

1. 5:2, 3.
2. *Midrash Shochar Tov*, Tehillim 16.
3. Shemos 15:2.

thers. As Rashi explains, "[The Jews were saying] 'This holiness did not originate with me. Rather, this *holiness* and His Godliness are established upon me from the days of the *forefathers*.' " They were saying that their holiness originated from the forefathers. Thus the book of Bereishis, which starts out with Purpose from its first word, continues with the patriarchs, who achieve this Purpose by establishing *kedushah* in the world. Indeed, the word בראשית in a different permutation spells the words ישר אבת, "the uprightness of the forefathers."

Additionally, the book of Bereishis is also referred to as the book of Avraham, Yitzchak, and Yaakov, since it deals with the deeds of the patriarchs,[1] which were the roots for what was to follow. This, of course, fits in nicely with the rabbinical dictum, מעשה אבות סימן לבנים, "the deeds of the fathers are a portent for the children."[2] What the forefathers spent their lives achieving has an effect for all time.

In the light of all of the above, we see that the book of Bereishis is the book of Purpose and preparation, concerned with the period Before the Jews emerged as a nation. Therefore, it is the stage of *kedushah* and Before, corresponding to the first stage of the tefillin and the Seder.

PAST

The second *parshah* of the tefillin and the second stage of the Seder deal with the forces of the Past: the forces of evil and destruction which try to reduce *kedushah* to a thing of the Past. The Egyptians were the epitome of these forces and were themselves eventually destroyed and relegated to the Past.

The second book of the Torah, the book of Shemos, also deals with the Past — the Exodus and destruction of Egypt. In

---

1. *Avodah Zarah* 25a and *Rashi* there.
2. See *Sotah* 34a; *Bereishis Rabbah* 40:6; *Parshas Derachim, derush chamishi*.

fact, even the second half of Shemos, which deals with the giving of the Torah at Mount Sinai and the building of the Mishkan, is actually the culmination of the Exodus. As the Ramban writes in his introduction to the book of Shemos:

> When the Jewish people left Egypt, even though they were liberated from the house of bondage, they were still considered exiles wandering in the wilderness. Only when they came to Mount Sinai and built the Mishkan, and the Almighty rested His Divine Presence in their midst, did they return to the greatness of their fathers, who had the secret of the Almighty upon their tents. Only then were they considered fully redeemed.

Thus, the Ramban informs us that there were three stages in the redemption from Egypt: the actual Exodus, the great revelation at Sinai, and the resting of the Divine Presence in the midst of the Jewish nation. It is therefore clear that the whole of Shemos deals with the Exodus wherein the Egyptians are reduced to the Past and Israel are separated from their midst, rising to great heights. Hence the book of Shemos corresponds to the second *parshah* of the tefillin and to *Maggid*, the second stage of the Seder.

PRESENT

The third *parshah* of the tefillin and the third part of the Seder both relate to the Present. The third book of the Torah, Vayikra, deals with the Present as well. Vayikra is primarily concerned with our obligations of the Present. It contains the details of the sacrifices and deals with the laws relating directly or indirectly to them,[1] and other methods of becoming attached to God

---

1. *Ramban.*

through worship. It also contains laws of *taharah* (ritual purity), dietary and marital laws, and the laws of the sabbatical and jubilee years.

Even though the Holy Temple no longer stands and we are presently unable to offer the sacrifices mentioned in the book of Vayikra, our rabbis tell us[1] that God says, "I have already established the order of the sacrifices. Whenever the Jewish people read them, I consider it as if they offer the sacrifices to me, and I forgive them for all their sins." Consequently, when we read the sections of the *korbanos*, they pertain to the Present in the same manner that the sacrifices themselves served at the time they were actually offered up. Thus the book of Vayikra is applicable in the Present even concerning the subject of the sacrifices.

The offering of the sacrifices in the book of Vayikra corresponds to the Meal, the third stage of the Seder. As the Gemara says, "As long as the Temple stood, the altar [i.e., the sacrifices] atoned for Israel. Now [that the Temple is destroyed] a man's table [i.e., the meals a person eats] atones for him."[2] This gives us a deeper insight as to why the third book, Vayikra, the book of the sacrifices, corresponds to the Meal, the third section of the Seder.

Even the laws of *shemittah* (the sabbatical year) and the laws of the jubilee year relate to the Present in that they represent the concept of accepting the Torah, which is embodied in the third *parshah* of tefillin, *Shema*. To understand this, let us first mention a unique aspect of the mitzvah of *shemittah* as it is written in the book of Vayikra.

We read: "Hashem spoke to Moshe on Mount Sinai, saying, 'Speak to the children of Israel and say to them: When you come to the land that I am giving to you, the land shall rest a Sabbath for God [in the seventh year].'"[3] In this verse, the laws of

---

1. *Megillah* 31b.
2. *Berachos* 55a. See also what we have noted previously in the name of Rabbi Chaim of Volozhin (p. 99).
3. Vayikra 25:1–2.

shemittah appear immediately after it says that God spoke to Moshe on Mount Sinai. Our rabbis ask, "Weren't all the mitzvos given at Sinai? If so, why is the sabbatical year alone singled out as having been commanded at Sinai?"[1] Chazal answer that even though all the mitzvos were indeed given at Sinai, we are informed of this specifically by the mitzvah of the sabbatical year in order for it to serve as a model, so that people will understand that just as the sabbatical year was said with all its details at Mount Sinai, so too were all the other mitzvos said with all their details at Mount Sinai. There is an obvious question to be asked: why was the sabbatical year chosen to be the example? With the answer to this question, we will see how *shemittah* is connected to the acceptance of the Torah.

From the words of our rabbis[2] we see that the sabbatical year is parallel to a whole year of accepting the Torah. Every seven years we again accept and renew our allegiance to the Torah. How is this so? When the Jewish people accepted the Torah they said, "*Na'aseh v'nishma* — We will do and we will hear." They said "we will do" before hearing what was required of them. The sabbatical year is a whole year of expressing *"na'aseh"* before *"nishma"* on the practical level. Just as our initial acceptance of the Torah was marked by having faith in God and saying "we will do," even before we could hear exactly what Hashem would command us, so too, every seven years a farmer accepts God's will — not to work the land — even though he does not know what the outcome will be. Unable to work his fields during the sabbatical year, the farmer does not know how he will sustain himself during that year and the following one. He is in the category of *"na'aseh* before *nishma,"* obeying before hearing and understanding what the future will hold. Thus *shemittah* is the prime example of *"na'aseh* before *nishma."* It was therefore chosen to be the para-

---

1. *Toras Kohanim* and *Rashi*, Vayikra 25:1.
2. *Midrash Shochar Tov*, Tehillim 103:20; *Yalkut Shimoni* 860.

digm for the rest of the mitzvos, showing that they, too, were given at Sinai with all their details.

With this in mind, we can now see the connection between *shemittah* and the acceptance of the Torah, as well as answer an incidental question that arises: since the sabbatical year was not operative until some time after the later entry of the Jewish people into the land, why doesn't it appear in Bamidbar, the book of the Future? The answer is, since *shemittah* is intrinsically bound up with the acceptance of the Torah — which is part of the Present — and it represents a continuous application of *"na'aseh v'nishma"* every seven years in the Present, it appears in Vayikra, the book of the Present.

Yovel, the jubilee year, also pertains to the concept of accepting the Torah. Occurring every fifty years, the jubilee alludes to the receiving of the Torah, which occurred fifty days after the Jewish people left Egypt.[1] Therefore *yovel* also corresponds to the *Shema*, which embodies the acceptance of the Torah.

We noted above that *shemittah* might have been expected to be included in Bamidbar, the book of the Future. There is another topic in Vayikra that we would expect to be in Bamidbar as well — the blessings and curses mentioned toward the end of the book.[2] In that section of Vayikra we are told what will befall the Jewish people depending on their deeds — Future results. If so, why are they mentioned in the book of Vayikra, the book of the Present?

The answer is that the blessings and curses are part of the receiving of the Torah. Indeed, immediately after the blessings and curses we are told, "These are the statutes, laws, and teachings that Hashem set between Him and the Jewish people *on Mount Sinai* through the hand of Moshe,"[3] i.e., these are the conditions

---

1. See *Kli Yakar*, beginning of *parshas Behar*.
2. Vayikra 26:3–46.
3. Ibid., 46.

whereby the Torah was given to us on Mount Sinai. Thus it is apparent that they are part and parcel of the acceptance of the Torah at Sinai, and remain so to this very day. It is clear, therefore, that the book of Vayikra relates to the Present in all its details.[1]

FUTURE

The fourth section of tefillin and the Seder deal with the Future and Results. This parallels the book of Bamidbar, which deals primarily with the consequences of the Jewish nation's actions — both reward and punishment — and their Future entry into the land.

There are numerous instances of punishment in Bamidbar appearing in the following episodes: The people complained, and the fire of God went forth among them;[2] those who craved meat and complained that they had none were struck by God with a plague;[3] Miriam was punished for speaking against Moshe;[4] it was decreed that the Jewish people wander in the desert for forty years and that they not enter the Holy Land, due to their acceptance of the slander of the spies;[5] the spies themselves died in a plague;[6] the people were defeated in battle for going against the word of God;[7] Korach, Dasan, Aviram, and their followers were punished, some swallowed by the earth and some consumed by a fire that descended from God;[8] 14,700 complainers were killed by a plague;[9] Moshe and Aharon were punished with a decree that they may not enter the land;[10] God sent poison-

---

1. See *Tefillin: The Inside Story*, pp.124–128, for a fuller account of the connection between the *parshah* of *Shema* and the book of Vayikra.
2. Bamidbar 11:1–3.
3. Ibid., 33.
4. Ibid. 12:10.
5. Ibid. 14:21–35.
6. Ibid., 36–37.
7. Ibid. 14:45.
8. Ibid. 16:23–35.
9. Ibid. 17:7–14.
10. Ibid. 20:12.

ous snakes against the people who spoke against God and Moshe;[1] the people sinned with the daughters of Midian and Mo'av, and God sent a plague which killed twenty-four thousand people.[2] There is also reward in Bamidbar, exemplified by Pinchas being elevated to the priesthood due to his zeal on behalf of God and for effecting atonement for the Jewish nation.[3] In no other book is the concept of reaping the consequences of our actions — either reward or punishment — stressed as much as in Bamidbar.

Aside from the emphasis on consequences, the chief concern of the book of Bamidbar is the Future entry into the land. As the Seforno explains in his introduction to Bamidbar, the camps and the banners of the tribes[4] were introduced so that the Jews would be able to travel in that formation and immediately enter the Holy Land. Then God introduced the various duties of the *Kohanim* and *Levi'im*.[5] He also commanded that whoever was ritually unclean be removed from the camp.[6] This was all so that the people would merit the anticipated entry. The laws of *sotah*[7] (a suspected adulteress) were also introduced so as to remove those who were not fitting from the nation. Similarly, the laws of the *nazir*[8] were introduced so that the people could elevate themselves to a higher level. By observing these latter two sets of laws, the Jews would merit the blessings of the *Kohanim*.[9] We then have the dedication of the altar,[10] the purification of the *Levi'im*,[11] and the Passover sacrifice.[12]

---

1. Ibid. 21:6.
2. Ibid. 25:9.
3. Ibid., 10–13.
4. See Bamidbar 2:1–34.
5. Bamidbar 3:1–4:49.
6. Ibid. 5:1–4.
7. Ibid., 11–31.
8. Ibid. 6:1–21.
9. Ibid., 22–27.
10. Ibid. 7:1–89.
11. Ibid. 8:5–26.
12. Ibid. 9:1–14.

All this was in order to facilitate the Future entry into the land. However, the Jews sinned by accepting the evil report of the spies, and the Result was death in the desert and exile for many generations to come.[1]

Immediately after this terrible decree God gives the people hope for the Future. Lest they despair of ever entering the land, He tells them that those who did not sin are still destined to enter Eretz Yisrael, and He immediately tells them of the sacrifices they are to offer in the land,[2] as if to say, "See, it's still important for you to know this, for it will become necessary as soon as you enter the land," even though it would be relevant only at the end of their forty-year wanderings in the desert. He also informs them[3] of the mitzvah of *challah*, separating a portion of their dough, which will be effective once they come into the land. They were then told how the land was to be distributed among the tribes,[4] followed by the laws of inheritance.[5] Later on, the members of the tribes of Reuven and Gad were told to pass before the nation to conquer the land, and they accepted this mission.[6]

Finally, in *Masei*, the last *sidrah* of Bamidbar, the Jews were told[7] of their Future occupation of the land. They were told to drive out the inhabitants and destroy their idols and places of worship. They were also told how to divide the land and what the borders of Eretz Yisrael were to be. Then Moshe was told who should conduct the Future division of the land.[8] He was also told that the *Levi'im* were to be provided with forty-eight cities in the Holy Land.[9] The people were also told to designate three cities of

---

1. Ibid., ch. 13–14.
2. Ibid. 15:1–16.
3. Ibid., 17–21.
4. Ibid. 26:53–56.
5. Ibid. 27:6–11.
6. Ibid. 32:20–32.
7. Ibid. 33:50–34:15.
8. Ibid. 34:16–29.
9. Ibid. 35:1–8.

refuge in the Holy Land. These cities were to provide protection for a person who accidentally killed someone and was being pursued by a surviving relative.[1] All of the above-mentioned matters pertain to the Jewish people's Future in the Land of Israel.

Additionally, the very name of the fourth book — Bamidbar — meaning "in the desert," alludes to the Future. Looking at the book of Hoshea,[2] we see that the Future redemption will have its beginnings in the desert. We read there:

> Therefore, behold, I will persuade her and lead her into the *desert*, and I will speak to her heart. And I will give her vineyards *from there*, and [I will give her] the valley of destruction for [i.e., to be] the opening of hope, and she shall dwell there as in the days of her youth and as in the day of her ascent from the land of Egypt... And I will make a covenant for them on that day with the beasts of the field and the birds of the sky and the creeping things of the earth. And the bow, the sword, and war I will break away from the land, and I will let them lie down in security. And I will betroth you to Me forever, and I will betroth you to Me in righteousness, justice, kindness, and mercy. And I will betroth you to Me with faith, and you shall know Hashem...
>
> (Hoshea 2:16–25)

Our rabbis explain that the verse "Therefore, behold, I will persuade her and lead her into the desert, and I will speak to her heart" refers to the Future redemption, which will begin from the *midbar* (desert).[3] The next verse tells us, "And I will give her vineyards from there, and [I will give her] the valley of destruction for [i.e., to be] the opening of hope." This verse stresses that from the

---

1. Ibid., 9–15.
2. See also *Rashi* on Yechezkel 20:35.
3. See *Targum Yonasan; Shemos Rabbah* 2:4; Rabbi Yosef Karo; *Metzudas David*.

desert they will be given their vineyards. Furthermore, the valley of destruction will be transformed into the opening of hope, and all the Future good that is mentioned in the subsequent verses will stem from there. This theme, of course, pertains to the fourth stage, with regards to transforming the negative into the positive.[1] Thus we see that in addition to the topics of Bamidbar themselves dealing with the Future, the very name of the *sefer* alludes to the Future redemption.

---

1. See pp. 69, 100, 120–121.

The Four Sons and the Four Species

On Seder night we are introduced to four sons, who ask four types of questions: the *chacham* (wise son), the *rasha* (wicked son), the *tam* (plain son), and the *she'eino yodea lishol* (one who does not know how to ask). On the festival of Sukkos we take the four species: *esrog* (citron), *aravos* (twigs of willow leaves), *lulav* (branch of date-palm leaves), and *haddasim* (twigs of myrtle leaves).[1]

DIAGRAM 18

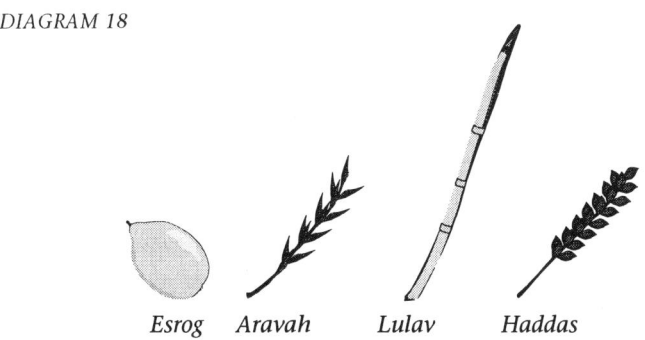

Esrog   *Aravah*   *Lulav*   *Haddas*

---

1. Vayikra 23:40.

These two groups of four correspond to each other:

TABLE 6

SON	Chacham	Rasha	Tam	She'eino yodea lishol
SPECIE	Esrog	Aravah	Lulav	Haddas

THE FOUR SONS

The four sons are mentioned in the Haggadah in an arrangement of opposite extremes. We are first introduced to the *chacham*. The Torah describes him not only as one who is wise, but also as one who wishes to be meticulous in the observance of mitzvos. He is thus learned in Torah and particular in the fulfilment of mitzvos.

The *chacham* is followed by his opposite, the *rasha*. He has no interest in learning the true reasoning behind the mitzvos and in fact has no intention of observing them at all. To the contrary, his only interest is to taunt and mock those who are observant.

We are then introduced to the *tam*. As the Ma'aseh Nissim tells us, the word *"tam"* here does not merely mean "simple," as it is usually translated. Instead, its meaning corresponds to its usage in the description of Yaakov Avinu as an *"ish tam"* (perfect person).[1] His perfection was a result of his being *"yosheiv ohalim* — one who dwells in tents [and learns Torah]."[2] Thus the *tam* is one whose recognition of God comes from learning Torah.

The *tam*, whose strong point is his study of Torah, is followed by his opposite, the *she'eino yodea lishol*. He is a person who does not think to inquire after the reasons of the mitzvos. Rather, he keeps them out of a sense of tradition, feeling it important to uphold the *minhagim* (customs) of his fathers.[3] Conse-

---

1. *Targum* on Bereishis 25:27.
2. Ibid.
3. *Ma'aseh Nissim*.

quently, his strong point is the observance of mitzvos, and his weak point is lack of Torah study. He is thus the opposite of the *tam*.

THE FOUR SPECIES

The four sons, with their different characteristics and the sequence in which they are referred to, correspond exactly to the characteristics and order in which we hold the four species on Sukkos. The four species are held in the following order:[1]

DIAGRAM 19

1	2	3	4
Esrog	Aravah	Lulav	Haddas

Let us explain briefly what these four species resemble and how they correspond to the four sons.

The *esrog* has a taste and a pleasant fragrance. It is symbolic of those who have both Torah, which is represented by taste (טעם), and mitzvos, represented by fragrance (ריח).[2] This parallels the first son, who both studies Torah and is meticulous in his mitzvah observance. The *esrog* and the *chacham* are also associated in another way: they both identify with the heart. The *esrog* resembles the heart,[3] and wisdom rests in the heart.[4]

The *aravah*, having no taste or smell, symbolises those who lack both Torah learning and observance of mitzvos. This corresponds to the *rasha*, who is neither studious nor mitzvah observant.

The *lulav* has a taste but no smell. It therefore represents

---

1. See *Mishnah Berurah, Orach Chaim* 651:12, and *Be'er Heiteiv* 651:4 in the name of the Shlah. This order is hinted at in the word אעלה, an acronym for אתרג, ערבה, לולב, הדס. (See *Zohar, Ki Seitzei* 283a, and *Tikunei Zohar, tikun* 13, p. 25b.)
2. *Rabbeinu Bachya*, Vayikra 23:40; *Vayikra Rabbah* 30:12.
3. *Vayikra Rabbah* 30:14.
4. See Mishlei 10:8 and Shemos 31:6.

those whose strong point is Torah learning more so than the fulfilment of mitzvos. The *lulav* thus corresponds to the *tam*, whose stronger point is his Torah learning.

This brings us to the fourth specie, the *haddas*, which has a smell but no taste. This represents those whose strong point is observance of mitzvos but lack Torah study. Therefore, the *haddas* corresponds to the fourth son, the *she'eino yodea lishol*, who is ignorant but who keeps the mitzvos he is familiar with by tradition.

THE FOUR STAGES

On a deeper level, the four species and the four sons also parallel the stages of Purpose, Past, Present, and Future that we have seen reflected in the four *parshiyos* of tefillin, the four stages of the Seder, the first four books of the Torah, and others. Let us examine this in detail.

Stage One

We have seen that *Kadesh, Kadeish,* and Bereishis all symbolise the idea of *kedushah* and Purpose. The *esrog* also personifies the concept of *kedushah*.[1]

Moreover, the *esrog* tree was the only fruit tree to fulfil God's will when He commanded that the trees themselves have exactly the same taste as that of their fruits.[2] It thereby fulfilled its Purpose.

Interestingly, another way in which the *esrog* and the *par-*

---

1. *Rikanti, Emor,* in the name of the *Bahir;* see also *Zohar, VaYechi* 220b, and commentaries there, which state that the *esrog* corresponds to *Atzilus,* the highest realm; see also *Hashmatos HaZohar* 1:267b; see also the liturgy before the *Shema* of the first day of Sukkos, where it says, "I take on the first day for the One Who is last and first the *fruit of a beautiful tree* [the *esrog*], to the One Who is exalted in *holiness."*
2. See *Rashi,* Bereishis 1:11, and *Sukkah* 35a.

shah of *Kadesh* are comparable to each other is in the fact that that both are situated on the left side — the right side of God.[1] The *parshah* of *Kadesh* in the head tefillin is located on the left side of the wearer, and the *esrog* is held in the left hand.

Finally, the *esrog* parallels *Kadeish* and the *parshah* of *Kadesh* in that they all represent the realm of Before and Above. The *Emek Berachah*[2] says:

> The *esrog* is the first of the four species to be mentioned in the Torah, because its taste is good and it has a pleasant smell. It is a whole entity and has no joining of separate segments [i.e., leaves on branches], which is not the case with the other three species. It therefore alludes to the Almighty, Whose existence does not depend on others. He is the First, from Whom the existence of all creatures is drawn. However, this existence [of all the creatures] is separate from the Almighty, and they are not bound with Him on the same level. Therefore, the *esrog* must be held Above the knot [which binds together] the other three species at the time one shakes them, in order to hint that He is Above all.

Thus we see that the *esrog* hints at the dimension of Before and Above, just as *Kadeish* and the *parshah* of *Kadesh* do.

The *chacham* also fulfils God's will, because the Purpose we were created for is to become *chachamim* in Torah.[3] Indeed, wisdom itself is *reishis*, First and Purpose.[4] Thus the *chacham*, who is filled with wisdom, is associated with *reishis*.

There is yet another connection between the *chacham* and Purpose. We have seen that Purpose parallels the dimension of

---

1. See p. 179.
2. Ch. 69.
3. *Avos* 2:8.
4. See Tehillim 111:10.

Before. The *chacham* is also associated with the dimension of Before. In order to understand this, let us first discuss what is behind the questioning of the Seder night.

We have previously discussed that Pesach is the time of our freedom — the anniversary of our Exodus from Egypt. However, true freedom is not only freedom from physical bondage and oppression; it is also a state of mind. Therefore, besides showing that we are physically free on the Seder night, there must also be a demonstration of mental freedom. This is achieved in the form of questioning. The Jewish people came out of Egypt after 210 years, during which for a long time they had not been given time to think.[1] Questioning shows that the mind is free from the slave mentality of accepting a master's commands without trying to find out their meaning. By asking questions, one frees oneself from his previous mindset and thereby reconsiders the matter. It is for this reason that even someone who performs the Seder by himself must still ask questions first, before relating *"Avadim Hayinu,"* the story of the Exodus,[2] for on the anniversary of our freedom we must demonstrate the freedom of our intellect. Therefore we have an obligation to ask questions.

However, everyone is different. Not everyone enjoys the same mental capabilities or the same philosophical bent; nor is there one all-encompassing answer that will suit everyone's question. For this reason, the Haggadah presents us with four archetypes — four different questions for four types of people. In addition, each question is given a tailor-made answer to address the specific needs of the questioner. Different messages are given to each of the four sons on the Seder night, in order to free each one in his own way. With this in mind, let us now return to the *chacham*.

Concerning the wise son, we read:

---

1. As seen previously, p. 80, in the name of *Mesilas Yesharim*, ch. 2.
2. *Shulchan Aruch, Orach Chaim* 473:7.

> When your son asks you in time to come, saying, "What is the meaning of the testimonies, and the statutes and laws, which Hashem our God has commanded you?"
>
> (Devarim 6:20)

He wants to know the significance of three categories of mitzvos — *eidos, chukim,* and *mishpatim.* We, however, only answer him about one, as we read further:

> Then you shall say to your son, "We were slaves to Pharaoh in Egypt, and Hashem brought us out of Egypt with a strong hand. Hashem placed signs and wonders, great and evil, upon Egypt, upon Pharaoh, and upon all his household before our eyes. And He brought us out of there, in order that He might bring us, to give us the land that He swore to our forefathers. And Hashem commanded us to do all these *statutes,* to fear Hashem our God, for our good, all the days, that He may keep us alive, like this day."
>
> (Ibid., 21–24)

Both the question the wise son asks and the answer given warrant examination. We see that the very manner in which he phrases his question indicates a connection to Purpose. He says, "What is the meaning of the testimonies...which *Hashem our God* has commanded you?" He thereby relates the mitzvos to their source — to God, Who came Before and Whose service is the ultimate Purpose of existence.

The answer given to the wise son is also tied in with Purpose. There is a striking difference between the question the *chacham* asks and the answer we give him. He asks about various types of mitzvos: testimonies, statutes, and laws. However, we respond concerning only one of them: statutes. Why do we respond to him only about the statutes? The answer is that we are talking to an intelligent son — the *chacham*. With his tremendous intellect, the *chacham* can acquire an incredible amount of Torah learning, the mark of a true Torah Jew. Indeed, so much importance is ascribed to the mitzvah of learning Torah that it is equated to all the other mitzvos combined. Our whole system of Torah learning is based on questioning — something the *chacham* excels at. The Gemara is replete with questions and answers. This intellectual challenge is what brings true freedom, even if one is physically oppressed.

However, there is a danger in priding oneself too much on one's intellect. Though we have described the wise son as having the most strengths of all the four sons, he has his pitfalls as well. The danger with this intellectual is that his very intelligence may lead him astray! When confronted with something that he does not understand or that does not fit with his line of thinking, his "wisdom" may cause him to deem it irrelevant, something he can reform or dispense with if need be. We therefore tell him that *Before* he delves into wisdom, he must realise that the *chukim* are the most important thing in the Torah, and that their observance is not to be taken lightly. The magnificent human intellect can comprehend a good deal about many of the mitzvos. However, the reasoning behind certain mitzvos is inaccessible to our finite minds. The wise son has to realise that there is a point where human intellect stops, as Shlomo HaMelech, the wisest of all men, said, "I thought I would become wise, but it is beyond me."[1]

The message we give the *chacham* is that even though he has an open, questioning mind, there is a danger that his intellectual freedom may end up enslaving him to his limited mind and desires. Though he may be wise, we adjure him not to be *too* clever. There are things that are Above human comprehension which he

---

1. Koheles 7:23. Indeed, the *chukim* demonstrate our loyalty to the King of kings by indicating that we don't perform the mitzvos because of the reasons that lie behind them, but solely because we were commanded to do so.

cannot and will not understand. He must realise that there is a Creator, Whose intellect towers Above ours.

Let us examine this in more depth. The true freedom of the wise son is achieved only when he subjugates his mind to the will and the statutes of God and not to his own limited understanding. We therefore say to him, "And Hashem commanded us to do all these *statutes, to fear Hashem* our God, for our good, all the days, that He may keep us alive, like this day." The wise son asked about the meaning of the various categories of mitzvos and is answered only concerning the statutes, which are a sign of fear of God. We tell him that God commanded us to fulfil the statutes, which are *Above* our intellect, in order to fear Him. We thereby tell him that fear of God takes priority and is something that is beyond and comes *Before* wisdom — both in calibre and in time. The wise son must realise that "fear of Hashem is the *beginning* of wisdom."[1] He must further understand that which we say in *Pirkei Avos*:[2] "Anyone whose fear of sin takes precedence over his wisdom, his wisdom will endure; but anyone whose fear of sin does not takes precedence over his wisdom, his wisdom will not endure."

The *chukim* correspond to the "highest" *parshah* of the tefillin, *Kadesh*, which also deals with the dimension of statutes, as it says there, "And you shall observe this statute in its correct time *miyamim yamimah*." Thus, through focusing on the statutes, the *chacham* becomes bound to the dimension of Before and Above, which is the dimension of *Kadesh* of the tefillin and *Kadeish* of the Seder.

We go on to tell the wise son, "And it will be considered a merit for us if we observe to do *all this mitzvah* before Hashem our God, as He has commanded us." Here we see the whole Torah viewed as one large mitzvah, and that we will be considered

---

1. Tehillim 111:10.
2. 3:9.

righteous if we keep it *before* God. This means we must serve Him whether we understand or not — simply *because* He commanded us to do so ("as He commanded us"). We do not perform mitzvos because we understand them; we perform them because He commanded us. This is exemplified by the *chukim*, which we fulfil simply because God commanded them. This means that we should fulfil the whole Torah as if it is a *chok*, observing it for no other motive than because God commanded it. We thus impress upon the *chacham* that the Purpose of our existence is simply to fulfil God's will, an unconditional observance. This can be truly accomplished only if we observe His commandments purely *because He told us to*, not because we understand them.

Consequently, both the question of the wise son and the answer we give him are related to Purpose, Before, and Above, which all belong to the realm of *Kadesh* of the tefillin and *Kadeish* of the Seder. Although he inquired about a variety of mitzvos, we tell him only about the statutes, so that he realises that the Purpose of life is to fulfil God's will solely because that is His desire.

This all parallels the level of the *yud* of the Tetragrammaton, which represents *Chochmah* (Wisdom) and the level of Above and Before.

Stage Two

We have seen how the *parshah* of *Vehayah Ki Yeviacha*, *Maggid*, and the book of Shemos symbolise the Past. The *aravah* and *rasha* also represent this dimension. Our rabbis say that one characteristic of the *aravah* is that it wilts before other species of plant life and therefore represents this world, which is temporary.[1] Accordingly, the *aravah* alludes to the Past. The *rasha*, who is symbolised by the *aravah*, has no Future. Additionally, he becomes a member of the Past very quickly, as it says, "...just a little longer, and there will be no wicked; and you will contemplate his place,

---

1. See *Seder HaYom* 49d.

and he will be no more."[1] Indeed, in *Maggid, Vehayah Ki Yeviacha*, and the book of Shemos the *wicked* Egyptians suddenly become members of the Past and are no more!

At this point, let us turn to the archetypal *rasha* of the Torah — Eisav. In the story of Yaakov and Eisav, we find that Eisav the *rasha* disappears into the Past, whereas Yaakov the *tam*, the one who seeks perfection, remains in the Present. Eisav occupies himself with material pursuits, attaching himself to that which is temporary, while Yaakov occupies himself with Torah, attaching himself to that which is eternal and gaining eternal life in the next world; therefore Eisav has passed away into the Past, while Yaakov still lives. Interestingly, Eisav was born before Yaakov. This in itself is symbolic of the Past preceding the Present.

We will analyse the verses describing the birth and personalities of these two antithetical brothers in depth.

> And the first came out red, all over like a hairy cloak, and they called his name Eisav. After that his brother came out, his hand clutching Eisav's heel, and he called his name Yaakov.
>
> (Bereishis 25:25–26)

The name עשו is derived from the word עשה, "made." This is because he came from the womb "made" — fully developed with hair like a boy several years old.[2] Because of his *physical* maturity he was considered *made* — in the Past — hinting to having "made it" in this world. On the other hand, Yaakov's name was given to him because he was holding on to the *eikev* (heel) of Eisav. This hinted that only later in history, after a lengthy and sustained struggle, would Yaakov be able to rise and take power from Eisav.[3]

We then read: "And the lads grew, and Eisav was a man who knew hunting, a man of the field, and Yaakov, a plain man,

---

1. Tehillim 37:10.
2. *Rashi*, Bereishis 25:25.
3. *Rashi*, Bereishis 25:26.

dwelling in tents."[1] In connection with Eisav, it states, "and Eisav *was*," in the Past tense, whereas with Yaakov it says, "and Yaakov, a plain man, *dwelling* in tents," in the Present tense. This is because Eisav went after worldly pursuits of wickedness, which are temporary and ultimately become things of the Past, whereas Yaakov aspired to Torah, that which is ever Present. In turn, the brothers acquired the same qualities as their different pursuits.

There is another difference in the Torah's description of the brothers vocations. Concerning Eisav it says, "...and Eisav was a man *who knew* hunting." However, in connection with Yaakov, nothing is mentioned of what he knew. This is because Eisav, true to his name, felt he already knew everything he needed to know and didn't need to learn more. He felt he was skilled in his field and accomplished with the knowledge he had gained in the Past, and he did not seek to know anything further. Consequently we are informed that he remained nothing more than "a man of the field."

In contrast, nothing is mentioned of Yaakov's knowledge, for those who understand true knowledge recognise that whatever they know needs to be explored, developed, and investigated still further. They realise that the quest for knowledge is an ever-Present search. Therefore it says of him, "and Yaakov, a plain man, dwelling in tents," which our rabbis[2] interpret to mean that Yaakov is a perfect man who learned in the tents of Torah. Interestingly, the verse says "tents" of Torah, in the plural. This shows that he did not feel accomplished with the knowledge he had attained in the Past, but always thirsted for more, going from one house of learning to the next.[3] His perfection came as a result of his continuous striving for the truth of wisdom, in the Present.

With the above in mind, we can understand another differ-

---

1. Bereishis 25:27.
2. See *Targum* and *Rashi*.
3. See *Rashi*.

ence between the two descriptions. Concerning Eisav, the Torah mentions the word "man" (איש) twice: "and Eisav was a *man* who knew hunting, a *man* of the field," whereas by Yaakov "man" is written only once: "and Yaakov, a plain *man*, dwelling in tents." By examining this closely, we see that the twofold expression of "man" in connection with Eisav is in reference (a) to himself, what he knew, and (b) to his occupation. By Yaakov the word "man" is mentioned only in reference to his character.

The reason for this difference is that Eisav's personality was not enhanced through his occupation, for physical pursuits do not improve the real person. Therefore he and his occupation were considered separate entities. This can be seen in contemporary society. Being accomplished within intellectual or physical fields such as mathematics, science, and athletics does not necessarily mean that these skills and talents have refined one's character. Very often the moral behaviour of those who have mastered these fields leave a lot to be desired. Yaakov, however, became a perfect man *because* of his being in the tents of Torah, which helps build the character of the real person.

Eisav and Yaakov's respective connections to the Past and Present are also reflected in the love their parents had for them. We are told, "And Yitzchak *loved* Eisav because there was deception in his mouth [i.e., he deceived Yitzchak into thinking that he was a righteous man[1]], and Rivkah *loves* Yaakov."[2] The love of Yitzchak for Eisav did not endure and was left in the Past. Therefore it says, "And Yitzchak *loved* Eisav," in the Past tense. In contrast, the love of Rivkah for Yaakov is ever Present. Therefore it says, "...and Rivkah *loves* Yaakov." Moreover, the Torah tells us that the reason for Yitzchak's love of Eisav was because Eisav deceived him. Falsehood cannot endure,[3] and therefore Yitzchak's

---

1. Ibid.
2. Bereishis 25:28.
3. See p. 185.

love for Eisav ultimately ceased. However, concerning the love Rivkah had for Yaakov, no reason is given. It simply says, "...and Rivkah loves Yaakov." Rivkah loves Yaakov, whose character is molded by the Torah, which epitomises the Present.[1] Therefore, her love for him is enduring, existing in the realm of the Present.

Eisav's association with the Past goes even further. In addition to the name Eisav, he was also known as "Edom" (Red). This was because of what ensued in the following episode: "Yaakov cooked a stew, and Eisav came from the field and he was faint. Eisav said to Yaakov, 'Pour into me from this red, red thing, for I am faint.' Therefore his name was called Edom."[2] The colour red symbolises bloodshed, when the murderer reduces his victim to the Past. This is the trait of Eisav and his descendants.[3] Furthermore, Eisav derives his power from the star of destruction Ma'adim (Mars), and that is why he is told, "And by your sword you shall live."[4] Yet again Eisav is associated with destruction and the Past. Eisav is also called Edom because of his affiliation with *adamah* (earth), for he was a man of the *adamah*.[5] Eisav is thus associated with the material earth — a passing and fleeting world.

Our rabbis[6] compare Edom — the kingdom of Eisav — to the *aravah*. The *aravah* has certain features that show it is genuine: it has a red stem, longish leaves, and a smooth "mouth" (the edges of its leaves are smooth).[7] These factors hint at the kingdom of Edom, for the longish leaves symbolise the prolonged exile of Edom, and the smooth "mouth" signifies their smooth and dishonest mouths, for they take after their ancestor Eisav, who was a smooth talker.

---

1. See pp. 132–133.
2. Bereishis 25:29–30.
3. *Rabbeinu Bachya*, Bereishis 25:28.
4. Bereishis 27:40; *Rabbeinu Bachya*, Bereishis 25:30.
5. *Rabbeinu Bachya*, Bereishis 25:25, 27.
6. Rabbeinu Bachya in *Kad HaKemach* on the subject of *lulav*; see also *Tzapachas HaShemen* there, os 31.
7. *Sukkah* 34a.

In the light of this, we can understand the words of our rabbis,[1] who tell us that in the merit of taking the four species on the first day of Sukkos, God will punish Eisav the wicked, of whom it says, "And the *first* came out red." In what way are the four species associated with the downfall of Eisav? The *aravah*, symbolic of Eisav, wilts and rapidly becomes part of the Past. Similarly, on the last day of Sukkos we take the *aravah* and beat it. All this shows that Eisav will be destroyed and left in the Past. Thus, Eisav, the paradigm of the *rasha*, who is lost to the Past, and the *aravah*, whose existence is fleeting and transient, are compared to one another.

There is another association between Eisav and the *aravah*. In the Torah, the *aravah* is referred to as ערבי נחל. This term has the same numerical value as the word עשו — 376.

We noted above that the smooth-edged leaves of the *aravah* are compared to the smooth-talking Eisav. Hence the *aravah*, which resembles the wicked, the Past, and *speech* of the *lips*, parallels the sphere of the second cup, the cup of *Maggid*, in which we have an obligation to tell of the destruction of the *wicked* in the *Past* with our *mouths*.

The wicked son's relationship to the transient Past can be seen from the very nature of his question. As the Malbim[2] explains:

> The *rasha* taunts those who are loyal to the Torah, saying, "What good is this service to you?" His is a twofold question:
> 1. The purpose of the *pesach* offering and the Seder is to serve as a remembrance of the Past Exodus. But why go to so much trouble? Isn't it enough to mark the event on the calendar, and we will thereby be reminded of it?

---
1. *Vayikra Rabbah* 30:16.
2. On *Shemos* 13:12.

2. What is this service to you — you who have already tasted of the fruit of the "tree of enlightenment"? Why don't you go along with the spirit of the times? Aren't you ashamed to hold on to these ancient practises, which are irrelevant and part of the Past?

The wicked son's twofold question relates to the Past. He first asks, "Since it is only a remembrance of the Past, why all this bother of practising mitzvos now? Let it just be written down as a remembrance." Secondly, "How can you do things that belong to the ancient Past which are now irrelevant or impractical?" We answer him, "Because of this did Hashem do for me when I left Egypt." Because of our keeping the mitzvos *now*, God took us out of Egypt in the Past.[1] Consequently, the Exodus in the Past depends on what we do now in the Present. Therefore, you, wicked son, are incorrect in saying that we should simply remember the Past by noting the date on the calendar and not bother to involve ourselves in the mitzvos, thus severing ourselves from the Past. The mitzvos we perform do not just belong to the Past, and therefore, "if you would *have been* [Past] there, you would not *have been saved*." You, *rasha*, look at the Past as an entity on its own without connection to the Present or Future. With that attitude God would never have taken you out of Egypt, for God determined that the Exodus was dependent on the observance of the mitzvos in later times. You choose to separate the periods and deny that there is a connection between them. Therefore you would not have merited to be saved.

The realm of the *rasha* is hinted at in the first *hey* of the Tetragrammaton, as it is a split letter alluding to duality. This symbolises the dual situation of the *rasha*, who on the one hand escaped through the bottom end of the *hey*, but on the other hand has the chance to change for the better. Since the letter *hey* has

---

1. See *Rashi*.

more than one part, it also hints at the plural form in which the wicked sons are introduced[1] when they ask their questions, whereas when the other sons ask their questions they are mentioned in the singular. The letter *hey* is made up of the letters 'י and 'ד to read the word די, "it is enough," hinting at our telling the *rasha*: "It is enough!" In the context of the *rasha*, this word hints at limitation, as he lives for the physical, which is limited and will be lost to the Past.

Stage Three

We have seen how the *parshah* of *Shema, Shulchan Oreich,* and *Vayikra* all symbolise the Present. The *lulav* and *tam* are also connected to this domain. The word לולב has the numerical value of sixty-eight, the same as the word חיים, "life." Life represents the Present, as the verse says, "You who cling to Hashem your God are all *alive today.*"[2]

We noted above, in the name of the Ma'aseh Nissim, that the *tam* parallels Yaakov, who is "*Yaakov ish tam.*" The *lulav*, which symbolises life in the Present, also parallels Yaakov, whose striving is for the ever-Present Torah, and who is mentioned in the Present tense.[3] Indeed, our rabbis tell us[4] that Yaakov is considered *bachayim* (living), as if he never died.[5] Therefore both Yaakov and the *lulav* represent continuous living in the Present.

In our discussion on the *aravah* and the *rasha*, we saw how Eisav and Yaakov parallel Past and Present respectively. Let us now return to Eisav and Yaakov, this time in relation to the *ara-*

---

1. See Shemos 12:26.
2. Devarim 4:4. The third *parshah* of tefillin also comprises the concept of today, as it says, "And these words which I command you *today* shall be upon your heart" (Devarim 6:6).
3. As mentioned above, pp. 161–162.
4. Ta'anis 5b.
5. "As his descendants live, so does he live." See also *Zohar, VaYishlach* 168a: יעקב אילנא דחיי הוה.

vah and the *lulav*. The Torah relates that during Rivkah's pregnancy her two children quarreled within her. Seeking the advice of a prophet, she was told, "Two nations are in your womb, and two races shall be parted from your bowels; and one race shall be stronger than the other race."[1] Rashi explains, "As soon as they leave your body each one will take a different course — one to his *wickedness* [לרשעו] and the other to his *perfection* [לתומו]."

As Rabbeinu Bachya explains,[2] Yaakov's perfection parallels the *lulav*. He comments that the Torah chose to describe Yaakov as a *tam* rather than as a man of *emes* (truth), which was his attribute,[3] in order to teach us two things: not only was he truthful, but he also possessed the trait of *tiferes* (glory), which is the twinning of two extremes.[4] This merging of both extremes, hinted at

---

1. Bereishis 25:23.
2. On Bereishis 25:27.
3. As he was always honest and upright. His honesty was based on the dictates of Torah, which is the epitome of truth, as our rabbis say, "There is no truth other than Torah" *(Pesichta Eichah Rabbasi 2)*.
4. Let us look for a moment at the attributes of the patriarchs in order to understand the words of Rabbeinu Bachya. Avraham Avinu excelled in the trait of *chesed* (kindness), as he practised deeds of kindness to mankind. Yitzchak, on the other hand, excelled in the trait of *gevurah* (strength and restraint). He negated his ego by allowing himself to be bound as a sacrifice upon the altar. This is *gevurah*, strength of the highest degree, as our rabbis say, "Who is strong [*gibor*]? He who overcomes his *yetzer*" (Avos 4:1). Yaakov combined both extremes of *chesed* and *gevurah*. This combination is known as *tiferes* (glory). This he achieved through the intense study of Torah. Torah shows us how to balance the two extremes of *chesed* and *gevurah* — how not to be so kind that it becomes detrimental, and how not to exert too much power. It is the true balance between them. Truth in one's traits means the correct balance between the two, the harmonious blending of the extremes. Therefore the letters of the word אמת are the first, middle, and last letters of the *alef-beis*, showing the two extremes joining in the middle, swaying to neither extreme. Yaakov, who toiled in Torah, combined and blended both of these extremes. Achieving this blend is the achievement of truth known as *temimus* (perfection), the *tiferes* of Yaakov. The Torah therefore tells us that Yaakov was an "*ish **tam** yosheiv ohalim*" (Bereishis 25:27), i.e., he became a perfect person as a result of his intense study in the tents of

in the תם of Yaakov, is also hinted at in the similar expression employed with the middle leaf of the *lulav*, which is called the תיומת. It is known thus because it is the leaf that connects the leaves of the two extremes of the right and left of the *lulav*.[1] A *lulav* in which the middle leaf is split is invalid.[2] In order for the *lulav* to be kosher, it must resemble Yaakov the *tam* — the perfect one — who blended the two extremes.

The blending — or Linkage — of extremes represented by the *lulav* and by Yaakov the *tam*, corresponds to the letter *vav*, the third letter of the Tetragrammaton, which represents the Present — the Link between the two extremes of Past and Future.

There is yet another way in which the *tam* relates to the Present. He asks: "What is this?" meaning, what is this in front of me *now* — in the Present. The Ma'aseh Nissim[3] explains our answer to him:

> The Torah tells us to say to him, "With a mighty hand God took us out of Egypt," in order to impress upon him that the very fact that the Exodus came about with God's *mighty hand* was good for us, and therefore we have to keep "this" as evidence to it being good for us now and as a thanksgiving. It helps us and is for our good — even in the Present. The Exodus, with its show of God's strength, was the greatest good that could have happened. This is because even though God had the ability to take us out of Egypt without revealing His mighty hand and strength to the nations, He did so, for our sake, so

---

Torah learning.
1. See also *Rashi, Sukkah* 32a, which says that "*teyumes*" is related to the word "*te'umim*" (twins). See also *Rikanti* 157a, which says that the *lulav* represents *tiferes* and unity.
2. *Shulchan Aruch, Orach Chaim* 645:3.
3. On the answer to the *tam* and on the section "*Avadim Hayinu*."

that "He may keep us alive, like this day" — in the Present.

[Why is it so good that the Almighty took us out of Egypt with a mighty hand?] Because everything is revealed before Him, and He knew that we would often sin in the future, thereby deserving destruction. He also knew that Moshe would not be able to pray for mercy if not for the fact that, if his prayer was not answered and the Jews would be destroyed, there would be a desecration of God's honour [as the nations would say that the initial strength which God showed had waned]. This came about only because the Exodus was undertaken with a mighty hand, whereby everyone could see that He was the One Who was taking them out and that we are His children [thus giving rise to the possibility of the desecration of His honour if He would destroy us]. This would not have been possible had the Exodus taken place without a show of God's strength...

Thus "the mighty hand" mentioned in the answer to the *tam* was in order that "He may keep us alive, *like this day*," and thus relates to the Present. It is to the *tam*, who symbolises the Present, that we relate this special kindness.

Stage Four

We have seen how the *parshah* of *Vehayah Im Shamoa*, *Hallel*, and the book of Bamidbar symbolise the Future. The *haddas* and the fourth son also relate to the Future. The change from the bitter and difficult Past to the Future good is represented by the *haddas*, as the prophet tells us: "For with joy you shall go out, and with peace you shall be brought; the mountains and the hills shall burst into song before you, and all the trees of the field shall clap hands."[1] This verse speaks of the Future redemption.[2] Immediately afterwards we are told: "Instead of the briar a cypress shall rise, and instead of the nettle a **haddas** shall rise."[3] This means that when the Jewish people return from the exile in the Future, these trees will replace the thorns that commonly grow in the desert.[4] Thus we see that in the Future a miracle will occur, and the *haddas* will sprout in place of the nettle in the desert. This indicates the connection between the *haddas* and the book of Bamidbar, which relates the events that happened to the Jews in their wanderings in the desert after the Exodus.

Rabbeinu Bachya[5] comments: "The bitter taste of the *haddas* and its sweet fragrance symbolise the pain a person experiences when he repents, for a person should grieve and chastise himself according to the measure that he sinned, and experience pain according to the measure of pleasure he derived from the sin. The pleasant odour that results will rise up to heaven." The myrtle thus hints at the Future transformation of bad to good. The sinning *rasha* becomes part of the Past (for he is on the plane of things that do not last, as we saw with the wicked Eisav). However, if he comes to his senses, he will feel remorse and think about his position in the Present. This will hopefully be followed by repentance. Once he has mended the wrong he has done, he will again merit the Future. Indeed, in the Future, the entire world will be prompted to do *teshuvah*, as we see from the prophets and as we recite in the *Aleinu* prayer.[6] Thus the *haddas*, which hints at repentance, parallels the Future.[7]

Rabbeinu Bachya commented on the *haddas*'s bitter taste on

---

1. Yeshayahu 55:12.
2. *Rashi*.
3. Yeshayahu 55:13.
4. *Redak*.
5. On Vayikra 23:40.
6. See p. 129.
7. See also *Rikanti* 157b.

the one hand and its sweet fragrance on the other. Let us examine this further.

These opposing characteristics hint at the transformation of the disadvantages and handicaps of the Past into accomplishment and success in the Future. Just as *marror* hints at the Future transformation of bad to good,[1] the stinging nettle will be transformed into a *haddas*.

The *haddas* is associated with Bamidbar in another way. Our rabbis tell us that "one who learns and teaches Torah in a place where there is no *talmid chacham* is like a *haddas* in the desert, which is beloved."[2] We see here that the *haddas* transforms the desolation of the *desert* into something beautiful.

For another connection between the *haddas* and the fourth stage, let us return to the matriarch Leah, who, as we learned before, corresponds to the fourth cup. Similar to the *haddas*, Leah's life incorporated elements of initial bitterness and final pleasantness. Concerning her we read, "Leah's eyes were tender."[3] Rashi explains that this was because she wept continuously, thinking that she was destined to be Eisav's wife. Leah is the only one among the matriarchs of whom we are told about her eyes. In this way she parallels the *haddas*, which is compared to the eyes.[4] Furthermore, Leah led a life of initial bitterness and rejection. She said of herself[5] that she was afflicted and hated, but she ended up having more children than all the other wives of Yaakov.[6] Moreover, from Leah will descend the *Mashiach*, who will bring the Future redemption and transform all sorrow and bitterness to sweetness once again.

In fact, the *Mashiach* is himself the embodiment of the trans-

---

1. See pp. 89, 174–177.
2. *Rosh HaShanah* 23a.
3. Bereishis 29:17.
4. *Vayikra Rabbah* 30:14.
5. See Bereishis 29:32–33.
6. See *Rashi*, Bereishis 29:35.

formation from bad to good. He is the scion of the Davidic line, whose origins were riddled with controversy and sordidness. First there was Lot, whose daughter tricked him into an incestuous relationship that resulted in the nation of Mo'av,[1] from whom David's ancestress Rus descended. Then there was the episode of David's forebears Yehudah and Tamar.[2] While both of these individuals were righteous, the circumstances surrounding the birth of Tamar's children seemed questionable. There was also the controversy surrounding Bo'az's marriage to Rus,[3] in which certain people were convinced that Bo'az's interpretation of the halachah that allowed him to marry Rus was incorrect — an argument bolstered by the fact that Bo'az died on their wedding night, something that the critics were sure indicated God's displeasure. Finally there was David's marriage to Bas Sheva,[4] from whom the *Mashiach* will be descended. There were those who felt that their relationship was of dubious origin, despite the fact that their marriage was within the confines of halachah and sanctioned by divine fiat. Thus the *Mashiach*, the most illustrious representative of David's line, who himself will be perfectly good and will herald the Future — the time when all will be good — has origins mixed with perceived bad and good and will rise from murky origins to flawless clarity.

Indeed, the *Mashiach* will eradicate the duplicity and wickedness in the world that was introduced by the snake when he offered the fruit of the tree of knowledge of good and evil to mankind. This is alluded to in the numerical value of the word משיח, which has the same numerical value as the word נחש, "snake" — 358.[5]

---

1. See Bereishis 19:30–37.
2. Ibid. 38:13–30.
3. See Ruth, ch. 4.
4. See Shmuel II, ch. 11.
5. See *Roke'ach*, Bamidbar 6:26, where he shows that opposing forces can have the same numerical value, demonstrating that they are opposed to one another.

The final stage of the Future is where Purpose and Result meet. *Kadeish* of the beginning, which was untainted by evil or bitterness, became spoiled through the first sin, which caused suffering and misery to descend into the world. In the end, all of this negativity will be transformed and enveloped in the initial Purpose of *kedushah*.

This phenomenon parallels the *she'eino yodea lishol*, the son who does not know how to ask. This son is hampered by his lack of Torah knowledge and a querying mind. It is our duty to transform this lack. We are therefore told in the Haggadah, "And the son who does not know how to ask, you must open up for him [i.e., start the discussion for him], as it says, 'And you shall tell your son on that day *leimor* [to say].' "

In the *Maggid Tzedek*[1] we are told that the word *"leimor"* seems superfluous. Therefore, its inclusion is coming to add something we might not otherwise have thought of, namely, that we should speak to the son in such a manner that he himself will come "to say" — to ask. We are told to answer the *she'eino yodea lishol* with an eye to the Future: "...tell your son on that day *to say*," i.e., that he *should say* — in such a manner "that he should be encouraged to say," so that his disadvantage of not being able "to have said" in the Past will be repaired, and he will aquire the skill to do so in the Future.

Of the Future we are told, "For the land will be filled with the knowledge [*de'ah*] of Hashem like water covers the sea."[2] At that time ignorance will be nonexistent, and the *she'eino **yodea lishol*** will be transformed into a ***yodea***, "one who knows."

The fourth *parshah* of the tefillin, which deals with the Future, is also concerned with education with a view to the Future. But there is a tremendous difference between the education of children spoken of in the third *parshah* of the tefillin and that

---

1. *Siddur HaGra*.
2. Yeshayahu 11:9.

spoken of in the fourth one. The third *parshah* says: "And you shall teach them to your children, and *you* shall discuss them..."[1] In contrast, the fourth *parshah* says: "And you shall teach them to your children so that they — your children — shall speak about them when you sit in your house and when you travel on the way, when you lie down and when you get up."[2]

The Ramban explains[3] the reason for this change of expression as follows: "In the third *parshah* we are told ושננתם and ודברת בם: that you should instruct and that you should speak of them at all times and wherever you may be. However, in the fourth *parshah*, the commandment is ולמדתם...לדבר בם — teach your children until they themselves speak the words of Torah at all times and wherever you [the father] may be, in such a manner that they will study Torah independent of where you are and what you are doing." We see from the Ramban that the ideal of the fourth *parshah* is to instruct our children with a specific Future goal in mind — having our children speak words of Torah and perform the mitzvos on their own, thus assuring their connection to Torah in the Future.

Let us now turn to the oft-commented fact that we answer the *rasha* and the *she'eino yodea lishol* with the same verse.[4] While this may be true, in reality we use different parts of the same verse. In connection with the *rasha* we do not quote the first part of the verse; we say only, "Because of this did Hashem do for me when I left Egypt." We explain this to mean "to me and not to him." However, by the *she'eino yodea lishol* we quote the first part of the verse: "And you shall tell your son on that day to say...," and from it we prove, as we have noted, "You must open up the conversation for him," i.e., since it says "to say," it means that we

---

1. Devarim 6:7.
2. Ibid. 11:19.
3. On Devarim 11:18.
4. Shemos 13:8.

should cause him to say — that we must open him up.

The part of the verse used to answer the *rasha* proves that "had he been there, he would not have been redeemed." This expression "He would not *have been redeemed*," is in the Past tense — the dimension of the *rasha*, who would have been left in the Past and not been redeemed. Conversely, the expression used in reference to the *she'eino yodea lishol* points to the Future — "And you *shall tell* your son on that day *to say*" — you should open him up so that he will be able to ask in the Future. This is the dimension of the *she'eino yodea lishol* — the Future transformation of all disadvantages.

The *she'eino yodea lishol* thus also relates to the final *hey* of the Tetragrammaton. Being a split letter and comprising two parts, it hints at the transformation of his situation, from a disadvantaged Past to a hopeful Future. The word די, "enough," which the *hey* is comprised of, hints at the limitation of his Past disability, whereby he becomes someone who can ask — in the Future. Thus, the *she'eino yodea lishol*, like the *marror* and *haddas* that we have discussed previously, represents the transformation of a disadvantaged Past into a brilliant Future.

We noted above that the fourth *parshah* of tefillin is concerned with education with an eye to the Future. It also relates to the transformation of bad to good. We read there, "Guard yourselves lest your hearts be seduced..." How do we guard ourselves? We are to "place these words of Mine upon your hearts..." Interestingly, we are also told in the third *parshah* that "these words...shall be upon your heart." However, there is a difference between the expressions used in the two *parshiyos*: in the third *parshah* we are told that "they shall be upon your hearts," whereas in the fourth *parshah* a special word is used, and we are told, "*v'samtem* — place [them] upon your hearts." Our rabbis[1] tell us that "*v'samtem*" may be broken up into two words and in-

---

1. *Kiddushin* 30b.

terpreted as *sam tam,* meaning that Torah is the "perfect medicine." Thus we see that the Torah is a life-giving medicine — the antidote of the *yetzer hara.* God says to us, "My sons! I have created the *yetzer hara,* but I have also given you the Torah as its spice [cure]. Toil in Torah, and you will not fall into the clutches of the *yetzer hara.*"[1] Just as a spice makes something bitter into something pallatable, so too the Torah transforms the negative desires that stem from the evil inclination into positive ones, using them for the service of the Almighty. Therefore the word "*v'samtem,*" implying the transformation of bad into good, is employed here.

This means that by learning Torah, the repercussions of Adam's sin can be rectified. The *yetzer hara* was brought into the hearts of mankind through the first sin, when Adam was expelled from Gan Eden and effected the fall of mankind. However, just as medicine can make the sick well, Torah frees us from the grasp of the evil inclination. All the tricks of the *yetzer hara* — sadness, laziness, desire for wealth, confusion, pride — will lose their hold over us if Torah is studied correctly. This is the transformation of transient bad into a lasting Future. It therefore appears in the *parshah* of the Future, for that is the time when all bad will be truly transformed into good.

This transformation includes the revival of the dead, which is also hinted at in this *parshah.*[2] This is also an example of the ultimate return to good and the rectification of the first sin, which caused death to be brought into the world. Indeed, the revival of the dead is associated with *kedushah* — the beginning phase — which will surface and prevail in the Future, in the end of days. As the Seforno explains:[3]

> One whose holiness is complete endures eternally, as

---

1. Ibid.
2. *Rashi,* Devarim 11:21.
3. On Shemos 15:11; see also *Seforno,* Vayikra 11:45.

the sages tell us:[1] "God will *return the dead to life*, and they shall never again be dust, as it says, 'And it shall come to pass that whoever is left in Zion, and whoever remains in Jerusalem *"holy"* shall be said of him, everyone inscribed for life in Jerusalem.' "[2]

The revival of the dead will thus bring about the fulfilment of "the end of the act of creation, yet the first in the plan of creation." At that time Purpose will shine forth, despite the many factors in the various stages of history which attempted to extinguish it. This corresponds to the circular *kodesh hillulim*[3] of the Haggadah, whereby the original perfection of creation is realised at the end.

In summary, we have the following relationship:

TABLE 7

STAGE	Purpose	Past	Present	Future
TEFILLIN	Kadesh	Vehayah Ki	Shema	Vehayah Im
SEDER	Kadeish	Maggid	Meal	Hallel
SPECIE	Esrog	Aravah	Lulav	Haddas
SON	Chacham	Rasha	Tam	She'eino yodea lishol
BOOK	Bereishis	Shemos	Vayikra	Bamidbar

THE SEQUENCE OF THE FOUR SPECIES AND TEFILLIN

We have seen how the four species correspond to the four *parshiyos* of tefillin. In addition to all we have mentioned, there is a further connection. We noted previously that the way we hold

---

1. *Sanhedrin* 92a.
2. Yeshayahu 4:3.
3. See pp. 120–122.

The Four Sons and the Four Species

the four species corresponds to the sequence in which the four sons are referred to in the Haggadah. This order also corresponds to the order in which the four *parshiyos* of the tefillin are written and set in the *batim*.

TABLE 8

STAGE	Purpose	Past	Present	Future
SPECIE	*Esrog*	*Aravah*	*Lulav*	*Haddas*
TEFILLIN	*Kadesh*	*Vehayah Ki*	*Shema*	*Vehayah Im*

We are taught that a person wearing tefillin faces God. Therefore, the *parshah* of *Kadesh*, which is on the wearer's left side, is on the right side of God, so to speak.[1] Likewise, the *esrog*, which hints at the realm of *Kadesh*, is held in our left hand — God's right side. The following picture thus emerges:

DIAGRAM 20

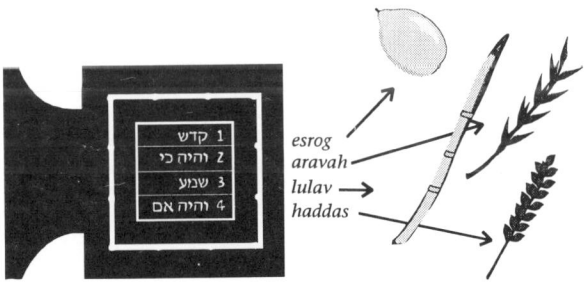

Furthermore, just as the *parshah* of *Kadesh* embodies the highest level, which is Above and separated from this world (whereas the other three *parshiyos* correspond to the lower three worlds), so too, the *esrog* embodies the highest level and is sepa-

---

1. See *Eliyahu Rabbah* 32:66.

rate from the other three species.

Interestingly, the Torah tells us that when we wear the tefillin "all the nations of the earth shall see that God's name is called upon you, and they will be afraid of you."[1] The same holds true for the four species. As the *Derech Hashem* tells us,[2] "[When the Jews take the four species,] the light of God radiates upon the heads of Israel and crowns them in such a way that the fear of them falls upon all their enemies." Thus, the tefillin and the four species effect the same phenomenon.

---

1. Devarim 28:10; *Berachos* 6a.
2. 4:8:2.

The Four Mitzvos of the Seder Night

We have seen[1] that the four central mitzvos of the Seder night — *korban Pesach*, the Passover sacrifice; the mitzvah of relating the events of the Exodus; the mitzvah to eat matzah; and the mitzvah to eat bitter herbs — correspond to the various stages of the time line. The Passover sacrifice represents the dimension of Purpose. The mitzvah of *sippur* is the telling of our Past. Matzah represents God's connection to us in the Present, and *marror* hints at the Future. Let us delve still further and see how this parallel extends to the other themes we have been discussing.

KORBAN PESACH

The *korban pesach* relates to the dimension of Purpose and the factors related to this realm in many ways. Our rabbis tell us[2] that when the *chacham* asks why we perform the various practises

---
1. Pages 88–90.
2. Haggadah.

on the Seder night "you shall then inform him of the laws of the [*korban*] *pesach*, that one may not eat anything after the Passover sacrifice."

As we discussed previously,[1] we must answer the *chacham* concerning the *chukim*, demonstrating that we do not keep mitzvos merely because we understand them but because God commanded us to fulfil them. Specifically we refer to the laws of the *pesach* sacrifice, which has *chukim* attached to it. Indeed, we see in the Gemara[2] that the mitzvah of *korban pesach* itself is considered a *chok*.[3] Thus the *korban pesach* has a special affiliation to the *chacham*.

In its relationship to *chok*, the *korban pesach* also corresponds to the *parshah* of *Kadesh* in the tefillin. This is because only in the *parshah* of *Kadesh* — which reflects the dimension of Above — is this service of the *pesach* offering and the fact that it is a *chok* mentioned.[4] This is because a *chok* is Above human comprehension.

There is another connection between the *pesach* offering and the *Kadesh* of tefillin and *Kadeish*, the first stage of the Seder. The *korban pesach* is the only one of the four mitzvos of the Seder night that embodies intrinsic *kedushah*, as it is *kodashim* (a holy sacrifice) and therefore pertains to the level of holiness. Matzah and *marror* do not embody intrinsic *kedushah*.

An interesting allusion to the *kedushah* of the *pesach* offering is that the letters of the word פסח are the same letters as the word חסף, which hints at the verse "Hashem has revealed [*chasaf*] His *holy* arm,"[5] for on Pesach God revealed His *holy* arm to deliver His

---

1. Pages 157–160.
2. *Menachos* 36b.
3. The Shlah explains that the *korban pesach* is a *chok* for the following reason: It is surprising that we are commanded to eat it only after we have already partaken of the meal, whereas other mitzvos connected with eating, such as matzah, must be eaten when one has an appetite.
4. *Shemos* 13:10.
5. *Yeshayahu* 52:10.

people.[1] A further connection between the *pesach* offering and *kedushah* can be seen in that the *pesach* offering shows that the reason why God took us out of Egypt was so that we would become "a kingdom of priests and a *holy* nation."[2]

Since the *pesach* sacrifice corresponds to the realm of Purpose, it is mentioned first in the order of the obligations of the night, when we recite later in the Haggadah: "Rabban Gamliel would say, 'Whoever does not explain the following three things on Pesach has not fulfilled his duty. They are the *pesach* sacrifice, matzah, and *marror.'* " The Haggadah then goes on to explain the reason for each of these mitzvos, again mentioning the reason for the *pesach* sacrifice first. This is because the *korban pesach* represents the realm of Before and Purpose.

However, the question arises, If the *pesach* sacrifice symbolises the beginning phase, the stage of Before, and therefore shows that God precedes all,[3] why is it eaten at the *end* of the Seder? Furthermore, the *pesach* offering is the only one of the three foods of the night which must be prepared and offered up beforehand — on the fourteenth of Nissan, before the night of the fifteenth[4] — yet it is the last thing to be eaten.

The answer is that these seemingly paradoxical aspects of the *korban pesach* merely represent one more example of the stage of Before, Purpose, and *kedushah* uniting with the stage of Future and Result, representing the fruition of Purpose, and the final achievement of *kedushah*, which will reign forever. Once again we see the axiom of "The end was conceived in the beginning" being fulfilled. Therefore, we prepare and offer up the *korban pesach* Before Passover, because it represents Purpose. However, of the three mitzvah foods, it is the last to be eaten, and after ingest-

---

1. *Haggadas Ba'alei HaTosafos*, p. 111.
2. Shemos 19:6; *Sefer HaChinuch,* mitzvah 7, 16.
3. As per the *Shlah* seen previously on p. 89.
4. See Shemos 12:6; Vayikra 23:5–6; Bamidbar 28:16–17.

ing the *kedushah* of the *pesach* sacrifice we may not eat anything else, so that the taste of *kedushah* will remain in our mouths. This parallels the fact that *kedushah* will prevail in the end — the Purpose having been achieved and remaining forever.

It is interesting to note that when we explain the reason for the *pesach* offering we say: "The *pesach* offering that our fathers ate at the time the Holy Temple stood — for what reason? Because the Holy One, blessed be He, passed over the houses of our fathers in Egypt."[1] This is the only one of the three foods discussed in this stage of the Haggadah that is mentioned in connection with the *Holy* Temple. This is because it is the only mitzvah of the Seder night that embodies intrinsic *kedushah*. Therefore, it can be eaten only when a house of *kedushah* exists, something that is not necessary in the case of matzah and *marror*.

Both the sanctity of the *pesach* offering and the Beis HaMikdash are in the realm of Purpose. Therefore they correspond to the book of Bereishis, the first book of the Torah, whose opening chapter hints at the *kedushah* of the Beis HaMikdash,[2] the Purpose that existed Before creation.

SIPPUR

The second of the four central mitzvos of the Seder night is *sippur yetzias Mitzrayim*, narrating the Exodus of the Past. This, of course, corresponds to all of the above-mentioned themes — the *rasha, aravah,* etc. — each of which relates to the Past, as we have already explained.[3]

MATZAH

The third mitzvah is matzah. In the Present, it is the only food whose obligation to be eaten at the Seder is from the Torah.[4]

---

1. Haggadah.
2. See pp. 137–138.
3. See pp. 160–167.
4. See Rambam, *Hilchos Chametz U'Matzah* 6:1; see also *She'eilos U'Teshuvos*

The Four Mitzvos of the Seder Night   185

As we do not have the Temple, the obligation of the *pesach* offering does not exist. Similarly, since the mitzvah of eating *marror* mentioned in the Torah is dependent on eating it with the *korban pesach*, it is currently only a rabbinical obligation.[1] Matzah thus relates to the Present. This, of course, fits in with the fact that matzah symbolises God's continuous Providence in the Present, as we mentioned previously.[2]

One who eats matzah becomes attached to life.[3] This parallels the *lulav*, which also represents life.[4] Conversely, one who eats *chametz*, the opposite of matzah, on Pesach, becomes connected to death.[5]

Matzah also relates to the *lulav*, as well as Yaakov the *tam*, in the following way: We have seen[6] that the *lulav* represents the *emes* (truth) of Yaakov Avinu and the Present, which is the fusion of the extremes of Past and Future. The Talmud points out[7] that the word אמת is comprised of the first, middle, and last letters of the *alef-beis*. The middle letter, 'מ, joins the letter 'א at the beginning of the *alef-beis* and 'ת at the end of the *alef-beis*. Thus, the Present (*mem*) links the extremes of the Past (*alef*) and the Future (*tav*). Additionally, the composition of truth from these three letters indicates that *emes* stands the test of time and endures from the beginning (Before), through the Present to eternity.

Furthermore, the letters of אמת each stand on two feet, representing the fact that אמת stands and endures, whereas the letters of falsehood, שקר, stand on one leg and are thus unstable, hinting that falsehood cannot stand.[8] Our rabbis further

---

Chasam Sofer, Choshen Mishpat 196, in *Hashmatos*.
1. Rambam, *Hilchos Chametz U'Matzah* 7:12.
2. Page 88.
3. *Zohar, VaYeitzei* 157a.
4. See p. 167.
5. *Zohar, Pinchas* 251a; see also *Zohar, Tetzaveh* 183b.
6. Pages 168–169.
7. *Shabbos* 104a.
8. Ibid.

tell us[1] that nine is the number of truth, for the *gematriah katan* of *emes* equals nine[2] and when multiplying nine by any number, the addition of the resulting numerals will always add up to nine.[3] This represents the lasting quality of truth, for it illustrates that truth stands forever. We see that matzah personifies truth in the same way, for its *gematriah katan* value is also nine.

DIAGRAM 21

מצה

mem	(מ)	= 40
tzaddi	(צ)	= 90
hey	(ה)	= 5
	135	= 1+3+5 = 9

אמת

alef	(א)	= 1
mem	(מ)	= 40
tav	(ת)	= 400
	441	= 4+4+1 = 9

Thus matzah epitomises truth. It is plain, uncomplicated bread that has not risen, remaining just as it was at the time it became mixed — a simple combination of flour and water. In turn, this parallels Yaakov, for as Rashi explains, the description of Yaakov as *tam* means that he was straightforward, unpretentious, uncomplicated, and simple in his ways, without falsehood.

As we have seen above,[4] Yaakov, whose trait is *emes* — which endures in the Present — is considered as still living in the Present. He therefore corresponds to the matzah and *lulav*, which represent life and truth. The connection between these two concepts is illustrated quite clearly in the word *"emes"* itself. With

---

1. See *Midrash Talpiyos* in *Anaf "Emes."*
2. *Gematriah katan* is derived by calculating the numerical value of a word, and then taking the individual digits of the numerical value and adding them together. Hence, the word *"emes,"* which has a numerical value of 441, has a *gematriah katan* value of nine. See diagram 21 on this page.
3. For example, nine multiplied by five is forty-five, and four added to five is nine.
4. Pages 162–164.

the *alef* at the beginning of the word we have אמת. Without it, we are left with מת, "dead," the opposite of life.[1] Someone who clings to the truth survives.

Both life and truth are related to each other in that truth *causes* life, as our rabbis tell us.[2] This is hinted at by the fact that the letters of אמת relate in a threefold manner to the Present: proximity-wise in the alphabet, structurally, and numerically, as mentioned previously — life for all Present time.

On the other hand, the similarity between *chametz* and falseness can be demonstrated in its own way. *Chametz* results when dough is allowed to rise, giving it a great outer appearance, when in fact it has merely been inflated with air. "Successful" falseness always contains a bit of truth that has been exaggerated and distorted to the liar's convenience.[3] Like *chametz*, it is big in appearance but lacking in real substance. Conversely, matzah is a symbol of truth — while *chametz* is less than it appears to be from the outside (being filled with air), matzah is more than it appears to be.

Chametz and *se'or* (leaven) also reveal themselves as symbols of falsehood in the following way: If we reverse the letters of these words, we see ideas that are the exact opposite of what *chametz* and *se'or* represent. חמץ spelled backwards is צמח, which means "growth." שאר spelled backwards is ראש, which means "top" or "uppermost." True growth brings one ever upwards. It is the opposite of the growth generated by *chametz* and *se'or*, which is false and filled only with air. Therefore the letters of *"chametz"* and *"se'or"* are the reverse of *"tzemach,"* true growth, and *"rosh,"* uppermost.

Furthermore, the word *"sheker"* is spelled *shin, kuf, reish*. Not

---

1. See also *Zohar* 251a, which says that the word מחמצת (leaven) begins and ends with the letters מת, hinting that if one eats *chametz* on Pesach one becomes attached to death.
2. See *Sanhedrin* 97a.
3. See *Rashi*, Bamidbar 13:27.

only are the letters disorganised and not in their proper sequence as they appear in the *alef-beis* (contra to *emes*), they are also neither the first, middle, nor last letters.[1] Indeed, the closeness of its letters in the *alef-beis* hints that while falsehood may take hold instantaneously,[2] it has no continuity or lasting power and will therefore collapse after a short time.

There is another connection between Yaakov, *lulav*, and matzah, in that they all represent the concept of a binding knot to *kedushah*. Binding with a knot, of course, joins two entities and thus represents unity.

Matzah is described as a knot that binds us with holiness.[3] The *lulav* represents the human spine, to which the ribs are *bound*, and therefore the other species are *bound* to the *lulav*.[4] Yaakov is associated with the concept of the knot of holiness, as our rabbis tell us[5] that Yaakov epitomises the knot of the tefillin which binds both extremities (*chesed* and *gevurah*).

Interestingly, the word מצה has the numerical value of קהל (gathering), whereas חמץ has the numerical value of חלק (disjointed part or division).[6] Thus we see again that matzah is related to the idea of unity.

Unity is also apparent in the word for truth, "*emes*." In the word "*emes*," the first and last letters of the *alef-beis* converge on the middle letter to unite and become one. Where there is genuine truth, there is true unity. Indeed, King David says about the Torah, the ultimate truth, "The judgements of God are true; they are *collectively* correct."[7] This means that all the laws of the Torah, even the most remote and seemingly unrelated subjects, are in-

---

1. See *Shabbos* 104a.
2. Ibid.
3. *Zohar, Emor* 95a–b.
4. *Menoras HaMa'or*, ner 3, klal 4, chelek 6, perek 4.
5. *Zohar, Yisro* 78b.
6. *Drashos Chasam Sofer* 256, 258.
7. Tehillim 19:10.

terlinked and united with one another. This is a clear sign that they are true. This perfection of truth is also synonymous with the unity of truth symbolised by matzah.

Yaakov may also be compared to matzah in the following way: We have seen that Yaakov is called "a perfect man."[1] This also means that he was born circumcised and had no *orlah* (foreskin) at birth.[2] This parallels matzah, which has no fermentation. Both *orlah* and *chametz* represent the evil inclination, which entered man after the first sin. Thus Yaakov — the perfect one — and matzah are the opposites of *orlah* and *chametz*, as both are untainted by the *yetzer hara*.

Finally, matzah, *lulav*, and the *parshah* of *Shema* all symbolise unity and God's ever-present Divine Providence. We have seen previously[3] how matzah alludes to Divine Providence and the Almighty's unity. The *lulav* also symbolises the unity of God. This is because the word כפת (palm branch), referring to the *lulav*, is written without a *vav* in the Torah in order to be understood in the singular — *kapas* — hinting at the oneness of God. This is explained in the following way: If the word *"kapos"* would have been written, with a *vav*, to be understood in the plural, we would have thought that one needs to take more than one branch. If, on the other hand, it would have said *"kaf,"* we would have thought that we need only take one leaf. It is therefore written *"kapas,"* without a *vav*. Consequently, since it is written this way, it indicates the singular — one branch; however, since it is read in the plural, *kapos*, it signifies that there must be more than one leaf. Thus there is a combination of both the singular and the plural,

---

1. Bereishis 25:27.
2. *Avos D'Rabbi Nassan* 2:5.
3. Page 88.

i.e., the unifying of many leaves on one branch.[1] The *parshah* of *Shema* also embodies the unity of God and the concept of Divine Providence. It symbolises the unifying of opposing and differing forces.[2]

MARROR

We have seen[3] that *marror* alludes to the Future, when bitterness will be transformed to compassion. *Marror* has three names: *marror*, *chazeres*, and *chassah*.[4] When looked at collectively, all these names hint at the Future — the time when *marror* (bitterness) will *chozer* (return) to *chassah* (compassion), the time when God will once again have compassion on us. *Chassah* (the preferred type of *marror*[5]) therefore represents bitterness being transformed into compassion. *Marror* therefore has a positive aspect. Indeed, the very *merirus* (bitterness) of the Egyptian exile is what finally evoked God's mercy and deliverance. Thus, *marror* shows that *merirus* itself is the very cause for the final sweetness and ultimate good. This is a step further than matzah and the perfection of Yaakov, for with Yaakov and matzah there was no *orlah* or *chametz* — which represent bad — from the outset, whereas *mar-*

---

1. See *Sukkah* 32a and *Rabbeinu Bachya*, Vayikra 23:40. The *lulav* also represents the twinning — and unification — of opposite extremes (as we have mentioned on pp. 168–169 in the name of Rabbeinu Bachya on Bereishis 25:27). The unity of the *lulav* is unlike the unity symbolised by the *esrog* that we have mentioned previously, in that the *esrog* is one single fruit and not the unity of separate parts as by the *lulav* (see p. 288, n.1, where we explain why this is so). See *Rabbeinu Bachya* in *Kad HaKemach*, *os lamed*, on the subject of *lulav*, where he shows that the leaves of the *lulav*, which lie one on top of the other, represent Divine Providence in the levels from Above to Below.
2. For more on the unity of the *Shema*, see *Tefillin: The Inside Story*, pp. 216–222.
3. Page 89.
4. See Haggadah, *Me'am Lo'ez*, on the subject of *marror*.
5. *Pesachim* 39a.

ror symbolises the dimension where evil and bitterness existed at the outset but are ultimately transformed into good and compassion.

Furthermore, eating *marror* on the night of Pesach serves to repair the blemish of the first sin (eating from the tree of knowledge), for the blessing recited over the *marror* and the eating of it transforms the curse that Adam received into a blessing.[1] Yet again *marror* signifies the transformation from bad into good, something which will happen in its fullest sense only in the Future.

The significance of *marror*'s transforming bad to good explains why it is mentioned and explained last in the words of Rabban Gamliel: "They are the *pesach* sacrifice, matzah, and *marror*.... This *marror* that we eat — for what reason? Because the Egyptians embittered the lives of our fathers in Egypt." The obvious question is, If *marror* is meant to commemorate the bitterness of the Egyptian slavery, and thus is a matter of the Past, then it should be mentioned before matzah, which represents the Present. The answer is that the purpose of *marror* is to show that the *very same* bitterness (מרור) we were subjected to in the Past will be transformed (חזרת) into compassion (חסא) in the Future.

Thus *marror* is analogous with the fourth stage and cup of the Haggadah, which also deals with the Future — the time when bad will be transformed to good and bitterness will be transformed to sweetness. This is reflected in the verses of the *Hallel* of this stage of the Haggadah. We begin by mentioning the evil, sorrow, and rejection that befell the Jewish nation. We then mention our deliverance from this evil:

> The ropes of death surrounded me, and the confines
> of the grave seized me. I found trouble and sorrow.
> Then I called upon the name of Hashem; O Hashem,

---

1. *Pri Tzaddik*, Pesach, *os alef*.

save my soul. Gracious is Hashem and righteous; our God is compassionate. Hashem guards the simple; I was brought low, and He saved me. Return to your rest, O my soul, for Hashem has dealt kindly with you. For You have saved my soul from death, my eyes from tears, and my feet from stumbling. I will walk before Hashem in the land of the living.

(Tehillim 116:3–9)

We continue with "From the restricted confines I called upon the Lord; He answered me with the breadth of freedom."[1]

Later verses in this chapter also refer to the conversion of bad to good, which, again, will occur in the Future. The verses state three times that enemies surround the Jewish nation. This refers to the three times that Amalek will come up against Yerushalayim in the Future.[2] The verses read:

All nations surround me; but in the name of Hashem I cut them off. They surround me; indeed, they surround me; in the name of Hashem I cut them off. They surround me like bees; they are extinguished like a thorn fire; in the name of Hashem I cut them off. You pushed me many times that I might fall; but Hashem helped me.

(Ibid. 118:10–13)

Verses 21 and 22 also speak of the transformation from bad to good: "I thank You, for You have answered me, and You have become my deliverance. The stone which the builders rejected has become the cornerstone."

Finally, in thanksgiving for the Future transformation of the bitterness of the exile we say: "Give thanks to Hashem, for He is

---

1. Tehillim 118:5.
2. *Yalkut Shimoni* on Tehillim 118:10–11.

good; His kindness endures forever."[1]

Thus the *Hallel* parallels the *haddas* and *marror* and the other aspects of this fourth section which embody the transformation from bitterness to sweetness.

In summary:

TABLE 9

MITZVAH	*Pesach*	*Sippur*	Matzah	*Marror*
STAGE	Purpose	Past	Present	Future
SON	*Chacham*	*Rasha*	*Tam*	*She'eino yodea lishol*
SPECIE	*Esrog*	*Aravah*	*Lulav*	*Haddas*
SEDER	*Kadeish*	*Maggid*	Meal	*Hallel*
TEFILLIN	*Kadesh*	*Vehayah Ki*	*Shema*	*Vehayah Im*
BOOK	Bereishis	Shemos	Vayikra	Bamidbar

---

1. Tehillim 118:29.

The Four Stages of *"Baruch HaMakom"*

DIAGRAM 22

1	2	3	4
ברוך המקום	ברוך הוא	ברוך שנתן תורה	ברוך הוא
"Blessed be the Master of place"	"Blessed be He"	"Blessed be the One Who gave the Torah"	"Blessed be He"

ברוך המקום —"BLESSED BE THE MASTER OF PLACE"

God is called המקום — literally, "the Place" — because "He is the Place of the world, whereas the world is not His place."[1] This means that God encompasses all space and is not limited by it. Thus the recital of this first expression corresponds to the *chacham* and *pesach sacrifice*, which both relate to the concept of place, as we shall see.

The *chacham* recognises God from the "place" — i.e., from

---

1. *Bereishis Rabbah* 68:9.

the wonders of the world.[1] The *pesach* offering commemorates the fact that God is Master over place — over the world — as we say in reference to the *pesach* sacrifice: "The *pesach* offering that our fathers ate at the time the Holy Temple stood — for what reason? Because the Holy One, blessed be He, passed over the houses of our fathers in Egypt, as it says, 'You shall say it is a *pesach* sacrifice for Hashem, because He passed over the *houses* of the children of Israel in Egypt when He smote the Egyptians and saved our *houses*.' "[2] God distinguished between the houses of Israel and the houses of the Egyptians more accurately than the most technologically advanced "smart" missile, which sometimes hits the wrong target! Thus, the *pesach* sacrifice demonstrates that God is Master over place.

Moreover, it was the very blood of the first *pesach* sacrifice that signified which houses were Jewish, God having said that He would pass over every house which had the blood of the *pesach* sacrifice on it.[3] The *pesach* sacrifice was thus instrumental in showing that God is Master over place.[4]

Similarly, God commanded that the *pesach* sacrifice be eaten only in one place, as it says, "In one house it shall be eaten"[5] — in one *place*, demonstrating again that He is Master over place.

Moreover, the *pesach* sacrifice is the only mitzvah of the Seder night which depends on a special *makom*, the Holy Temple in Jerusalem,[6] which itself is referred to as *"makom,"* as we read in connection with Avraham going to the binding of Yitzchak, "And he saw the *place* from afar."[7] Similarly with Yaakov, it says,

---

1. *Ma'aseh Nissim.*
2. Shemos 12:27.
3. Ibid., 13.
4. God did not need this as a sign; rather, it was a sign signifying that the Jews were fulfilling God's will and thereby merited redemption (*Rashi*, Shemos 12:6, 13).
5. Shemos 12:46.
6. For a sacrifice is only permitted there (*Zevachim* 112b, 119a).
7. Bereishis 22:4.

"And he reached the *place*,"[1] which Rashi explains is the place of the Holy Temple (מקום המקדש). It says further in this episode with Yaakov, "...and he took from the stones of the *place*...and lay down in that *place*."[2] The Beis HaMikdash is also referred to as "the *place* that God will choose."[3] Thus the *place of holiness* is the Beis HaMikdash, and the *pesach* sacrifice depends on this place. Additionally, the Purpose of creation — which was to put *kedushah* into *makom*, the world, by means of the Holy Temple — is hinted at in the word "*bereishis*."[4] Therefore, the *pesach* sacrifice requiring the holy *makom* corresponds to *Kadeish* of the Seder and *Kadesh* of the tefillin and the book of Bereishis, which embody *kedushah* — Purpose.

Furthermore, the word מקום has the numerical value of 186, the same as the letter קוף when it is spelled out. The Gemara tells us that this letter symbolises *kedushah*.[5] Consequently we have yet another example of *makom* corresponding to *Kadeish*.

The confluence of Above, Before, Beis HaMikdash, and "*Baruch HaMakom*" within the dimension of *Kadeish* can be explained in light of the verse, "A glorious throne exalted from the beginning is the *place* of our holy sanctuary."[6]

We have seen[7] that the Beis HaMikdash was conceptually established Before the world was created. Our rabbis base this fact on the above-mentioned verse, which refers to the designated *makom* of the Beis HaMikdash ("holy sanctuary"), which is a "throne of glory" that is Above ("exalted"), from the "Beginning" — meaning, from Before creation.[8]

---

1. Ibid. 28:11.
2. Ibid.
3. Devarim 12:5.
4. See pp. 137–138.
5. *Shabbos* 104a.
6. Yirmeyahu 17:12.
7. Page 138.
8. See *Redak*.

The Four Stages of "Baruch HaMakom"

DIAGRAM 23

                            Above   Start and Before
A glorious throne **exalted** from the **beginning**

        "Baruch HaMakom"   Kadeish
is the **place** of our **holy sanctuary**.

Therefore, Above and Before are the same dimension in reference to the *makom* of the Beis HaMikdash. This is because the Beis HaMikdash is the place of *kedushah* in the world, and *kedushah* is both Above and Before. This *kedushah* of *place* thus parallels ברוך המקום, in which we ascribe God as the Master of place.

ברוך הוא — "BLESSED BE HE"

The word *"hu"* (he) refers to God in a nonspecific, vague manner, showing that He is *nistar* (hidden). This parallels the *rasha*, from whom God is hidden.[1] It also parallels the Past, which is hidden and can no longer be seen. The *rasha* also becomes part of the hidden Past if he does not repent of his ways.

Both the second stage of the Haggadah and the second *parshah* of the tefillin deal with the hidden Past and the wicked becoming lost in the Past. Therefore, they parallel the hidden aspect of *"Baruch Hu —* Blessed be He."

ברוך שנתן תורה לעמו ישראל — "BLESSED BE THE ONE WHO GAVE THE TORAH TO HIS PEOPLE, ISRAEL"

This represents the Present. We have seen[2] that the giving of the Torah is timeless and that it is a continuously occurring

---

1. *Ma'aseh Nissim.*
2. Pages 132–133.

event, for the Torah is always being bestowed upon us in the Present. Thus the words ברוך שנתן תורה לעמו ישראל correspond to the Present.

The *tam*, the third son of the Seder night, also corresponds to the Torah being given in the Present, as he is like Yaakov Avinu, of whom it says, "And Yaakov, an *ish tam*, who sits in the tents of Torah."[1] We have seen that this is written in the Present tense, as Yaakov continuously seeks perfection and the knowledge of Torah. The one who seeks perfection always looks for Torah in the Present, and he goes from tent to tent in order to continuously receive the Torah that is continuously being given in the Present. This, of course, corresponds to matzah and the *parshah* of *Shema*, which both pertain to the Present, as we have explained previously. What is more, we see that in the *Shema*, the giving of the Torah is spoken of in the Present, as it says there, "And these words which I command you *today* shall be upon your heart."[2] We learn here that the words of Torah should always be looked upon as if they are being given to us today— in the Present.[3] Furthermore, we received the Torah on the sixth day of Sivan. We have seen[4] that the letter *vav*, which has the numerical equivalent of six, symbolises the Link between the extremes of Past and Future. Torah has the power of uniting the extremes of Past and Future, as it is continuously being given in the Present.

There is another correspondence, between "Blessed be the One Who gave Torah" and matzah. Pesach is called "the feast of the matzos, the time of our freedom." The matzos symbolise freedom from the evil inclination, for they have not reached the stage of fermentation, which represents the evil inclination.[5] To-

---

1. Bereishis 25:27.
2. Devarim 6:6.
3. *Rashi*.
4. Page 65.
5. *Berachos* 17a.

rah also causes freedom, as our rabbis tell us, "There is no freer man than one who engages in the study of Torah."[1] Thus, Torah is the medium with which we can attain freedom. Therefore, both Torah and matzah symbolise freedom.

ברוך הוא — "BLESSED BE HE"

Again we have the word *"hu"* (he) referring to God in a non-specific, vague manner, showing that He is hidden. This expression appears by both the Future and the Past because both of these stages are hidden factors that we are not experiencing in the Present. In contrast, the Present is revealed, and therefore when referred to in the Present, God is not described as *"Hu,"* hidden. The *she'eino yodea lishol* (the fourth son) is one from whom God is hidden, for he neither searches nor yearns for an attachment to the Almighty.[2] He therefore parallels the concept of God being *"Hu"* — hidden.

In summary:

TABLE 10

	1 ברוך המקום "Blessed be the Master of place"	2 ברוך הוא "Blessed be He"	3 ברוך שנתן תורה "Blessed be the One Who gave the Torah"	4 ברוך הוא "Blessed be He"
STAGE	Purpose	Past	Present	Future
SEDER	*Kadeish*	*Maggid*	*Meal*	*Hallel*
TEFILLIN	*Kadesh*	*Vehayah Ki*	*Shema*	*Vehayah Im*
MITZVAH	*Pesach*	*Sippur*	*Matzah*	*Marror*
SON	*Chacham*	*Rasha*	*Tam*	*She'eino yodea lishol*
SPECIE	*Esrog*	*Aravah*	*Lulav*	*Haddas*
BOOK	Bereishis	Shemos	Vayikra	Bamidbar

---

1. *Avos* 6:2.
2. *Ma'aseh Nissim.*

The First Four Tribes

We read concerning the birth of the first four tribes of Israel:

> Leah conceived and bore a son, and she called him Reuven, for she said, "Surely Hashem has seen my affliction now; therefore my husband will love me." And she conceived again and bore a son and said, "Because Hashem has heard that I was hated, He has therefore given me this, too," and she called him Shimon. And she conceived again and bore a son and said, "Now this time my husband will become attached to me, because I have born him three sons"; therefore he called him Levi. And she conceived and bore a son, and she said, "This time I will thank Hashem"; therefore she called him Yehudah. She then stopped having children.
>
> (Bereishis 29:32–35)

As we shall see, these tribes correspond to the four stages in time and what they represent.

REUVEN AND PURPOSE

Reuven is *reishis* — the Start — as it says, "Reuven, you are my firstborn, my strength and the *reishis* [beginning] of my might."[1] Therefore, Reuven corresponds to *Kadesh* of the tefillin, which deals with the sanctification of the firstborn. Consequently, he also corresponds to the first book of the Torah, Bereishis, which deals with Purpose.

SHIMON AND PAST

The name "Shimon" is based on the fact that God heard that Leah was hated.[2] However, the name has a darker connotation as well — that of שם עון, "there lies sin," hinting at a flaw in Shimon's descendants. Leah foresaw through Divine inspiration that Zimri, the prince of the tribe of Shimon who sinned with the Midianite princess toward the end of the Jews' sojourn in the wilderness, would descend from her son.[3] Zimri, of course, was killed and left in the Past. Thus the "*sham avon*" of Shimon corresponds to the Past, the *rasha* of the Seder, and *aravah*. Also, the name "Shimon" itself is associated with the second stage of the Seder and tefillin, which relate to the destruction of the wicked.

LEVI AND PRESENT

Leah says after the birth of Levi, " 'Now [Present] this time will my husband become *attached* [Linked] to me, because I have born him *three* sons'; therefore he called him Levi." Thus Levi represents the Present.

The name "Levi" means "attached" or "joined."[4] He is thus associated with the dimension of Link. He is also the *third* son of

---

1. Bereishis 49:3.
2. Ibid. 29:33.
3. *Midrash HaGadol* loc. cit.
4. See *Targum*.

Leah, and in this way parallels the third stage, which is the Link between the Past and the Future, and Above and Below. Indeed, the tribe of Levi Link the upper and lower through their service of the sacrifices and their teaching of Torah, as it says of them, "They shall teach Your judgements to Yaakov and Your Torah to Israel; they shall place incense before You and burnt sacrifices upon Your altar."[1] He thus parallels ברוך שנתן תורה, "Blessed be the One Who gave Torah," of this stage, as the Torah which they are designated to teach is itself the Link between heaven and earth, and was handed down from heaven to earth.

The tribe of Levi are further associated with Torah in that they are the ones who carried the Ark which held the Torah. Thus, Levi corresponds to the third stage — the Present.[2]

---

1. Devarim 33:10.
2. With the tribes there is also a similarity between the first and third tribes, a pattern we will see in other areas (see pp. 273–279).

   With the birth of the first tribe, Reuven, we are told, "And she called him Reuven...'Now therefore *my husband* will *love* me.' " (Bereishis 29:32). Similarly, with the third tribe it says "And she conceived again...and said, 'Now this time will *my husband* become *attached* to me' " (ibid., 34). There are three points emphasised in reference to both the first and third tribes: (a) "now," (b) "love" and "attachment," and (c) "my husband."

   a. Concerning Reuven the expression "now" connotes a new Start, as he was the first of the tribes. With the third son, Levi, the "now" denotes continuation in the Present.

   b. The concepts "love" and "attachment" relate to the unity within the first and third realm (see pp. 273–279).

   c. "My husband" expresses unity again relating to the first and third sectors.

YEHUDAH AND FUTURE

We have seen[1] that Leah's calling her son Yehudah, with the name's allusion to thanksgiving, evokes an association with the Future, the fourth stage in history. Thanksgiving pertains especially to the *Hallel* said in the fourth section of the Haggadah, which is replete with *hoda'ah*. *Hallel* — the fourth section — therefore corresponds to the Future, the time when there will be proper thanksgiving to God.

Yehudah parallels the *marror* changing to *chassah*, the bitter changing to sweet. This began when he admitted[2] and said, "She has been more righteous than I,"[3] in relation to Tamar. He thereby transformed the bad that he had said and thought about her to good. He also changed her fate from death to life. He was *chas* — he had compassion on her — and therefore parallels the *chassah*. Indeed, this transformation from bad to good — the reversal of his decree to have Tamar burnt — saved the progenitor of the *Mashiach* that she carried within her, and if she would have been burnt, the *Mashiach* would have been lost as well. Consequently, the *Mashiach* himself — who will bring the final redemption, which will change all bitterness to ultimate sweetness — comes from a situation of bitterness transformed to sweetness.

Accordingly, Yehudah, the fourth son, represents the Future, as does the fourth section of the Haggadah and the fourth section of the other themes we have discussed.[4]

---

1. Pages 60–62.
2. "Admission" in Hebrew is "*hoda'ah*," also related to the name "Yehudah."
3. Bereishis 38:26.
4. Interestingly, the grammatical structure of the name יהודה, which has a *yud* at the beginning, indicates the Future. In Hebrew grammar, when a *yud* is added to a verb as a prefix, it transforms it into the Future tense.

Four Transgressions

According to Torah law, there are three cardinal sins — idolatry, immorality, and murder — for which one must give his life rather than transgress.[1] There is another transgression that is classified on a similar level to these three cardinal sins — the transgression of *lashon hara* (evil speech, which includes slander, gossip, talebearing, and the like). Our rabbis tell us, "Anyone who speaks *lashon hara* propagates sins as severe as idolatry, immorality, and bloodshed."[2] In addition, they tell us, "*Lashon hara* is worse than idolatry, immorality, and bloodshed."[3] Furthermore, "For four things God punishes a person in this world with the 'interest' and leaves the 'principal' as punishment in the World to Come: idolatry, immorality, and bloodshed; and *lashon hara* is worse than all of them."[4] We thus see that these four sins are rated as the most severe in the Torah. Upon close examination, we will see that they are the converse of the four stages we have been discussing.

---

1. See *Pesachim* 25a–b; *Sanhedrin* 74a; and *Shulchan Aruch, Yoreh De'ah* 157:1.
2. *Arachin* 15b and *Maharsha* there.
3. *Tanchuma, Metzora* 2.
4. *Yerushalmi, Pe'ah* 1.

IDOLATRY VERSUS PURPOSE

Idolatry is the reverse of the Purpose of the creation of man, which is to be subservient to the Almighty and to serve Him. One who serves anything aside from the Almighty goes against the Purpose of his existence.

The reverse of *avodah zarah* is the *pesach* offering. The Jewish people in Egypt were told to take the *pesach* sacrifice in order to counter idolatry.[1] This returned them to their Purpose. By their simultaneous action against idolatry and serving of God with the *pesach* sacrifice — which is intrinsically *kadosh* — they became attached to *kedushah*.

Furthermore, the laws of the *pesach* sacrifice also hint that God is One. It is for this reason that one may not break any bone of the *pesach* sacrifice and leave it whole. Additionally, it must be roasted and not cooked, as the cooking process causes expansion, detachment, and separation, whereas roasting consolidates that which is roasted. It must also be eaten in *one* place.[2] This all hints that we are serving the One God and is the reverse of *avodah zarah*, which represents duality.

We saw earlier[3] that the book of Bereishis at the opening of creation also speaks of the unity of God, as it says, "And there was evening and there was morning, the day of the *One*," i.e., the One God. By subduing the Egyptian idolatry (the lamb) and using it for a *pesach* sacrifice, the Jews showed that God is the One and only true God, and thereby became attached to the realm of *reishis*. Additionally, the book of Bereishis shows that God is *reishis*, the first cause, whereas idolatry is the reverse. By eradicating idolatry one demonstrates one's return to the *reishis*, the Start of this first stage.

We have noted that the *pesach* sacrifice alludes to the unity of God, and it therefore belongs to the realm of Above, where

---

1. *Rashi*, Shemos 12:6.
2. See *Gevuros Hashem*, ch. 60.
3. Page 139.

nothing else but the unity of God exists. This corresponds to the first letter of the Tetragrammaton, the *yud*, which is the most unified of all the letters and the only letter that does not reach the bottom line, alluding to Above. The *pesach* offering, which is the only obligatory food on the Seder night that is *kodashim* (holy food), attaches the Jewish people to the realm of the letter *yud*, which relates to *kedushah* and the unity of Above.[1]

There is a further connection between the Passover offering and the unified realm of Above.[2] Concerning the *korban pesach* we say, "The *pesach* offering that our fathers ate at the time the Holy Temple stood — for what reason? Because the Holy One, blessed be He, passed over the houses of our fathers in Egypt." Thus the Passover sacrifice alludes to the Holy One, Who is Above, and to Him passing *Above* the Jewish houses, which showed His unity, in that no other power could stand against Him.[3] Thus it is the converse of *avodah zarah*, which is the opposite of unity and One God.

Let us conclude this section by noting one more connection between *avodah zarah* and the themes of stage one. The sin of idolatry is principally associated with the heart.[4] This corresponds to the *esrog*, which our rabbis tell us represents the heart and the first stage.[5]

LASHON HARA VERSUS POSITIVE PAST

Lashon hara — a sin committed through speech — is a hei-

---

1. See p. 288, n. 1.
2. See also the *Shlah* quoted on page 88, which says that the *pesach* sacrifice alludes to God being Above.
3. Conversely, the matzah and *marror* allude to the dough of our fathers and to the bitterness that our fathers lived through respectively, as we say, "This matzah that we eat — for what reason? Because the dough of *our fathers* did not have time to rise," and, "This *marror* that we eat — for what reason? Because the Egyptians embittered the lives of *our fathers* in Egypt."
4. See *Kiddushin* 39b and *Kli Yakar*, Shemos 28:6.
5. See p. 153.

nous transgression, and one should be zealous to refrain from speaking it. On the other hand, relating the Exodus from Egypt — a mitzvah performed through the agency of speech — is praiseworthy, and we are told that the more one relates the story of the Exodus the more "praiseworthy" one is.

In the second stage of the Seder we have a mitzvah to tell of Past history. Similarly, in the second *parshah* of tefillin, the Past history of the Exodus and the downfall of Egypt are detailed, and we are told there to relate it to our children. However, one who speaks *lashon hara* transgresses by telling what someone else did in the Past. On a final note, *lashon hara* also corresponds to the *aravah*, which represents the lips.

IMMORALITY VERSUS POSITIVE PRESENT

Immorality is a pleasure a person experiences in the Present, but which has no positive value in the Future. As we have seen, matzah represents the Present[1] and counters immorality,[2] which is the pleasure of the Present. Immorality is the inflation of pleasure — the inflation of the evil inclination (שאר שבעיסה). When, however, the pleasure subsides, it is deflated. Matzah is not inflated by the *se'or* — the evil inclination — and is therefore the opposite of desire.

The Meal, the third part of the Seder, is where the body has pleasure whilst performing the mitzvos of God — the converse of the forbidden bodily pleasure of immorality. This concept of the negation of forbidden pleasure is also embodied in the *lulav*, which represents the spinal cord.[3] The desire of immorality has its root in the spine, for a person desires and the brain sends impulses down the spine to the body.[4] Therefore, the performance

---

1. See p. 88.
2. See p. 50.
3. *Ramban*, Vayikra 23:40.
4. *Sefer HaBahir*.

of a mitzvah with the *lulav* negates the impulse toward forbidden pleasures. Thus the *lulav* is also the reverse of immorality.

BLOODSHED VERSUS POSITIVE FUTURE

The fourth transgression — bloodshed — is referred to in the fourth stage of the Haggadah, which relates to the Future. Immediately following the blessings after the meal we begin the recitation over the fourth cup and say, "Pour out Your wrath against the nations that do not recognise You and upon the kingdoms that do not call upon Your name, for they have devoured Yaakov and destroyed his habitation." This line of the Haggadah is taken from verses in Tehillim (79:6,7), and refers to the punishment that the nations will receive in the Future for the Jewish blood they shed. We read there[1] that the nations *poured* the blood of the Jewish people like water, and we therefore request[2] that God respond מדה כנגד מדה, "measure for measure": "Pour out Your wrath..." We further make a request there[3] that we witness "the avenging of the blood of Your servants which has been poured."

This section of the Seder further parallels chapter 79 of Tehillim, for in the *Hallel* we say: "Why should the nations say, 'Where is their God?' " This echoes verse 10 in our chapter of Tehillim, where it says, "Why should the nations say, 'Where is their God?' Let it become known among the nations, before our eyes, the avenging of the blood of Your servants which has been poured."

Thus when we recite the same words in *Hallel* — "Why should the nations say, 'Where is their God?' " — we are saying to God that if He does not avenge the spilled blood of His people, the nations will taunt and say, "Where is their God?" We therefore request in the Haggadah, "Pour out Your wrath against the nations that do not recognise You."

---

1. Verse 3.
2. Verse 6.
3. Verse 10.

In addition to what we've noted, the *Hallel* hints at the revival of the dead, which is the opposite of bloodshed. We read, "I will walk before Hashem in the land of the living."[1] The Roke'ach explains that this refers to the revival of the dead and means: "I will walk before God in the Land of Israel, which is called the land of the living, because its dead will be revived first."[2]

The fourth *parshah* of tefillin also hints at the revival of the dead,[3] when those whose blood was spilled will be revived. It says there, "In order to increase your days and the days of your children on the land that Hashem swore to your fathers to give to them, as the days of the heaven on the earth." The words "to your fathers to give to *them*," instead of "to give to *you*," hint at the Future revival of the dead, when *our fathers* will be given the land.

The fourth *parshah* of tefillin also has a relationship with bloodshed in that it deals with the *adamah* (ground).[4] One who commits murder is considered as if he has spilled the blood of the murdered one and all his Future generations over the ground.[5]

The spilling of blood is in opposition to *chassah* — *marror* — which hints at compassion, the opposite of the cruelty of bloodshed, which removes the Future of a person and his potential descendants. Furthermore, let us note that the ground — the Lowest place — is where the dead will rise up from in the fourth stage of time, the Future. This parallels the *marror*, which is a *pri ha'adamah*, something that grows from the ground.

Additionally, bloodshed is associated with bitterness; in the book of Shmuel there is a reference to the "bitterness of death."[6]

---

1. Tehillim 116:9.
2. See also *Pesachim* 118a.
3. *Rashi*, Devarim 11:21.
4. See Devarim 11:17, 21.
5. See *Bereishis Rabbah* 22:9 concerning the episodes of Kayin killing Hevel and Achav killing Navos.
6. Shmuel I 15:32; see also Amos 8:10, where the day of death is called "a bitter

Therefore, bloodshed, which causes death, relates to *marror* — the bitter herb.

We have thus seen that *Hallel* and the fourth *parshah* both deal with the ultimate Future — revival of the dead. In this, they parallel the *marror*, which is *chazeres* and *chassah*, the reversal of the bitterness of *marror* through the compassion of God with the removal of the *bitterness* of death. These three themes are in opposition to bloodshed.

Bloodshed is caused by jealousy, as we see with Kayin and Achav,[1] who set their eyes on the wealth of others and murdered to obtain what they wanted. This relates to the *haddas*, which is compared to the eyes and thereby hints that a person must not be tempted by his eye.[2] Concerning one who is not satisfied with his lot and continuously seeks more, it says, "Also his eyes are not satisfied with wealth."[3] The fourth *parshah* of the tefillin also deals with material wealth, and so it, too, is connected to bloodshed.

The *haddas* further corresponds to the fourth *parshah* of the tefillin in the following manner: Our rabbis tell us, "If one sees a *haddas* in a dream, this presages success for his possessions, and if he has no possessions, it is an omen that an inheritance will fall to him from somewhere."[4] Thus the *haddas* alludes to material success, as does the fourth *parshah* of the tefillin, and therefore relates to bloodshed, which is a result of the pursuit of wealth.

We mentioned previously that the fourth *parshah* of the tefillin and *marror* are connected to bloodshed in that all three have a relationship to the ground, which is related to the dimension of Lowest. The *haddas* also relates to this level. Our rabbis tell us that the *haddas* is a very low tree and is therefore compared

---
day," and Koheles 7:26.
1. Bereishis, ch. 4; Melachim I, ch. 21.
2. *Sefer HaChinuch*, mitzvah 324.
3. Koheles 4:8; see *Sha'arei Kedushah* 1:2.
4. *Berachos* 57a.

to the element of earth.[1] The fourth book of the Torah, Bamidbar, also corresponds to this dimension, since this book deals with the *midbar* (desert), which is filled with sand.[2]

In summary:

TABLE 11

SIN	Idolatry	Slander	Immorality	Bloodshed
STAGE	Purpose	Past	Present	Future
SEDER	*Kadeish*	*Maggid*	Meal	*Hallel*
TEFILLIN	Kadesh	Vehayah Ki	Shema	Vehayah Im
MITZVAH	Pesach	Maggid	Matzah	Marror
SON	Chacham	Rasha	Tam	She'eino yodea lishol
SPECIE	Esrog	Aravah	Lulav	Haddas
BLESSING	"Baruch HaMakom"	"Baruch Hu"	"Baruch shenasan Torah"	"Baruch Hu"
BOOK	Bereishis	Shemos	Vayikra	Bamidbar

FOUR LEVELS OF PHYSICALITY

Looking at this from a different angle we see that these four transgressions advance according to the order of the four levels from Above to Below:

---

1. *Menoras HaMa'or*, ch. 149, and *Emek Berachah* in *Kavanas Arba'as HaMinim*, *kavanah hachamishis*.
2. See *Shem MiShmuel*, *Hoshana Rabbah* 5678 and *Shabbos Chol HaMo'ed Sukkos* 5681, which shows the association of the four species with the four major sins in the same order but from a different viewpoint.

TABLE 12

SIN	Idolatry	Slander	Immorality	Bloodshed
DIMENSION	Above	Higher	Lower	Below
PHYSICALITY	Thought	Speech	Body	Ground

The four transgressions advance from the finest level of physicality, thought, which can neither be seen, felt, nor heard, to the coarsest, earth, the most material level. Idolatry is principally regarded as a transgression of the thoughts of the mind (מחשבה).[1] Thoughts, of course, cannot be apprehended in the physical realm. Idolatry is thus a transgression of the highest level. Since idolatry is a direct affront to God, it goes against the Purpose of our existence, which is our submission to Him.

Next comes *lashon hara*, which is a transgression committed with the speech of the mouth (דבור). *Lashon hara* is not hidden in the heart; it is articulated with the mouth and can be heard. It therefore involves more physicality than the thoughts of idolatry, and so is on a lower plain. Furthermore, the mouth is physically positioned on a lower place on the body than the brain, which is associated with the thought process.

After *lashon hara* comes immorality. This transgression involves physical pleasure of the body (גוף), as opposed to *lashon hara*, where no physical pleasure is involved,[2] and therefore belongs to a lower dimension. Additionally, the organs involved in this sin are positioned lower on the body than the mouth. Here the Link between Past and Future generations is forged in the Present. Through male and female becoming Linked here, progeny are incepted, joining soul and body. If misused in the form of immorality, the *kedushah* thereof is negated.

Finally, there is bloodshed, the fourth transgression. It is per-

---

1. *Kli Yakar*, Shemos 28:6.
2. See *Ta'anis* 8a.

petrated with the hands, as it says, "Our hands did not spill this blood."[1] The hands extend lower down than the organs on the previous level. Bloodshed is connected to the Lowest dimension. This may be seen in the story of the murder of Hevel and in *parshas Masei*, where the Torah discusses various types of murderers and their punishments. The element of earth (ארץ), which is connected to the Lowest level, is referred to in both places.

By the murder of Hevel, God said to Kayin (the murderer) that the voice of the blood of his brother screams to Him from the *earth*.[2] God then curses Kayin from the earth, which opened its mouth to swallow the blood of his brother, Hevel.[3] Kayin is told that as a result of his action, the *adamah* will no longer give of its strength to him. He is also doomed to wander the *earth*.

Similarly, in *parshas Masei*[4] we learn that bloodshed defiles the *land*, and the land is not atoned for except through the blood of the one who spilled it. Thus, bloodshed is directly associated with the ground, as the blood is poured on and swallowed up by the ground, which is cursed as a result. The ground is below and not part of man. Therefore, the transgression of bloodshed, which is associated with the ground, is the Lowest of the transgressions. We now have the following pattern:

DIAGRAM 24

Thought	Above	Idolatry
Speech	Higher	Slander
Body	Link	Immorality
Ground	Lowest	Bloodshed

---

1. Devarim 21:7.
2. Bereishis 4:10.
3. Ibid., 11.
4. Bamidbar 35:33–34.

THE FOUR EXILES

The four most severe sins correspond to the four exiles the Jewish nation would experience.

Babylon and Idolatry

The Babylonians were deeply involved in idolatry (e.g., Nevuchadnetzar tried to convince Chananyah, Mishael, and Azaryah to bow to his idol.[1])

Persia and Media and *Lashon Hara*

Our greatest adversary during the time of the Persian and Median empires was the wicked Haman. Haman's slanderous tongue was the cause of Achashveirosh's decree against the Jews. Indeed, our rabbis tell us[2] that no one could speak *lashon hara* like Haman. They further say that it was he and his sons who slandered and wrote false accusations against the Jews, trying to prevent them from rebuilding the Beis HaMikdash.[3] In the end, of course, he was unsuccessful, killed, and left to the Past.

Greece and Immorality

The emphasis of Greek culture was on bodily gratification and enjoyment of the Present. Furthermore, Greek culture still abounds in the Present — mathematics, geometry, aesthetics, sports, and science all play an important role in the culture of the Present.

Edom and Bloodshed

Edom means "red one," as this nation is bloodthirsty.

The above may be summarised as follows:

---

1. See Daniel, ch. 3.
2. *Megillah* 13b.
3. See *Rashi* on Esther 9:10.

TABLE 13

EXILE	Babylon	Persia and Media	Greece	Edom
SIN	Idolatry	Slander	Immorality	Bloodshed
STAGE	Purpose	Past	Present	Future
DIMENSION	Above	Higher	Link	Lowest

ABOVE TO BELOW AND THE FOUR MITZVOS

The four principal mitzvos of the Seder night are directly opposed to these four transgressions, following the order from Above to Below.

The *pesach* sacrifice is the rectification for idolatry perpetrated with the mind Above, as we were distanced from idolatry in Egypt by means of the *pesach* sacrifice, as we saw above.[1] The mitzvah of *Maggid*, performed with the mouth, is the antithesis of slander, perpetrated with the mouth, which is lower than the brain. Matzah, which has no "yeast in the dough," counters the drive for immorality, stemming from desire, which tends to grow until it is uncontrollable, and it is perpetrated still lower down on the body. *Marror* is opposed to the bitterness of bloodshed and death, associated with earth, the Lowest level.

Thus we have the following:

DIAGRAM 25

Thought	Above	Idolatry	*Pesach*
Speech	Higher	Slander	*Maggid*
Body	Link	Immorality	Matzah
Ground	Lowest	Bloodshed	*Marror*

---

1. Page 205.

The confluence of the two themes of Purpose to Future and of Above to Below in reference to the above-mentioned four sins may be illustrated in the following way:

DIAGRAM 26

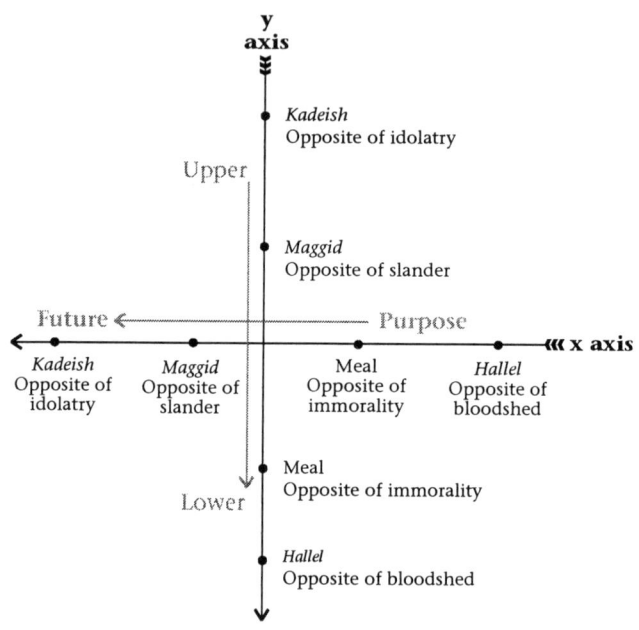

x = *Purpose to Future (time)*
y = *Upper to Lower (direction)*

The Four Elements

The composition of the physical world is based on materials that consist of and display characteristics which may be divided into four categories — earth, water, air, and fire — generally referred to as the four elements.[1] These four elements progress in ascending order.[2] Earth is the lowest. It is followed by water, which falls from heaven and rests on the earth. Next comes air, followed by fire, which rises upwards.

The four mitzvos of the Seder night correspond to these four elements. As we have mentioned, the *pesach* offering must be roasted with fire. It therefore corresponds to the element of fire, which rises Above. The mitzvah of *sippur*, telling of the Exodus, is performed with the power of speech, which involves the air that comes from the mouth. Next is matzah, which is a mixture of water and flour. Water, which descends from heaven to earth, is the element that Links Above and Below. It also blends with flour, Linking the individual particles together. Finally, there is *marror*, which is *"pri **ha'adamah**,"* grown from the ground, earth being the lowest element.[3]

---

1. See *Ramban*, Bereishis 1:1.
2. See *Rabbeinu Bachya*, Bereishis 1:2, and *Sha'arei Kedushah* 1:2.
3. This also corresponds to the four levels from Above to Below of the tefillin *parshiyos*.

DIAGRAM 27

Fire rising upwards	Above	*Pesach*
Air going forward	Higher	*Maggid*
Water from Above to Below	Link	*Matzah*
Earth Below	Lowest	*Marror*

THE FOUR NEGATIVE CHARACTERISTICS

We have seen that the four basic elements — fire, air, water, and earth — ascend in order, going from the Lowest, which is earth; to water, which falls from heaven downwards; to air; and finally to fire, which rises upwards. These four elements relate to four elemental, negative human characteristics. They are pride, negative speech, desire, and depression.[1]

Fire and Pride

Pride and haughtiness stem from the element of fire, for it is the lightest of the four elements and *rises Above* them. Anger is also in this category, for a person becomes angry only because of his pride; if he would be humble and recognise his shortcomings, he would not become angry at all.[2]

Air and Speech

Air is associated with speech, including negative speech and slander.[3]

Water and Desire

Water is associated with the desire for pleasure, for water

---

1. See *Sha'arei Kedushah* 1:2.
2. Ibid.; see also *Nefesh HaChaim*, *sha'ar* 1, ch. 5, which says that pride and anger stem from the element of fire.
3. Ibid.

causes growth and increase. Desire, which increases and becomes uncontrolled and misdirected, is considered negative.[1]

Earth and Depression

Earth, the lowest of the four elements, is associated with melancholy and depression, which draw a person downwards. The result of depression is lethargy in the fulfilment of Torah and mitzvos, because one is unhappy with his lot. One will also be distracted, because he is not satisfied with his wealth and he is unhappy with his inability to acquire the vanities of the world.[2]

THE FOUR SPECIES

The four species parallel the four elements and serve to negate the four negative characteristics. The *Sefer HaChinuch*[3] tells us that the *esrog* is similar to the heart. Additionally, the *Nefesh HaChaim*[4] states that the element of fire — which, as we have seen, is associated with haughtiness and anger — is predominant in the heart. Thus we see that, through the heart, there is a connection between the *esrog* and fire and these negative traits. Furthermore, both pride and anger are also directly associated with the heart, as it says, "haughty heart,"[5] and, "Remove anger from your heart."[6] Anger is a result of pride, as mentioned above. The *esrog* is the opposite of pride, as can be seen from the verse, אל תבואני רגל גאוה, "Let not the foot of the arrogant come to me."[7] The first letters of the verse spell אתרג.[8] Thus the *esrog* opposes pride and resultant anger.

1. Ibid.
2. Ibid.
3. Mitzvah 324.
4. *Sha'ar* 1, ch. 5.
5. Mishlei 16:5.
6. Koheles 11:10; see also Tehillim 131:1.
7. Tehillim 36:12.
8. See *Yalkut Shimoni* on Tehillim 36, and *Chasam Sofer*, Bereishis 1:11.

The *Chinuch* tells us further[1] that "the *aravah* is compared to the lips, hinting that one must control one's lips and speech." Thus the *aravah* serves to counteract the tendency to speak *lashon hara*, which is articulated with the air of the mouth.

The *Chinuch* further says that "the *lulav* resembles the spine." The desire of immorality has its root in the spine, for a person desires and the brain sends impulses down the spine to the body. The *lulav* represents the negation of desire for pleasure, which is related to the element of water.

The *Chinuch* concludes, "The *haddas* is compared to the eyes, hinting that a person should not stray after his eyes." Straying after the eyes is connected to the depression and envy one feels upon seeing the possessions of others. Therefore, the *haddas*, which represents the eyes, relates to the element of earth[2] and negates depression, which is related to this element.

Upon further analysis we see that the above-mentioned order of characteristics and elements corresponds exactly with the sequence we have seen with the four major sins. Arrogance relates to idolatry,[3] negative speech parallels *lashon hara*, desire relates to immorality, and jealousy relates to bloodshed. The following picture emerges:

TABLE 14

SPECIE	*Esrog*	*Aravah*	*Lulav*	*Haddas*
CORRESPONDS TO	Heart	Lips	Spine	Eyes
ELEMENT	Fire	Air	Water	Earth
NEGATIVE TRAIT	Pride	Speech	Desire	Depression

---

1. Mitzvah 324.
2. Since it is the lowest specie, as we have seen previously on p. 210.
3. See *Sotah* 4b.

Furthermore, the sequence of the four elements, which relate to the four negative characteristics and the four species, correspond to the order which Rabbeinu Bachya[1] gives to the four elements. Firstly, the element of fire, embodied by the *sun*, revolves around the *air space*, which makes up the heaven. Then we have the element of *water*, which surrounds the fourth element, *earth*. We thus have the following picture:

DIAGRAM 28

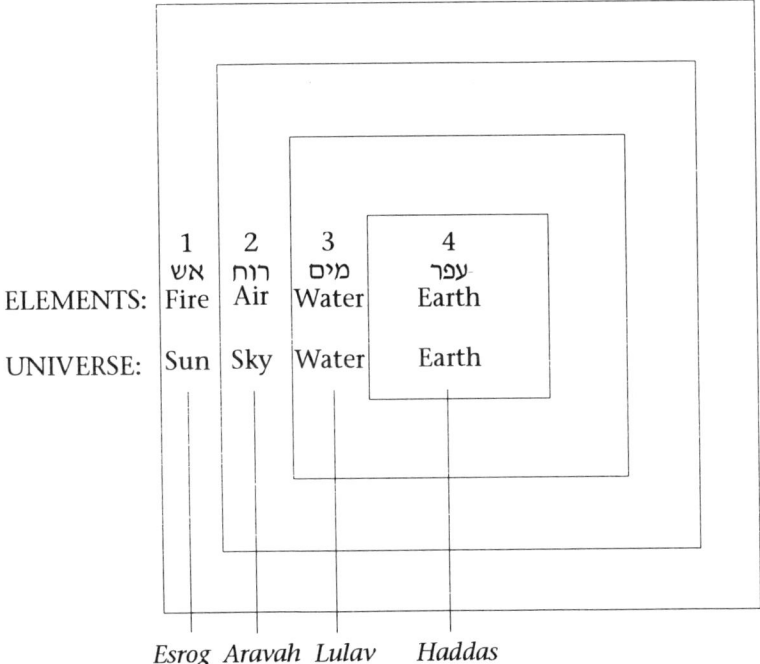

The four species thus correspond to the four principal elements of the universe, and one who holds these four species in his hands on Sukkos, in the order that they appear in the universe, has great influence on the universe.

---

1. On Bereishis 1:2.

We now have some inkling as to why our rabbis relate the verse, "There are four small creatures on the earth; however, they are exceedingly wise."[1] They explain: " 'There are four small creatures on the earth' — these are the four species. 'However, they are exceedingly wise' — they are great before God." This means that even though the four species may seem insignificant in the eyes of man, who looks at things simplistically, they are great in the eyes of God, for they are based on "mountains" of secrets and deep reason.[2] Thus, while they may seem insignificant, they in fact embody great profundity.

TWO HIGHER LEVELS AND TWO LOWER LEVELS

The four elements and the factors that they correspond to follow the pattern of two higher levels and two lower levels that we have seen previously.[3] The first two elements are fire and air, both of which are in the higher realm, as fire rises Above, and air is that which blows; they are both light and do not weigh down. The latter two elements — water and earth — weigh down and are therefore in the lower strata. Water is on a level higher than earth, for it is the lighter of the two. However, since it is drawn down from a high place to a low place,[4] it is in the lower realm. Earth, which is the heaviest, is the lowest level.

---

1. Mishlei 30:24.
2. *Eitz Yosef.*
3. Pages 102, 106–107, 111.
4. *Ta'anis* 7a.

The Scroll of Esther

Let us now shift our attention to the Purim story, for these four levels of upper and lower may be traced there as well. In turn, we will see how the Purim story relates to many of the themes we have been discussing until now. In the book of Esther we read:

> Letters were sent by the hand of the runners to all the king's provinces, to destroy, to kill, and to annihilate all Jews, young and old, children and women, on one day, the thirteenth day of the twelfth month, which is the month of Adar, and to plunder their possessions.
>
> (Esther 3:13)

Commenting on this verse, the Vilna Gaon says that a man has four parts to his existence: (a) the upper soul *(neshamah)*, (b) the middle spirit *(ruach)*, (c) the body *(guf)* and lower soul *(nefesh)*,[1] and (d) possessions *(mammon)*. Haman's plan was to uproot these four components of our existence. He intended "to

---

1. The lower soul and body are considered one (Vilna Gaon), because the bodily desires stem from the lower soul.

destroy, to kill, to annihilate...and to plunder." "To destroy" refers to Haman's wish to rid the Jews of all their mitzvos. This corresponds to the upper soul, which is connected to the spirituality of mitzvos. "To kill" refers to his intent to take away their middle spirit. "To annihilate" is a reference to his plan to destroy their bodies, to rid them from this world, so that not a single Jew should remain. "To plunder" refers to his desire to blot out the very name of Jews from the world by taking their possessions.

Accordingly, we were given four mitzvos on Purim, which serve to strengthen these four elements: the reading of the megillah, happiness, drinking wine and feasting, and giving gifts and charity.[1]

The reading of the megillah was an entirely new mitzvah. Its purpose was to counter Haman's plot to rid us of the spirituality of our souls (*neshamah*). The mitzvah to be happy corresponds to the spirit (*ruach*), which Haman tried to kill. Drinking wine and feasting is what the body *(guf)* enjoys. Therefore, the mitzvah of eating and drinking relates to the salvation of the body, which Haman wanted to annihilate. Finally, there are the mitzvos of giving gifts and charity. Haman wished to plunder our possessions. However, his plan did not succeed, and we demonstrate this by giving gifts and charity from our possessions to the poor on Purim.[2]

TABLE 15

MAN	*Neshamah*	*Ruach*	*Guf* and *nefesh*	*Mammon*
HAMAN'S DECREE	"To destroy"	"To kill"	"To annihilate"	"To plunder"
PURIM	Megillah	Happiness	Drinking wine and feasting	Giving gifts and charity

1. Vilna Gaon.
2. Ibid.

Further on in the megillah we read, "To the Jews there was light, happiness, joy, and honour."[1] This verse also contains four factors. The Talmud explains:

> Rav Yehudah said, " 'To the Jews there was light' — this means Torah, as it says, '...and Torah is light.'[2] 'Happiness' refers to the festivals, as it says, 'Be happy in your festivals.'[3] 'Joy' is *milah*, as it says,'I rejoice over your word...'[4] 'Honour' is tefillin, as it says, 'And all the nations of the earth shall see that God's name is called upon you, and they will be afraid of you.' "[5] Rabbi Eliezer the elder said this refers to the head tefillin.
>
> (*Megillah* 16b)

Rashi explains that Haman decreed that the Jews could not involve themselves in these above-mentioned activities; they were prohibited from learning Torah, from observing the festivals, from performing circumcision, from putting on tefillin. When Torah, festivals, circumcision, and tefillin were reinstated, they brought in their wake "light, happiness, joy, and honour," respectively.

The Gaon says that these four factors correspond to the previously mentioned list of Haman's intentions and the countering mitzvos. We thus have the following elements of Purim, along with the stages of the Seder and tefillin, corresponding to the elements of man:

---

1. Esther 8:16.
2. Mishlei 6:23.
3. Devarim 16:14.
4. Tehillim 119:162; see *Rashi, Megillah* 16b.
5. Devarim 28:10.

TABLE 16

HAMAN'S DECREE	"To destroy"	"To kill"	"To annihilate"	"To plunder"
MAN	Neshamah	Ruach	Guf	Mammon
"TO THE JEWS THERE WAS"	Light (Torah)	Happiness (festivals)	Joy (circumcision)	Honour (tefillin)
PURIM	Megillah	Happiness	Drinking wine and feasting	Giving gifts and charity
SEDER	Kadeish	Maggid	Meal	Hallel
TEFILLIN	Kadesh	Vehayah Ki	Shema	Vehayah Im
DIMENSION	Above	Higher	Link	Lowest
STAGE	Purpose	Past	Present	Future

STAGE ONE

TABLE 17

"To destroy"	Neshamah	Light (Torah)	Megillah	Kadeish	Kadesh

The first level is soul (*neshamah*), that part of man which is a portion of God Above and which rests Above the body.[1] The soul is all light.[2] Haman wanted to extinguish this light, and therefore banned us from learning our holy Torah, which helps us obtain that radiant light. However, his plans were thwarted, and "to the Jews there was light" — the light of Torah, which is of the level Above and which existed Before creation.

Megillas Esther was written as a result of the events surrounding Purim and was added to the books of the Torah. This

---

1. *Nefesh HaChaim* 1:15.
2. *Da'as Tevunos*, ch. 78.

was contrary to Haman's plan to take away the Torah from the Jews. The scroll was written with *ruach hakodesh* (divine inspiration). This was in answer to Esther's prayer that the megillah should have the same status as the other *holy* books of the Bible.[1] Consequently, we see that this aspect of Purim and all its details correspond to *Kadeish* of the Seder and *Kadesh* of the tefillin, the *parshah* of *kedushah*, the level from which the light of God's holiness descends to the world.

STAGE TWO

TABLE 18

"To kill"	Ruach	Happiness (festivals)	Happiness	Maggid	Vehayah Ki

The second level is spirit (*ruach*). This level is lower than the soul but higher than the body. In addition, this level includes the festivals. As the Talmud explains, "To the Jews there was happiness" refers to the reinstating of the festivals. This is also the stage of Past, since the essence of "be happy in your festivals"[2] is to commemorate Past events and to rejoice in the fond memories of God's Past intervention and miracles.[3] Therefore, this stage corresponds to *Maggid* and *Vehayah Ki Yeviacha*, which are related to the Past.

STAGE THREE

TABLE 19

"To annihilate"	Guf	Joy (circumcision)	Drinking wine and feasting	Meal	Shema

---

1. *Megillah* 7a.
2. Devarim 16:14.
3. *Sefer HaChinuch*, mitzvah 488.

The third level is that of "body" *(guf)*. It is a lower level and constitutes the Link between the upper and lower worlds. Haman decreed that the practise of circumcision was to be terminated. He also intended to destroy the body of every Jew. Haman's actions were intended to cheapen and negate the notion that the physical body can be elevated to a level of sanctity. This sanctity is most clearly evident through circumcision, which connects (Links) the limb of man's most base desire to the most sublime holiness. When Haman's plan was thwarted, the mitzvah of *milah* was reinstated with great joy. The mitzvah of drinking wine and feasting on Purim also relates to the idea of sanctifying ourselves. Man can take the otherwise unsavoury act of becoming intoxicated and utilise it in his divine service.

The joy of circumcision is the joy of the Present, more so than any other mitzvah. Rashi explains[1] that when we perform *milah*, we rejoice greatly, because unlike tefillin, mezuzah, and *tzitzis*, whose fulfilment is evident only at certain times — e.g., when wearing the tefillin or *tzitzis*, or when one is in a room that requires a mezuzah — the mitzvah of *bris milah* is continuously manifest. This joy is what the Psalmist was referring to in Tehillim. King David was distressed at being in the bathhouse, shorn of mitzvos. He therefore declared, "I am naked of all mitzvos." However, when he remembered the mitzvah of *milah*, he was comforted.[2] Therefore he said, "I rejoice over your word like one who *finds* [Present] great spoil."[3]

There is yet another connection between *milah* and the Present. The Talmud records, "Rabban Shimon ben Gamliel said, 'Any mitzvah the Jewish people accepted with joy — like circumcision, as it says, "I rejoice over your word..." — they *still* perform

---

1. On *Shabbos* 130a.
2. *Menachos* 43b.
3. Tehillim 119:162.

with joy.' "[1] Despite Haman's machinations, the joy of *milah* and its function as our Link with Above continues in the Present. It thus corresponds to the Meal of the Seder and to the *parshah* of *Shema*, which relate to the Present and our Link with Above.

STAGE FOUR

TABLE 20

| "To plunder" | Mammon | Honour (tefillin) | Giving gifts and charity | Hallel | Vehayah Im |

The fourth phase of Haman's plan was "to plunder their possessions." Money and wealth are material and therefore the Lowest aspect of man's existence. When Haman's plans were thwarted, we were given a mitzvah to perform on Purim even with this, the Lowest aspect of our existence.

In addition, we mentioned above that the fourth part of Haman's decree forbade the donning of tefillin. We further noted that with the reinstitution of this mitzvah, our honour was restored, giving rise to the fourth part of the verse "To the Jews there was light, happiness, joy, and *honour*." The Talmud[2] proves that the "honour" of this sentence refers to tefillin from a verse in the book of Devarim: "And all the nations of the earth shall see that the name of Hashem is called upon you, and they shall be afraid of you."[3] This means that the nations will see the tefillin upon you and will be afraid of you, awestruck by the glory of the tefillin.

This verse is actually part of a larger section, all of which has to do with Future and Result:

---

1. *Shabbos* 130a.
2. *Megillah* 16b.
3. Devarim 28:10.

> *And it shall come to pass, if you will* truly listen to the voice of Hashem your God, to observe and to do all His commandments which I command you today, that Hashem your God *will set you* supreme above all the nations of the earth. All these blessings *shall come upon you* and reach you, *if you will listen* to the voice of Hashem your God. Blessed *shall you be* in the city, and blessed *shall you be* in the field. Blessed *shall be* the fruit of your womb, and the fruit of your ground, and the fruit of your beasts, those cast forth by your cattle [i.e., their offspring], and the flocks of your sheep. Blessed *shall be* your basket and your kneading trough. Blessed *shall you be* when you come in, and blessed *shall you be* when you go out. Hashem *shall cause* your enemies that rise up against you to be smitten before you; *they shall* come against you on one way, and *they will* run away before you in seven ways. Hashem *shall command* the blessing upon you in your storehouses and in all the sending forth of your hand. And He *shall bless* you in the land which Hashem your God gives you. Hashem *shall set* you as a holy people to Himself, as He has sworn to you, if you observe the commandments of Hashem your God and go in His ways. And all the nations of the earth shall see that the name of Hashem is called upon you, and they shall be afraid of you.
> (Devarim 28:1–10)

Interestingly, these verses deal with Results in the same way that the fourth tefillin *parshah* does, and even begin with a similar expression: "if you will truly listen."[1] In any event, we see

---

1. See *Sukkah* 46b, where the Talmud interprets the words "if you will truly listen," which are written here in exactly the same way that the *Sifri* interprets the expression "if you will truly listen," written in the fourth tefillin *parshah*: "If you listen to the old, you *will* understand the new," in the Future.

from this whole section that the fulfilment of the blessing "And all the nations of the earth shall see that the name of Hashem is called upon you, and they shall be afraid of you," which refers to the tefillin, will only be fully realised in the Future, for only then will the fulfilment of the fourth stage come to its true and total fruition.

We have seen that the tefillin relate to the Future and are connected to the Lowest level, imbuing it with *kedushah*. Tefillin also relate to the Lowest level in the following way:

Close scrutiny of the verse "To the Jews there was light [Torah], happiness [of the heart], joy [circumcision], and honour [tefillin]," reveals a progression of sanctification from Above to Below. The light of Torah is the spiritual dimension of Above.[1] The next level is happiness, hidden in the thoughts expressed by the *heart*. The realm of thought, which is within man, is not tangible and still Higher than the remaining two levels. It is the level of *yom tov*, the festivals. The festivals are associated with time, which is the finest level of physicality. The appellation *"yom tov"* (good day), i.e., a segment of time, reflects their connection with this dimension. Following happiness is joy, referring to circumcision, which is on the physical body and Links the physical to the spiritual. Finally, there is the Lowest level, honour, referring to tefillin, which are made from animal hide, something from the Lowest world, completely outside of man and not part of him.[2]

Thus, the reinstatement of the mitzvah of tefillin, which are

---

1. See p. 90.
2. Honour, which corresponds to the tefillin made from animal hide on the Lowest level, corresponds to the fourth and lowest level of the *Aleinu* prayer, where we say, "We therefore put our hope in You, Hashem our God, to soon see the glory of Your might...to perfect the world with the kingdom of *Shaddai*, and all humanity will call upon Your name... Before You, Hashem our God, they will bend their knees and fall, and to the glory of Your Name they will give *honour*..." Thus the honour of the tefillin (the fourth level in Megillas Esther) and the honour of the *Aleinu* prayer parallel each other.

part of our possessions, countered "to plunder their possessions," in which Haman planned to rid us of our possessions — the Lowest level. As we noted previously, the fourth *parshah* of tefillin, which deals with the material world and our wealth, also relates to this level.[1]

From all of the above we have seen:

DIAGRAM 29

Light (אורה)	Above	Kadesh	Kadeish	Fire rising
Happiness (ושמחה)	Higher	Vehayah	Maggid	Air going forward
Joy (וששון)	Link	Shema	Meal	Water from Above to Below
Honour (ויקר)	Lowest	Vehayah Im	Hallel	Earth Below

FOUR LEVELS OF LIGHT

Torah, the festivals, *milah*, and tefillin each comes to influence and convey spiritual light to the Jewish nation. The light invested in these levels descends from the highest to the lowest world in a distinct pattern. The spiritual light of Torah, which is Above the physical world, is followed by happiness of the spirit, which is a light that dwells in the heart of a person.[2] Here the light has reached a lower level — it is within man. The next level, the joy of *milah*, causes spiritual light to radiate.[3] This light has descended still further to the lower, external part of the physical body as opposed to the previous level, happiness, which is internal. Furthermore, the light of *milah* is associated with the skin. The Hebrew word for skin, עור, is similar to the word אור (light). However, skin is material, whereas this light is spiritual. We remove the foreskin to reveal the spiritual light.[4]

---

1. The last two levels — body and wealth — are in the physical realm, whereas the first two, dealing with Torah, the soul, and the spirit and joy of the heart, are in the spiritual realm. This is consistent with the pattern seen previously (pp. 102, 107, 111, 222; see *Tefillin: The Inside Story*, p. 455, n. 1).
2. See Tehillim 97:11 and the *Malbim* there; see also Mishlei 13:9 and *Malbim*.
3. See *Tefillin: The Inside Story*, pp. 269–270.
4. Ibid.

The light then descends to the final and lowest level through the tefillin, which is more external than the previous level of *milah*, the tefillin being a separate entity and not part of the body itself. It is also lower in that on this level the light of spirituality enters the hide (skin) of an animal, whereas in the previous level it was revealed in the actual body of the person. Furthermore, in the previous level it was the removal of skin that revealed the light, i.e., the removal of some of the physical in order to reveal the spiritual, whereas in the fourth level it is an infusion of spiritual light into the animal hide. Thus we see that the spiritual light descends from Above to the internal, down to the Lowest external.

Thus we arrive at the following picture:

DIAGRAM 30

Light (אורה)	Torah	Most spiritual light	Above
Happiness (ושמחה)	*Yom tov*	Light in heart	Higher
Joy (וששון)	*Milah*	Light to body	Link
Honour (ויקר)	Tefillin	Light to animal skin	Lowest

Here we also have two upper and two lower levels, reflected by an amazing sequence of אור and עור: The first two are levels that are associated with *light* (spiritual) itself, whereas the latter two deal with *skin* (physical) and are thereby on a lower level.

The Four Rivers

We have seen that the four stages of deliverance in Megillas Esther correspond to the order of the four stages of the Seder and of the *parshiyos* of the tefillin. This pattern is also apparent in connection with the four rivers that are enumerated in the account of creation. We read:

> A river goes out from Eden to water the garden, and from there it separates and becomes four heads. The name of the first is Pishon; that is the one which encompasses the whole land of Chavilah, where there is the gold. And the gold of that land is good; there is the *bedolach* and the *shoham* stone. The name of the second river is Gichon; that is the one which encompasses the whole land of Kush. The name of the third river is the Chidekel; that is the one which flows to the east of Ashur. The fourth river is Peras.
> (Bereishis 2:10–14)

In his commentary on these verses, the Malbim tells us:

> God established four rivers, each one surrounding a particular country. Every one of these countries

nurtures a different quality and characteristic. After Adam ate from the tree of knowledge of good and evil, people were divided into four categories that encompass all the characteristics of humanity, every person according to the qualities of the lands in which he lives. The river that watered the garden was itself the river of Peras. This river surrounds the Holy Land, which has the ability to develop wise men and prophets possessing the spirit of God, but "from there [the Garden] it separates" from its source, "and becomes four heads" surrounding four territories whose dispositions and qualities differ from one another.

There are people who pursue riches and wealth in order to fill their houses with silver and gold and the treasures of kings, thinking that this is their life's sole purpose and success. There is a second group who pursue sensual desires and pleasure; and yet a third group who pursue honour, admiration, and prestige. The latter three pursuits are the source of mankind's evil. They are jealousy, lust, and the desire for honour. Our rabbis tell us[1] that these three traits remove a man from the world, for the root and origin of mankind's evil stems from these three. From the quest of wealth sprouts jealousy and the pursuit of attractive belongings. From the desire for the sensual stems immorality. The quest for an elevated position leads to wars, murder, and the destruction of the masses.

The strength of these bad traits is dependent on the location. The place where one finds gold, the *bedolach*, and the *shoham* stone develops the desire for wealth. The place where it is very hot promotes

---

1. *Avos* 4:21.

burning sensual desire. The people living in the place which produces strong and mighty-hearted people arouse wars. However, the fourth river alone is "holy to the Eternal," representing the one who busies himself with wisdom and the fear of God, despising the vanities of the world.

Let us discuss each of these rivers in turn.

THE FIRST RIVER

The name of the first river is Pishon; that is the one which encompasses the whole land of Chavilah, where there is the gold...the *bedolach* and the *shoham* stone.

The name Pishon has the connotation of "increase."[1] This name, plus the fact that this river encompasses land that contains precious mineral resources, indicates that it epitomises the pursuit of material wealth.

THE SECOND RIVER

The name of the second river is Gichon.

The name "Gichon" is associated with the snake, which is described as the one who slithers on its *gachon* (belly).[2] The snake is the symbol of lust. Therefore, this river and the land that it spans represent lust.

THE THIRD RIVER

And the name of the third river is the Chidekel; that is the one which flows to the east of Ashur.

---

1. The root פשה means increase (as in ופשו פרשיו in Chavakuk 1:8).
2. Vayikra 11:42, and *Rashi* there.

The inhabitants of Ashur were warlike. The name "Ashur" means power,[1] and specifically here it has the connotation of the power of war. The river Chidekel which relates to this land has the connotation of *chad v'kal*, "sharp and light,"[2] hinting at the cunning and swiftness of the people of Ashur in battle.[3] Therefore this river and the land it is associated with represent the drive for power and honour.

THE FOURTH RIVER

The fourth river is the river Peras.

This last river is in fact the same as the first one mentioned. It is the one which "goes out from Eden to water the garden"[4] and which then divides into four rivers. It is the source of all the other rivers and is associated with *kedushah*, as it is the river affiliated with the holy Land of Israel.[5]

THE RIVERS AND MEGILLAS ESTHER

These rivers and what they represent follow the pattern seen in the Scroll of Esther:

---

1. See *Rashi, Gittin* 34a.
2. *Rashi.*
3. See Chavakuk 1:8, which shows that "light" and "sharp" are expressions defining the powers used in battle.
4. Bereishis 2:10.
5. *Malbim.*

TABLE 21

RIVER	Peras	Chidekel	Gichon	Pishon
HAMAN'S DECREE	"To destroy"	"To kill"	"To annihilate"	"To plunder"
MAN	Neshamah	Ruach	Guf	Mammon
"TO THE JEWS THERE WAS"	Light (Torah)	Happiness (festivals)	Joy (circumcision)	Honour (tefillin)
PURIM	Megillah	Happiness	Drinking wine and feasting	Giving gifts and charity
SEDER	Kadeish	Maggid	Meal	Hallel
TEFILLIN	Kadesh	Vehayah Ki	Shema	Vehayah Im
DIMENSION	Above	Higher	Link	Lowest
STAGE	Purpose	Past	Present	Future

The first level in Megillas Esther relates to the upper soul (*neshamah*), the light of Torah, *Kadeish*, *Kadesh*, Above, and Purpose. These factors relate to the river Peras, which is associated with the holiness of the Land of Israel and its Torah. It is thus Above the level of the other rivers and consequently relates to the stage of Purpose.

The next level down in Megillas Esther relates to the middle spirit (*ruach*) and the Past, and thus to *Maggid* and *Vehayah Ki Yeviacha*. This relates to the second river, Chidekel, which corresponds to the concept of war, wherein one intends to reduce the enemy to the Past. This level relates to the seeking of honour. Even though it is lower than the level of *kedushah*, it is still higher than the next two levels down, as pride is not a physical desire. It is therefore on the level of Higher.

The third level of Link and the Present in Megillas Esther relates to the Meal, *Shema*, the body *(guf)*, and circumcision — the antithesis of immorality and bodily desires, which are associated with the third river. Since this level relates to the physical body, it is lower than the previous one.

The fourth and lowest level of Megillas Esther relates to possessions (*mammon*), giving gifts, *Hallel,* and *Vehayah Im Shamoa.* This all corresponds to the river Pishon and the land of Chavilah, where there is gold and precious stones. These rare articles are outside man and lower than him. They thus symbolise the level of Lowest.

Yotzer Ohr

In the morning daily prayer service we recite the following blessing:

ברוך אתה ה׳...יוצר אור ובורא חשך עושה שלום ובורא את הכל.

Blessed are You, Hashem...Who forms light and creates darkness, makes peace and creates all.

The source of this blessing is the verse:

יוצר אור ובורא חשך עשה שלום ובורא רע אני ה׳ עשה כל אלה.

Who forms light and creates darkness, makes peace and creates evil; I am Hashem, Who makes all these.

(Yeshayahu 45:7)

A cursory examination reveals that the blessing differs somewhat from the verse: the last part of the verse is *"u'vorei ra* — and creates evil,"* whereas the blessing ends with *"u'vorei es hakol* — and creates all."* Rabbi Yaakov Emden, in his siddur, *Beis Yaakov*, explains the difference. He notes that even though the verse tells us that God created *ra* (evil), the blessing tells us "and creates all," because evil exists not for its own sake, but for our sake, that we may overcome it and thus amplify the good. We will thereby receive the ultimate good as a reward in the Future. Thus evil serves good and is part of the master plan of creation, part of the all-encompassing "and creates *all*" stated in the blessing. Therefore, "and creates all" includes the creation of evil mentioned in the verse.[1]

This blessing may be divided into the following parts: (a) "Who forms light," (b) "and creates darkness," (c) "makes peace," (d) "and creates all." These four concepts correspond to the four stages of the Seder and the tefillin *parshiyos*.

---

1. "*U'vorei*" is mentioned in connection with both darkness and evil. *Beriyah* is the first crude stage of creation ("something from nothing") but does not include the forming (יצירה) or completion (עשייה) of the thing created. Since the two factors of "darkness" and "evil" incorporate negativity, they are considered as still being in the stage of incomplete creation (בריאה).

    Evil and darkness were not created as an end in themselves; rather, they were created to be overcome and crushed, thus letting the light of spirituality break forth and shine through. Consequently, the negativity of darkness and evil in their original state is only the initial stage of their creation (*beriyah*), and hence the term "*beriyah*" is used. Only once they have been overcome and transformed do they fulfil their ultimate purpose. These forces of darkness and evil must be acted upon day and night in order to achieve this end. Therefore, the Menorah of the Beis HaMikdash, epitomising the light of Torah shining through the darkness of "creates darkness" was kindled each night, symbolising the expulsion of darkness. Likewise, the Mizbei'ach HaKetores, which transforms the negative of "creates evil" (hinted at by the inclusion of *chelbenah*, a malodorous spice) to good, had to be kindled each day. See also pp. 268–270.

TABLE 22

YOTZER OHR	"Forms light"	"Creates darkness"	"Makes peace"	"Creates all"
VERSE	"Forms light"	"Creates darkness"	"Makes peace"	"Creates evil"
STAGE	Purpose	Past	Present	Future
SEDER	*Kadeish*	*Maggid*	*Meal*	*Hallel*
TEFILLIN	*Kadesh*	*Vehayah Ki*	*Shema*	*Vehayah Im*

יוצר אור — "WHO FORMS LIGHT..."

The first part of the blessing is concerned with the formation of light. This particular spiritual light is in the realm of *Atzilus*, the realm of Purpose and Above.[1] It is the light of holiness,[2] which was the Purpose of creation. Therefore, it corresponds to the first level of the Seder and tefillin.

This is the realm of the holy *pesach* sacrifice, which must be offered in the Beis HaMikdash, the place of holiness, which itself was the Purpose of creation, and relates to the *light* of holiness.[3]

This is also the domain of the *chacham*, the wise son, for wis-

---

1. *Siddur Beis Yaakov*. Our rabbis tell us (*Sha'arei Kedushah* 3:1) that there are four levels through which God lowered Himself, so to speak, from the highest of the heavens to this, the lowest of worlds, in order to create the physical plane.The four levels are *Atzilus* (Emanation), *Beriyah* (Creation), *Yetzirah* (Formation), and *Asiyah* (Completion). These four stages are derived from the words of the prophet, "All that is called by My Name *for My glory*, I have *created* it, I have *formed* it, and I have *made* it" (Yeshayahu 43:7). The first level, *Atzilus*, is the conceptualisation of creation. *Atzilus* is derived from the word "*etzel*," meaning "next to." This is because *Atzilus* is the level that is closest to God. The second level is the initial actualisation of creation, the ex nihilo creation of primal matter. Third is Formation, taking the amorphous matter and energy of the previous stage and giving it shape and form. The final stage is Completion, in which the final product is perfected.
2. See p. 138; see also *Da'as Tevunos* 78.
3. See p. 138.

dom is likened to the advantage light has over darkness.[1] Wisdom lights up the face of the *chacham*.[2] Moreover, the *chacham* referred to here is also a *tzaddik*, for his strong points are his Torah learning and his good deeds,[3] and our rabbis tell us, " 'And God called the light day' — these are the deeds of the righteous."[4] Thus the *chacham* is included in the light and Purpose of creation.

Additionally, the book of Bereishis is the book of the forefathers,[5] who brought down the spiritual light of God to the world and whose entire lives were centered around building a nation that would bring down the Divine light of the "One Who forms light" into the world.

This is also the domain of the *esrog*, which is yellow, the color of light. It thus corresponds to the element of fire, which is *ohr* (light).[6] Interestingly, an *esrog* which is green is invalid unless it will eventually turn yellow off the tree. Moreover, it is preferable not to purchase an *esrog* unless it has begun to turn yellow.[7]

ובורא חשך — "AND CREATES DARKNESS..."

The second part of the blessing states that God "creates darkness." The concept of darkness relates to physicality itself, as spirituality increases light, whereas physicality increases darkness.[8] The darkness of the blessing thus parallels *Maggid* of the Seder and the second *parshah* of tefillin, which both deal with darkness — the *chomer* (materialism) of Egypt and its destruction.

---

1. See Koheles 2:13.
2. Ibid. 8:1.
3. Compared to the taste and smell of the *esrog*, as mentioned previously, on p. 153.
4. *Bereishis Rabbah* 3:8.
5. See *Avodah Zarah* 25a and *Rashi* there.
6. *Menoras HaMa'or*, ch. 149.
7. See *Shulchan Aruch, Orach Chaim* 648:21, and *Mishnah Berurah* 64 and 65.
8. See *Da'as Tevunos* 78.

Consequently, we see that the first and second stages depict two extremes: light of Purpose and darkness of the Past, respectively.

Darkness is the realm of the *rasha*, the wicked son, for he is steeped in darkness, as our rabbis tell us, " 'And to the darkness He called night' — these are the deeds of the wicked."[1]

In the Future, darkness and all that is related to it will vanish[2] and become a thing of the Past.

עושה שלום — "MAKES PEACE"

Peace is the fusion of two extremes — the coming together of opposing forces. This corresponds to the stage of Present and Link, which is the meeting point of the extremes of Purpose and Future, and Above and Below. It parallels the Meal of the Seder and the *parshah* of Shema, in which these and other extremes are unified.

Yaakov also relates to peace, as he created peace between two extremes when he synthesised the extremes of Avraham's *chesed* and Yitzchak's *gevurah*.[3] This synthesis is exemplified by the Meal and *Shema*, the *parshah* of unity, where extremes become united in the service of God.

Furthermore, Yaakov is called, "Yaakov, the perfect one [*shelimah*]."[4] Both the concepts of *shaleim* (perfection) and *shalom* (peace) relate to one another, as both represent perfection: *shaleim* is the perfection of the self, through the blending of extremes, and *shalom* is the perfection of one's relationship with others. Additionally, Yaakov is called *"tam,"* which the *Targum*

---

1. *Bereishis Rabbah* 3:8. See also *Mishlei* 4:19, 13:9, 24:20, and *Iyov* 18:5, 21:17. Additionally, see *Tanchuma Yashan, No'ach* 8. See also *Kol Eliyahu*, p. 98, concerning the connection between the righteous and the wicked and light and darkness.
2. See p. 139.
3. See pp. 168–169 and n. 4.
4. Selichos.

translates to mean *"gevar shelim,"* a perfect person. Thus "makes peace" parallels the *tam*.

The third book of the Torah, Vayikra, is also concerned with unity in the service of God and therefore relates to Linkage and peace. Vayikra's central theme deals with our obligations toward God whereby we can become connected to and be one with Him.[1] Similarly, peace corresponds to the letter *vav*, the third letter of the Tetragrammaton, which represents unity.

Peace also parallels the *lulav*, which is the blending of opposite extremes.[2] Indeed, the *lulav*'s blending of extremes is why the *aravah* and *haddas* — which represent Past and Future respectively — are bound to the *lulav*, which represents the Present, the middle path between them. The *lulav*'s connection to Link also explains why it is the only species mentioned by name in the blessing over the four species, for the *lulav* is the Link that binds them together.

There is also a correspondence between peace and matzah, which is a symbol of unity.[3] Looking at Yaakov, *lulav*, and matzah together, we see that they represent unity and life.[4] Both of these concepts of unity and life coincide with "makes peace," for life depends on peace and harmony, whereas death results when there is friction and conflict between extremes.[5]

"Makes peace" also parallels ברוך שנתן תורה לעמו ישראל — "Blessed be the One Who gave Torah...," for our rabbis tell us, "Anyone who learns Torah for its own sake, it is as if he makes peace..."[6] Since the giving of the Torah is an event that is constantly taking place in the Present it "makes peace" between the

---

1. See *Tefillin: The Inside Story*, p. 126, for a detailed acount of how the sacrifices in the book of Vayikra effect unity with God.
2. See pp. 168–169.
3. See pp. 88 and 189.
4. See pp. 88, 167–169, 185–189.
5. *Seforno*, Bamidbar 25:12.
6. *Sanhedrin* 99b; see also Mishlei 3:17.

extremes of Past and Future by Linking them.

Let us conclude our discussion on peace by noting that in the section on darkness we said that evil and darkness are destined to vanish. In contrast, this stage emphasises the submission of physicality and evil to spirituality. It is the realm of "makes peace," Linking and making peace between the extremes of light and dark[1] rather than destroying darkness.

ובורא את הכל — "AND CREATES ALL"

The fourth part of the blessing, "and creates all," incorporates the transformation of bad into good in the Future, when we will be able to see clearly that "all" was for the good. Consequently, it parallels *marror, she'eino yodea lishol, haddas, Hallel, Vehayah Im Shamoa,* and Bamidbar, all of which relate to the transformation from bad to good that will occur in the Future.

TABLE 23

YOTZER OHR	"Forms light"	"Creates darkness"	"Makes peace"	"Creates all"
STAGE	Purpose	Past	Present	Future
SEDER	Kadeish	Maggid	Meal	Hallel
TEFILLIN	Kadesh	Vehayah Ki	Shema	Vehayah Im
MITZVAH	Pesach	Maggid	Matzah	Marror
SON	Chacham	Rasha	Tam	She'eino yodea lishol
SPECIE	Esrog	Aravah	Lulav	Haddas
BLESSING	"Baruch HaMakom"	"Baruch Hu"	"Baruch shenasan Torah"	"Baruch Hu"
SIN	Idolatry	Slander	Immorality	Bloodshed
BOOK	Bereishis	Shemos	Vayikra	Bamidbar

1. See *Tefillin: The Inside Story,* pp. 246–248, for a more detailed account.

The Tetragrammaton

We have already seen[1] that the four letters of God's name correspond to the stages of Purpose to Future, and of Above to Below. We have also seen[2] that the four cups of the Seder and the four tefillin *parshiyos* correspond to the four letters of the Tetragrammaton. Let us now see how they parallel the various other themes we have been discussing.

THE FIRST LETTER

We have seen that the first part of the Seder and the first *parshah* of tefillin comprise the concept of *kedushah*, which in turn corresponds to the concepts of Purpose and Above — the beginning of all. This is hinted at by the letter *yud*, the first letter of the Tetragrammaton, which encompasses the other three concepts of time within itself.[3]

The numerical value of the letter *yud* is ten. The number ten portrays *kedushah* in many areas.[4] It is well known that a group

---

1. Pages 63–67.
2. Page 69.
3. See pp. 78–79.
4. See *Tefillin: The Inside Story*, pp. 206–214, for a fuller treatment of this subject.

must consist of at least ten men to be considered a minyan. The Talmud says, "Any *holy* matter may not be executed with less than *ten* people present."[1] Interestingly, the Torah tells us in *parshas Kedoshim*, the *parshah* of *holiness*, "Hashem spoke to Moshe saying, 'Speak to the entire community of Israel and say to them, You must be *holy*, since I, Hashem your God, am *holy*.' "[2] The Ba'al HaTurim points out that this verse refers to the Jewish people specifically as an *eidah*.[3] The Gemara tells us that *"eidah"* implies a group of at least *ten* people.[4] This group is to be told, "***Kedoshim** tiheyu —* You must be *holy*," a clear connection between the number ten and holiness. Moreover, the Ba'al HaTurim observes that the sentence "I am Hashem your God" is mentioned *ten* times in *parshas **Kedoshim***. Again, the number ten is associated with *kedushah*. The commandments in *parshas Kedoshim* also embody the Aseres HaDibros, the *Ten* Commandments.[5] Thus we see that the section in the Torah dealing primarily with the *holiness* of the Jewish people has a marked association with the number *ten*.

Ten is also the number which represents a new Start in many areas representing a Start of *kedushah*.[6] Let us examine some of the areas where ten is seen as a Start in relation to Pesach.

The number ten and Start correspond to the actual *pesach* sacrifice. The Jews performed this *first* mitzvah as a nation on the *tenth* of the month of Nissan, as it says, "On the tenth of this month every man shall take a lamb..."[7] Thus, the *Start* of the redemption from Egyptian slavery was on the tenth of Nissan.

Incidentally, the significance of this mitzvah as the Start of

---

1. *Megillah* 23b.
2. Vayikra 19:1–2.
3. As opposed to the more common "Speak to the children of Israel."
4. *Megillah* 23b.
5. *Vayikra Rabbah* 24:5; *Ramban*, Vayikra 19:2.
6. See *Tefillin: The Inside Story*, pp. 207–213.
7. Shemos 12:3.

the redemption is more than just the fact that it was the first step of the process that culminated in the offering of the *korban pesach* and the Exodus. This mitzvah demonstrated the freedom of the Jews in and of itself, for when the people displayed their freedom by tying a lamb (which the Egyptians considered a god) to their beds, the Egyptians could do nothing to stop them.

The verse states regarding this mitzvah that Moshe shall tell "the whole community of Israel"[1] to take a lamb on the tenth of the month. Here, too, the term *"eidah,"* meaning a community of at least ten, is employed. It is mentioned here, in connection with the *kedushah* of the *pesach* sacrifice, as this was the first time the Jewish people would be involved in *kedushah* as a community. Thus, the *eidah* was to perform its *first* act of *kedushah* on the *tenth* of Nissan.

The Rambam states, "The sacrifices of the firstborn cattle, tithes [tenth of one's animals], and the Passover offering all need one pouring of blood. The blood of each of these is poured on the foundation of the altar."[2] The reason the blood of these sacrifices is poured on the *foundation* is because they relate to the idea of Start. The Passover sacrifice marks the Start of the Jewish nation. The *first*born is also a Start, for obvious reasons. The tithes are given to God to remind us that He is the source — the Start — and first cause of our flock, and indeed of all our possessions. The blood of all three is therefore placed at the foundation of the altar — as the Start is the foundation, and it effects the outcome. Consequently, we see that *ma'aser* (tithe) is associated with the *pesach* sacrifice and *bechor* (firstborn), which all represent Start.

We are told to bring a tenth of our produce and the *bechor* to the Beis HaMikdash in order to learn the fear of God. The Torah says, "And you shall eat before Hashem your God *in the place He*

---

1. Ibid.
2. *Mishneh Torah, Hilchos Ma'aseh HaKorbanos* 5:17; see also Mishnah, *Zevachim* 5:8.

shall choose to put His name there: the *tenth* of your grain, your wine, and your oil, and the *firstborn* of your herds and your flocks, that you may learn *to fear Hashem* your God always."[1]

The combination of these factors — tenth, firstborn, Temple, and fear of God — relates to the concept of Start in the following way: The Holy Temple is the first and Start, as we are told by the prophet, "A glorious throne exalted from the *beginning* is the place of our *holy sanctuary*."[2] Fear of God is also considered a beginning, as it says, "Fear of Hashem is the *beginning* of wisdom."[3] Consequently, tenth and *bechor*, which are in the category of Start, cause the fear of Hashem, which is also a Start, when brought to the Temple, which is a Start as well.

Let us look once again at the association between the firstborn, the tenth, the Passover offering, and Start. When God smote the firstborn Egyptians on the first night of Passover, He saw the blood of the *pesach* lamb on the houses of the Jewish people and passed over them.[4] However, it was not merely the blood of the Passover lamb which God beheld. Rather, through the Passover sacrifice, God recalled another lamb which played a key role in our history — the lamb of the *akeidah*, the binding of Yitzchak.[5] There, too, the word "*seh*" (lamb) is used (אלקים יראה לו השה), as it is with the *korban pesach*. Hence, it was the merit of the binding of Yitzchak, the *tenth* trial of Avraham, which stood on behalf of the Jewish people at this point. Moreover, the *korban pesach* was selected on the *tenth* of the month and was now functioning at the time of the *tenth* plague. It was at this very moment, when all these tens converged, that the wicked firsts — the firstborn of Egypt — were destroyed. At that instant a new beginning came about for the Jewish nation, and the firstborn of Yisrael were se-

---

1. Devarim 14:23.
2. Yirmeyahu 17:12.
3. Tehillim 111:10.
4. See Shemos 12:13.
5. *Mechilta, parshah 7.*

lected for their holy mission — to serve in the Holy Temple. All this was in the merit of the binding of Yitzchak, the *peter rechem* (firstborn) of Sarah, which was recalled through the *korban pesach*. Yet again we have firstborn, *pesach*, and tenth sharing an association.

Now that we have seen the association of *kedushah*, Start, and the number ten in relation to Pesach, let us turn to the first *parshah* of tefillin. The text of this *parshah* mentions the Start of the Jewish nation. It also deals with the beginnings of *kedushah* in Judaism. It is therefore the *first parshah* of the tefillin. In it, Moshe Rabbeinu is told, "Sanctify to Me every firstborn, the first from every womb, among the children of Israel...it is Mine." Rashi explains that "it is Mine" because "I acquired the firstborn of Israel for Myself when I destroyed the Egyptian firstborn [during the tenth plague]."[1] Consequently, it is also apparent from the first *parshah* that the number ten plays a significant role at this moment, for the tenth plague marked the *Start* of the *kedushah* of the Jewish *bechor* (in itself a Start). Thus, Start and ten again coincide.

In fact, *parshas Kadesh* includes the association of the *peter rechem*, firstborn of the mother, the tenth plague, and the Passover offering. Here, too, the tenth trial of Avraham; Yitzchak, the firstborn of Sarah; the *korban pesach* taken on the tenth of the month; the tenth plague; the new beginning for the Jewish nation; and the firstborn of Yisrael are all united to make a holy Start. This is similar to the association of the firstborn cattle, tithes, and the Passover offering, the sacrifices of which need their blood poured on the *foundation* of the altar.

We mentioned previously[2] that the letter *yud* epitomises Start. Not coincidentally, its numerical value is also ten. Since the *yud* represents *kedushah* and Start, it is stressed in the first *parshah* and not

---

1. See also Bamidbar 3:13.
2. Page 63.

in the other *parshiyos* of the tefillin. In the verse והיה כי יביאך, "And when Hashem brings you...," which appears in the first *parshah*, the word יביאך is spelled with an extra *yud*, something not found in the same word when it appears in the second *parshah*.

It is apparent that the number ten corresponds to holiness and Start. It is therefore associated with *Kadesh*, the *parshah* of holiness, and Start. In addition to the above, the number ten also relates to the concepts of Before and preparation.[1] It was on the tenth of Nissan, four days prior to the actual sacrifice, that the Jews in Egypt had to *prepare* the Passover sacrifice. This was done by selecting a lamb from the flock and making sure it had no blemish — a preparation done Before the actual sacrifice. It was also a preparation for the redemption, as we are told that the Jews were delivered in the merit of taking the lamb on the tenth and preparing it.[2] Moreover, the *pesach* sacrifice is also associated with the letter *yud* in that it is *kodashim*, and therefore it is in the realm of the holiness of *yud*, which personifies the concepts of Before and preparation.

God warned the Egyptians of the tenth plague Before any of the other plagues.[3] Therefore, ten has its influence Before in order to facilitate the Result at the end. This is similar to the *yud* of Olam Haba,[4] the two *yud*s mentioned in connection with the creation of man[5] and the ten sayings of creation.[6]

As we have seen before,[7] the tenth plague — the slaying of the firstborn — is also connected to the level of Above. This is because the firstborn of Israel received their own special *kedushah* at this point, and the plague was directly executed by God, Who is

---

1. See *Tefillin: The Inside Story*, pp. 102–104.
2. *Rashi*, Shemos 12:6.
3. See Shemos 4:23 and *Rashi*.
4. See p. 64.
5. See *Tefillin: The Inside Story*, p. 110.
6. Ibid.
7. Pages 110–111.

Above. This parallels the fact that *yud*, which has the numerical value of ten, is the only letter which does not reach down to the point where all the other letters extend. It is Above everything. In fact, our rabbis say[1] that the Divine presence never descended to a point lower than *ten tefachim* (handbreadths) from the ground. Additionally, the *yud* is in the realm of *"Baruch HaMakom* — Blessed be the Master of place," which refers to God being Above place.

It turns out that the number ten, which is associated with the smiting of the firstborn, simultaneously represents the realm of Before and the realm of Above. This is consistent with the *yud* of the Tetragrammaton, which relates to the level of Before and to the level of Above at the same time.

The *yud* also represents the realm of *Chochmah* (Wisdom)[2] and therefore corresponds to the *chacham*, the wise son.

Finally, let us turn our attention to the *esrog*: It is the smallest of the four species and thereby resembles the letter *yud*.[3]

THE SECOND LETTER

The second letter of God's name is *hey*, which represents the Past and the second level down.[4] This parallels the second *parshah* of the tefillin. Indeed, whereas the first *parshah* encompasses the dimension Above, the second *parshah* is concerned with the first stage of our physical time zone. It also deals with the redemption of a firstborn *chamor* (donkey), which in turn represents the redemption of the *chomer*. In order to redeem the physical, we have to deal with it directly. Thus the second *parshah* is connected to this world and not to what is Above. The alternative to redeeming the donkey is breaking its neck, which

---

1. *Sukkah* 5a.
2. See p. 68 and n. 1.
3. See also p. 288, n. 1.
4. As explained above, p. 64.

symbolises breaking the *chomer*. Therefore, the second *parshah* touches the physical world in order to break its hold over us.

The second *parshah* of the tefillin is also concerned with the wicked, for the breaking of the neck of the *chamor* is also symbolic of the breaking of Pharaoh's power. The commentators point out[1] that the Hebrew word פרעה has the same letters as הערף (nape of the neck). This is why it is written in the second *parshah* of the tefillin: "*Va'arafto...* — And you shall break the nape of the neck of the donkey,"[2] and then we are told that we do this because Pharaoh stiffened his neck and did not let us go.

The *hey* of God's name has an opening at its base, representing this world, through which the *rasha* may "go out" and leave God. The breaking of the neck of the *chamor* and the killing of the firstborn mentioned in the second *parshah* serve as a warning to him.

The *hey* represents this dark world, from which the primordial light was taken and hidden for the World to Come. As Rashi explains,[3] it was hidden from this world because of the *resha'im* who would misuse it. The *hey* with which this passing world was created also resembles the retribution of the *rasha*, who is interested in the passing desires of this world and is eventually lost to the Past and blotted out (and who, if he wishes to repent, will be helped by God, which is alluded to by the opening in the side of the *hey*).

Thus, the *hey* is associated with the *rasha*, "creates darkness," *lashon hara*, "*Baruch Hu*," *sippur*, *aravah*, *Maggid*, *Vehayah Ki Yeviacha*, and *Shemos* — all of which are in the second domain, as we have previously explained at length.

---

1. See *Asarah Ma'amaros, Ma'amar Eim Kol Chai* 3:27, and *Yad Yehudah* there.
2. Shemos 13:13.
3. On Bereishis 1:4.

THE THIRD LETTER

We have seen[1] that the *vav*, the third letter of God's name, is the letter of joining and that it is like a hook. It therefore represents the Present. The same is true for *Shema*, the third *parshah* of the tefillin. It is the *parshah* of the Present and unity in every respect.[2]

We are told in this *parshah* to merge the spiritual Torah of Above with the physical world Below, as it says, "And these words...shall be upon your heart...and you shall teach them to your children and discuss them...and you shall bind them as a sign..." This also relates to the *vav* of God's name, which symbolises the Link between Above and Below, i.e., the extension of the *yud* that is Above down to the world Below, which results in a bridge between the upper and lower. In addition, the *vav* parallels *matan Torah*, the giving of the Torah (which this *parshah* represents), which was a bridge between the spiritual and the physical. Moreover, the Torah is the unifying element that binds the Jewish people to God and also to each other, and so is closely connected with the letter *vav*, which represents these two functions.

The *vav* as the elongated *yud* is alluded to at *matan Torah* in two ways: (a) the Ten (*yud*) Commandments were given on the sixth (*vav*) of Sivan, and (b) the Ten (*yud*) Commandments were written on tablets that were six (*vav*) handbreadths long.[3] These both symbolise the *yud* being lowered down by means of the *vav*.

The *Shema* also symbolises the lowering of the *yud* by means of the *vav*. The *Shema* alludes to the Ten Commandments.[4] At the same time, this *parshah* has a great affinity to the letter *vav*, which resembles the attachment of Torah to Below.[5]

---

1. See p. 65.
2. See *Tefillin: The Inside Story*, pp. 216–222, for a detailed explanation.
3. *Shemos Rabbah* 28:1.
4. *Zohar, Va'eschanan* 268a; *Siddur HaGra*.
5. See *Tefillin: The Inside Story*, pp. 219–220.

The *Shema*'s relationship to the *vav* can be seen in the following manner: *Vav* has the numerical value of six. There are six words in the first verse of the *Shema*. There are also six verses in the *Shema*. Moreover, the *Shema* represents the giving of the Torah, which occurred on the sixth of Sivan at the sixth hour, when God made His sixth descent to this world.[1] Thus the whole chapter relates to the *vav* and the giving of the Torah.

The third blessing, *"Baruch shenasan Torah l'amo Yisrael —* Blessed be the One Who gave Torah to His people, Israel," also corresponds to the letter *vav* of the Tetragrammaton, which represents God extending and giving the *yud* of Torah to the Lower world. Consequently, whereas *"Baruch HaMakom"* represents the *kedushah* of God Above, which corresponds to the letter *yud*, *"Baruch shenasan Torah"* represents God lowering His Torah to His people, Israel.

Man was created on the sixth day of Creation, having physical faculties yet possessing a lofty soul. Thus man is a bridge between the physical world, on the one hand, and the spiritual world on the other. The sixth day itself was the Link between the first days, in which the material world was created, and the seventh day of creation, the holy Shabbos. Again the sixth is the Link between the physical and the spiritual.

The function of the letter *vav* as a Link, along with the third *parshah* of tefillin, corresponds to "makes peace" of *Yotzer Ohr*, as peace is the fusion of extremes. This in itself corresponds to Yaakov and the *tam*, which both relate to unity, as we explained previously. "Makes peace" also corresponds to the Meal of the Seder, which is the joining of the Past of *Maggid* and the Future of *Hallel*, and Above with Below. Furthermore, the third book of the Torah, Vayikra, matzah, and *lulav* are also the fusion between extremes.

Additionally, the *lulav* looks like the *vav*, which is an exten-

---

1. See *Pirkei D'Rabbi Eliezer*, ch. 41 and 46.

sion of the *yud*, and thus the *esrog*, which looks like a *yud*, has its extension in the *lulav*.[1]

THE FOURTH LETTER

The fourth letter of God's name, the *hey*, parallels the fourth *parshah* of tefillin and *Hallel*, the fourth section of the Seder. This *hey* represents Olam HaZeh in its Future state of perfection, when all bad will be transformed into good. It also represents the penitent returning through the side opening of the *hey*.

The fourth *parshah* of tefillin also relates to the transformation of bad to good, as we noted earlier[2] in the discussion of the Torah being a *sam tam* (perfect medicine). This therefore relates to the last *hey* of the Tetragrammaton.

The revival of the dead hinted at in the end of this *parshah*[3] is also an example of the ultimate return to good and the correction of the first sin, which caused death. At that time, when the world will have changed into the perfect *hey*, man will regain his previous state of perfection.

The final *hey* of the Tetragrammaton also parallels the last words of this *parshah*, "heaven on earth," referring to the bringing down of physical rain from Heaven.[4] This is a Result of our connecting the spirituality that stems from Above to ourselves down Below, as commanded in the *Shema*, the third *parshah* of the tefillin. The *parshah* of *Shema* is *our* Linking the lower world to the upper one *in the spiritual sense* — through the observance of the mitzvos mentioned therein. Conversely, the *parshah* of *Vehayah Im Shamoa* — "And if you will listen..." — represents *God* joining the upper world to the lower one *in the physical sense*, His reciprocating our behaviour by showering us with *physical* bless-

---

1. See p. 288, n. 1, concerning the *lulav* being an extension of the *esrog*.
2. Page 177.
3. Ibid.
4. See *Rashbam*, Devarim 11:21.

ing from the heavens Above to this world Below. This is the concept of the final *hey* of the Tetragrammaton, which represents the perfection of this lower world.

We thus see that the Tetragrammaton spans the dimensions and levels from Purpose to Future and from Above to Below and relates to the themes we have mentioned.

TABLE 24

TETRAGRAMMATON	Yud	Hey	Vav	Hey
YOTZER OHR	"Forms light"	"Creates darkness"	"Makes peace"	"Creates all"
STAGE	Purpose	Past	Present	Future
SEDER	Kadeish	Maggid	Meal	Hallel
TEFILLIN	Kadesh	Vehayah Ki	Shema	Vehayah Im
MITZVAH	Pesach	Maggid	Matzah	Marror
SON	Chacham	Rasha	Tam	She'eino yodea lishol
SPECIE	Esrog	Aravah	Lulav	Haddas
BLESSING	"Baruch HaMakom"	"Baruch Hu"	"Baruch shenasan Torah"	"Baruch Hu"
BOOK	Bereishis	Shemos	Vayikra	Bamidbar

The Mishkan

While the Jews were in the wilderness, God commanded them to build a Mishkan (Tabernacle). The Mishkan served to emulate the Heavenly Chariot, and through it God would come to dwell among us. This is also the secret of the tefillin.[1] Thus the tefillin have a direct connection with the Mishkan. Based on our entire discussion up to this point, it is therefore apparent that the Mishkan is connected to the Pesach Seder as well. Indeed, looking at the four principal inner vessels of the Mishkan, we see that they correspond to both the four *parshiyos* of the tefillin and the four stages of the Pesach Seder.

The four principal vessels within the Mishkan (and later in the Temple in Jerusalem) are the Aron (Holy Ark), Menorah (Candelabra), Shulchan (Table), and Mizbei'ach HaKetores (Incense Altar).

---

1. *Midrash HaNe'elam, Chayei Sarah* 129a.

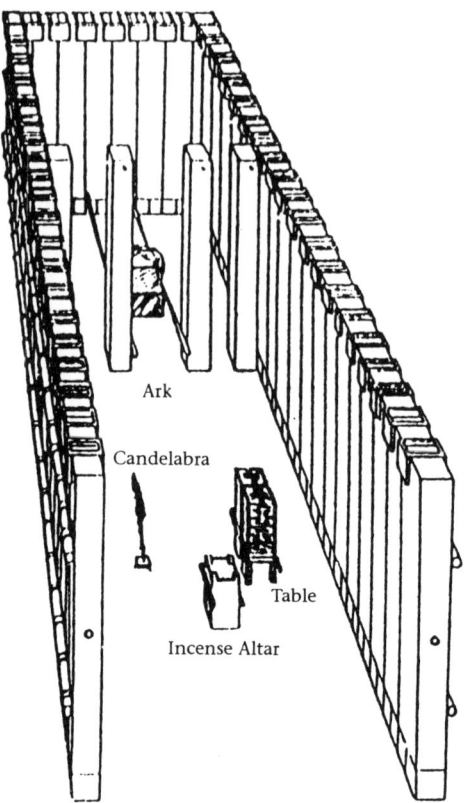

DIAGRAM 31

THE ARK

The Aron is the first vessel of the Mishkan to be mentioned in *parshas Terumah*, the portion of the Torah that discusses the Mishkan, the vessels, and the materials from which they were to be built. It is mentioned first because it is the vessel with the most *kedushah*. This is because it housed the Torah, which represents the Purpose of the world and contains the highest degree of *kedushah* in the world.[1] It is for this reason that the Ark was the

---

1. As explained above on p. 90.

only vessel housed in the Holy of Holies.

The Aron is the Start of all *kedushah* in the Sanctuary, reflected by the fact that the cloud of the *Shechinah* (Divine Presence) did not enter the Sanctuary until the Aron was brought in.[1] In this way it parallels the first stage of the Pesach Seder and the first *parshah* of the tefillin, which are the Start and the domain of *kedushah*. The Aron also hints at *Chochmah*, the sphere of Godly wisdom that is Above our comprehension.[2] The Aron was therefore separated from the rest of the vessels and kept hidden from the eye, behind the dividing curtain.[3] The Aron is called *"Aron HaKodesh."*[4] Thus it corresponds to *Kadeish* of the Seder and *Kadesh* of the tefillin, which represent the level of *kedushah*, which is Above everything.

As we shall see, the Aron has multiple connections with the number ten, and therefore with the letter *yud* of the Tetragrammaton. One connection lies in the fact that it housed the Ten Commandments. In turn, this demonstrated the connection of Torah to creation, which came about through *ten* sayings. These ten sayings were not complete until the Ten Commandments were uttered at Mt. Sinai. Regarding the ten sayings of creation, the expression *"ma'amaros"* is employed, whereas the ten statements[5] of Sinai are called *"dibros."* The word *"dibbur"* indicates a more intense form of speech than the word *"amirah."* This alludes to the fact that the Ten Commandments are the completion of the ten sayings of creation. They are thus a reinforcement of the Start and Beginning.

---

1. See Melachim I 8:6–10.
2. *Malbim*.
3. See *Malbim* in *Remazei HaMishkan*, which notes that the Mishkan was constructed in such a way that its various parts matched the organs of a human being. The Aron in the *Kodesh Kodashim*, separated from the other vessels that stood without, parallels the brain (the highest location of the body).
4. See Bamidbar 31:6 and *Rashi* there.
5. Although generally translated as "commandments," the word "statements" is a more accurate translation.

Kedushah spread from the Aron, which housed the Ten Commandments, to the rest of the Mishkan. It was therefore the Start of *kedushah* for the Mishkan. This Start embodied multiples of *ten*: The Aron was ten *tefachim* (handbreadths) tall.[1] It supported the *keruvim*, which were ten *tefachim* tall, and their wings spread over the Aron at a height of ten *tefachim*[2] and housed the Tablets with their ten statements. Furthermore, the Holy of Holies which housed the Aron, was ten *amos* (cubits) long, ten *amos* wide, and ten *amos* deep. The Holy of Holies was also the tenth and most elevated level of *kedushah* in the Land of Israel.[3] Thus, the Aron is associated with the holiness hinted at by the number ten.

Each year on the *tenth* of Tishrei — Yom Kippur — the *Kohen Gadol* would enter the Holy of Holies, which housed the Ten Commandments in the Aron, to signify a new commitment to the Torah. The *tenth* day of the year, which Starts the year with a *new* slate, was the only day the *Kohen Gadol* could enter the Holy of Holies and advance to the Aron, the centre of all the above-mentioned tens. He thereby gained a *new Start* imbued with the *kedushah* of ten for the entire Jewish nation.

The Aron corresponds to "Who forms light" in *Yotzer Ohr*, in that the letters of the word ארון are the same as אורן, "their [Israel's] light." This is because the Ark housed the Torah, which is the light of Israel.[4] Moreover, just as God hid the light of "Who forms light,"[5] so is the light of the Torah hidden within the Aron.

The Aron's association with light also connects it to the book of Bereishis, in that the word "*bereishis*" deals with the light of *kedushah* and the Beis HaMikdash, as we have seen above.[6] This light of *kedushah* emanates from the Torah housed in the

---

1. *Sukkah* 4b.
2. Ibid. 5b.
3. *Keilim* 1:6–9.
4. *Ba'al HaTurim*, Shemos 25:10.
5. See *Tefillin: The Inside Story*, p. 245, n. 3.
6. Page 137.

Aron, which is also hinted at in the word *"bereishis"* — "for the sake of the Torah which is called *reishis.*" Additionally, the Ark is associated with *Chochmah* and thus relates to the *chacham,* who has the light of the wisdom contained in the Aron.

Finally, there is the *esrog,* which symbolises the level of *Kodesh Kodashim* and the Aron.[1] Interestingly, the Aron stands separate from the other three vessels in the Sanctuary, behind the dividing curtain[2] in the same way that the *esrog* stands apart from, and unattached to, the other three species.

THE CANDELABRA

There was a special relationship between the Aron and the Menorah in the Mishkan. The Aron, which represents the hidden light of the Torah, was secreted in the Holy of Holies. However, the Menorah, which also represents light, was on the other side of the curtain and radiated its light to the world outside. The reason for the difference is because whereas the Aron's light represents *Chochmah* — the sphere of Godly wisdom that is Above our comprehension — the Menorah's light represents *Binah,* the discerning of the Torah, the section of Torah that is within our reach.[3] *Binah* is the realm of the *hey,* the second letter of the Tetragrammaton.[4] The Menorah was outside the Holy of Holies because it is in our realm. It is on a Lower level than the Aron, which embodies the hidden light of Torah that is Above our comprehension. The Menorah, on the outside of the dividing curtain, radiates the hidden Torah of the Aron within the Holy of Holies to the outside world.

The relationship between the Menorah and the Aron is mirrored by the relationship between the second stage of the Seder,

---

1. *Rikanti, parshas Emor* and *parshas Terumah.*
2. See diagram 31 on p. 260.
3. *Malbim.*
4. See p. 68, n.1.

Maggid, to the first one, *Kadeish*. Just as the Menorah is the revelation of the hidden light of the Aron, *Maggid* elaborates and explains *Kadeish*. In the first part of the Seder we mention the Exodus, including the fact that this is where our *kedushah* stems from. However, no mention is made of the details. Thus they are hidden — the realm of *Chochmah*. The second part of the Seder, with its questions, answers, and explanations, is the realm of *Binah*, in which the Exodus mentioned in *Kadeish* is illuminated and elucidated. This parallels the relationship between the Aron and the Menorah, the Menorah being the revelation of the holy light of the Aron and the understanding of that light within the level of *Binah*.

The Menorah and Aron share yet another relationship. The Torah in the Aron represents *Torah shebiksav*, the Written Torah. This was the written text that the Almighty gave to Moshe. However, the Written Law cannot be understood without being explained by *Torah sheba'al peh*, the Oral Law that was given alongside the written text. The Menorah symbolises the radiance and illumination that the Oral Law sheds on the Written Torah.

Paradoxically, the *light* of the Oral Law parallels the level of "creates darkness" of *Yotzer Ohr*, for the Oral Law is compared to darkness. This is because one cannot see the radiant light embodied in the Oral Law without toiling over it. Before achieving understanding of *Torah sheba'al peh* — which is only arrived at after tremendous struggle — one can only see the prodigious difficulty inherent in the struggle itself. However, through the pain experienced in the toil over the Oral Law, one removes the darkness and reveals the light that is hidden within.[1] Thus the Menorah represents the revelation of the light from within the darkness.[2]

---

1. *Tanchuma, No'ach*, ch. 3.
2. There is an allusion to the paradoxical "light from the dark" represented by the Menorah in the tefillin. The two *shin*s of the head tefillin have a total of seven branches (one *shin* with three branches and the other with four). These seven branches represent the seven branches of the Temple's

Although the light of the Menorah could be seen on the outside, it required constant attention, needing to be kindled *every night* (as opposed to the light of the Aron, which no one kindled). This hints at the light of the Oral Law, which cannot be attained without continuous toil. A person must first experience a degree of darkness — night — and only then is he rewarded with illumination. Thus the Menorah parallels the concept of "creates darkness" in this respect as well.

The light from darkness represented by the Menorah is also reflected in the oil that was used to kindle it, which was obtained by beating and squeezing the olive. The oil represents the Torah,[1] and since it was obtained only through beating it out of the olive, it illustrates that one can reach the light of Torah only through great toil.

This light of the Oral Law "was kindled" and rose to great heights during the period of the Greek Empire. The Greek Empire is described as *choshech* (darkness).[2] Amazingly, the miracle of Chanukah, the time when the Menorah remained lit for eight days even though there was enough oil only for one, surfaced in the very darkness of Greece. Thus "creates darkness" corresponds to the Menorah in this way as well, for at the very moment of "creates darkness" — the Stygian darkness of the Hellenist kingdom — the light of the Menorah was rekindled.

Chanukah is the only festival not mentioned explicitly in the Written Law. Rather, its existence stems from the Oral Law.

Menorah (*Zohar, parshas Pinchas, Ra'aya MeHeimna* 254b). Consequently, "the light of the Menorah" is situated on the head tefillin, which represents the *Aron HaKodesh*, as they hold *parshiyos* of the written Torah within (see *Tefillin: The Inside Story*, pp. 280–282). This Menorah of the tefillin, along with the remainder of the outside of the tefillin, is painted black. This hints at the fact that the light of the Menorah (representing the Oral Law) shines forth from the darkness of the night of this world (see *Tefillin: The Inside Story*, pp. 268–270, 282, and 298–300, for more details).

1. *Shir HaShirim Rabbah* 1:2, on Shir HaShirim 1:3.
2. *Bereishis Rabbah* 2:4.

Therefore, Chanukah is the festival of the Menorah, which represents the Oral Law. Furthermore, since Chanukah, the festival of lights, stems from the Oral Law, which is considered darkness, it represents the light shining forth from the darkness.

This second section of the Seder and the second *parshah* of the tefillin deals with the forces of evil and darkness, their destruction, and the emergence of the light of Israel. Likewise, the darkness of the Greek Empire was overcome, and in its place emerged the light of the Jewish Menorah.

Finally, let us add that the Menorah, which represents the Oral Law, corresponds to the *aravah*, as it represent the lips of the *mouth*.

THE TABLE

The Shulchan, along with its showbread, represented the sustenance of the Jewish nation emanating from the *kedushah* of the Aron within. It therefore symbolised the fusion, or Link, between the upper and the lower, the spiritual and the physical. Furthermore, a portion of *levonah* incense, of which it says, "a memorial portion for Hashem,"[1] was kept on the Table. Thus the Table held both the bread that was laid before God and then eaten by man (the *Kohanim*), and the *levonah*, which was offered up to God. The Shulchan thus represents the Link between the spiritual and the physical. Moreover, there was a miracle performed in conjunction with the Shulchan in the Mishkan, in that each batch of showbread stayed fresh and warm for the entire week it was displayed[2] — a spiritual miracle performed on the physical bread.

The Table of Showbreads held twelve breads divided into two rows of six.[3] The Shulchan therefore corresponds to the *par-*

---

1. Vayikra 24:7.
2. *Chagigah* 26b.
3. See Vayikra 24:6.

shah of *Shema*, which has six words in the first verse and contains six verses, and which also represents the Link between Above and Below. It also corresponds to the Meal of the Seder, in which many mitzvos involving food are performed, thereby Linking Above with Below. Additionally, the bread on the Table in the Mishkan was matzah, which appears on the Seder table as well.

The third section of the Seder includes *Tzafun*, the eating of the hidden *afikoman*. This corresponds to the Shulchan in the Mishkan, which was on the northern side, which is called "*tzafon*," because the sun sometimes appears to be hidden there.[1]

The book of Vayikra also relates to the Link between Above and Below, and thus parallels the Table. This all relates to *temimus* of the *tam* and "makes peace" of *Yotzer Ohr*, which are the fusion between the two extremes. The Shulchan with the showbread made of wheat corresponds to "makes peace" in another way as well, for when there is wheat in the home, there is *shalom*.[2]

THE INCENSE ALTAR

The Incense Altar is the last of the inner vessels of the Mishkan to be mentioned,[3] as it represents the final stage — the Future. The Malbim tells us that this altar hints at the Future and the Result which transpires from the service of the other vessels, the tying together of all the worlds and levels. Furthermore, the crown that borders the top of the Incense Altar hints at the crown that the righteous will wear in the Future, as our rabbis say, "In the Future, the righteous will sit with adornments on their heads."[4]

This Incense Altar also represents the transformation from

---

1. As mentioned previously, p. 53.
2. *Bava Metzia* 59a, based on Tehillim 147:14.
3. See Shemos 30:1.
4. *Berachos* 17a; *Kli Yakar*, Shemos 30:1; see also *Peirushei HaTorah* of the Ba'alei HaTosafos, Shemos 30:2.

bad to good, for our rabbis explain[1] that the *ketores* (incense) contained the *chelbenah* spice, which had an unpleasant odour. However, when combined with the other spices, it became part of the overall pleasant odour. This hints at the combination of the wicked with the righteous in our prayers.[2]

As we have noted previously, the transformation from bad to good will transpire completely only in the Future, as we say in the fourth section of the *Aleinu* prayer, "We therefore put our hope in You, Hashem our God, to soon see the glory of Your might...to perfect the world with the kingdom of *Shaddai*, and all humanity will call upon Your name, *to turn all the wicked of the world toward You..."*

The dimensions of length, breadth, and height of the Incense Altar were all *one* cubit. This also alludes to the Future, when all bad will be transformed to good, and God will be *One*.[3] This also corresponds to the fourth section of the Haggadah, wherein we express the Future unity of God.[4] Returning to the fourth stage of the *Aleinu* prayer, we see this unity expressed there as well, as it says, "And it is said, 'And Hashem shall be King over the whole world; on that day Hashem will be One and His name will be One.' "[5]

The *Zohar* informs us[6] that the incense has the power to break the *yetzer hara* (evil inclination). Furthermore, the incense removes death and counters the Angel of Death.[7] Indeed, we are further informed by the *Zohar*[8] that Death has no dominion over a place in which one recites the section dealing with the incense.

---

1. *Krisos* 6b.
2. Ibid.
3. See *Kli Yakar*, Shemos 30:1.
4. See pp. 123–124.
5. Zechariah 14:9.
6. *Shemos* 218b.
7. See *Rashi*, Bamidbar 17:11, 13.
8. *Shemos* 219a.

Both these functions of the incense — the neutralisation of the evil inclination and of the Angel of Death — are actually one and the same, as the evil inclination and the Angel of Death are synonymous.[1] This parallels the fourth part of the Seder, which heralds the Future elimination of the Angel of Death. Additionally, this negates bloodshed, the fourth transgression.

In this respect, the Incense Altar also parallels the fourth tefillin *parshah*, which deals with the transformation of the *yetzer hara* to good[2] — something which will truly occur only in the Future. The fourth *parshah* also deals with the revival of the dead — the time when the Angel of Death will have no dominion, and his function will be overturned with the revival of those he killed.

We mentioned previously that the sweet-smelling incense included the *chelbenah*, which represents the wicked, hinting that we should include the wicked in our service to God. In this capacity, the Incense Altar also corresponds to "creates *all*," the fourth stage of *Yotzer Ohr*, which incorporates "creates evil."

The pleasant odour of the Incense Altar also corresponds to the *haddas* (the fourth specie), as the chief characteristic of the *haddas* is its fragrance. Furthermore, the Incense Altar is instrumental in transforming the bad odour of the *chelbenah* into a sweet smell. This parallels the fact that the *haddas* relates to the transformation of bad to good.[3]

---

1. *Bava Basra* 16a.
2. See p. 177.
3. See p. 172.

TABLE 25

VESSEL	Ark	Candelabra	Table	Incense Altar
STAGE	Purpose	Past	Present	Future
TETRAGRAMMATON	*Yud*	*Hey*	*Vav*	*Hey*
YOTZER OHR	"Forms light"	"Creates darkness"	"Makes peace"	"Creates all"
SEDER	*Kadeish*	*Maggid*	Meal	*Hallel*
TEFILLIN	*Kadesh*	*Vehayah Ki*	*Shema*	*Vehayah Im*
MITZVAH	*Pesach*	*Maggid*	*Matzah*	*Marror*
SON	*Chacham*	*Rasha*	*Tam*	*She'eino yodea lishol*
SPECIE	*Esrog*	*Aravah*	*Lulav*	*Haddas*
BLESSING	"Baruch HaMakom"	"Baruch Hu"	"Baruch shenasan Torah"	"Baruch Hu"
SIN	Idolatry	Slander	Immorality	Bloodshed
BOOK	Bereishis	Shemos	Vayikra	Bamidbar

Stages One and Three versus Stages Two and Four

Unity versus Multiplicity

Until this point, we have primarily discussed each of the four stages individually and shown how the components of the various groups of four fit in with their respective stages. We will now see how the different stages within every individual set of four may be further divided into two groups of two in a profound way: stages one and three, and stages two and four. These two sets of two represent various concepts, and each set (of stages one and three) serves to contrast the other set (stages two and four).

The first division we will discuss is between positivity and unity on the one hand, and negativity and multiplicity on the other. This contrast is particularly apparent in the blessing of *Yotzer Ohr*, from which it can also be shown to exist in the Tetragrammaton. It also appears in the four *parshiyos* of the tefillin, and in the four stages of the Seder, as well as other areas.

IN *YOTZER OHR*

We have discussed the verse יוצר אור ובורא חשך עשה שלום ובורא רע אני ה' עשה כל אלה, "Who *forms light* and *creates darkness*, makes *peace* and *creates evil*; I am Hashem, Who makes all these."[1] We have also seen the blessing based on this verse: ברוך אתה ה׳... יוצר אור ובורא חשך עושה שלום ובורא את הכל, "Blessed are You, Hashem...Who *forms light* and *creates darkness, makes peace* and *creates all*." The first and third components of this verse and blessing correspond to each other, and the second and fourth components correspond to each other. The Tetragrammaton follows the same pattern. In the above-mentioned verse itself, it says that "I am Hashem [*Y-k-v-k*]," Who brought these four factors into existence. Consequently, these four factors have a special affinity with the four letters of the Tetragrammaton, whence they stem. The four components of the blessing can be divided into two groups, and the corresponding letters of the Tetragrammaton also divide into these two groups.

DIAGRAM 32

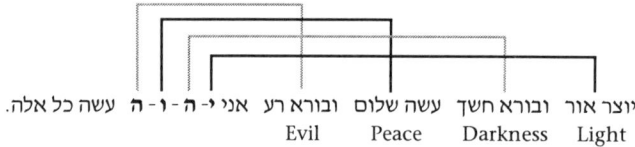

| יוצר אור | ובורא חשך | עשה שלום | ובורא רע | אני י-ה-ו-ה עשה כל אלה. |
| Light | Darkness | Peace | Evil | |

Let us see how the first and third factors correspond to each other, and how the second and fourth factors correspond to each other, and how this pattern may be traced in the letters of the Tetragrammaton as well.

---

1. Yeshayahu 45:7.

DIAGRAM 33

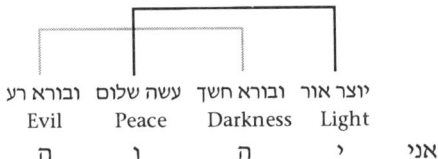

Factors one and three are light (אור) and peace (שלום), aspects of positivity and unity. Light here is the light of *Atzilus*,[1] the highest level, where all is one. Peace, we have seen, is on the third level, which results from unity in this world. Positivity and unity stem from the will to give and impart, which is the essence of all existence.[2] On the other hand, factors two and four are darkness (חשך) and evil (רע) — aspects of negativity and disunity.

These concepts relate to receiving and taking without the will to give, opposing the essence of all existence, and are thus considered external and not the true essence.

The first and third and the second and fourth letters of the Tetragrammaton have a connection to this pattern as well, as we will see. Let us now turn to the four *parshiyos*.

IN THE FOUR *PARSHIYOS*

DIAGRAM 34

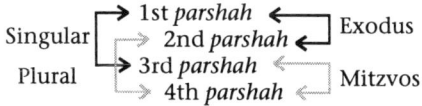

In the first two *parshiyos* we are told to explain the mitzvos and their relationsip to the Exodus. However, the crucial differ-

---

1. See n. 1. on p. 242.
2. See Tehillim 89:3 and *Michtav MeEliyahu*, vol. 1, p. 144.

ence between them is that in the first *parshah* we are addressed in the singular and are told to relate the explanation for the mitzvos in the singular, whereas the second *parshah* is expressed in the plural. The first *parshah* mentions "me" (singular) and "you" (singular). We read: "And you shall tell your son on that day saying, 'It is because of this that God did for *me* when *I* left Egypt. And it shall be for *you* as a sign...because with a strong hand God brought *you* out of Egypt.' "

The second *parshah* presents the same idea in the plural: "And when your son asks you in time to come, saying, 'What is this?' that you shall say to him, 'With a strong hand Hashem brought *us* out of Egypt...and it came to pass, when Pharaoh was stubborn and would not let *us* go, that Hashem killed all the firstborn in the land of Egypt... And it shall be a sign...because with a strong hand Hashem brought *us* out of Egypt.' "

Similarly, the essence of both the third and fourth *parshiyos* is the observance of mitzvos, but in the third *parshah* it is portrayed in the singular and in the fourth it is portrayed in the plural. In the third *parshah* we read:

> *Hear* [singular], O Israel, Hashem our God, Hashem is One. And *you* [singular] shall love Hashem your God with all *your heart* and with all *your soul* and with all *your* possessions. And these words which I command *you* today shall be upon *your heart*. And *you shall teach* them to *your* children, and *you shall discuss* them when you sit in *your* house and when *you travel* on the way, and when *you lie down* and when *you get up*. And *you* shall bind them as a sign on *your* arm, and they shall be as *totafos* between *your* eyes...

This passage addresses the individual and thus uses the singular form in the Hebrew.

The very same commandments are expressed in the plural in the fourth *parshah*:

And it shall be that *if you truly listen* [plural] to My mitzvos that I command *you* this day, to love Hashem *your* God and to serve Him with all *your* hearts and with all *your* souls... *Place* these words of Mine upon *your* hearts and upon *your* souls, and *bind* them as a sign upon *your* arm, and they shall be as *totafos* between *your* eyes. And *you shall teach* them to *your* children that they shall speak about them...

It thus emerges that the first and third *parshiyos* are in the singular, and the second and fourth are in the plural. The first and third *parshiyos* therefore point to the dimension of unity, and the second and fourth point to the domain of duality and plurality.

The difference between unity and multiplicity as expressed in the third and fourth *parshiyos* is apparent in yet another way. In the third *parshah* it says, "And you shall love Hashem your God with all your heart and with all your soul and with all your *possessions.*" In the fourth *parshah*, where we are again commanded to love God, it says only, "to love Hashem your God and to serve Him with all your heart and with all your soul," with no mention made of possessions.

The Vilna Gaon[1] explains that the reason for this difference is because the fourth *parshah* (written in the plural) is addressing the community and not the individual. An individual can reach the level where he subjugates his entire being to the Almighty. Such a person is prepared to give up everything he has for Him. This is demonstrated in the third *parshah*, which is written in the singular and therefore addresses the individual. The fourth *parshah*, however, addresses the community as a whole. Not everyone in the community is necessarily prepared to give up all of their possessions for the sake of God. Therefore, the fourth *par-*

---

1. *Aggados* on *Berachos* 6:2.

shah, addressing the community, does not mention the necessity to love God with all of one's wealth. Consequently, the third *parshah* deals with total submission to God — the unifying of everything one has to Him. However, the fourth *parshah* does not embody the total unity of dedicating every aspect of life to God.

Based on the fact that the first and third *parshiyos* are expressed in the singular, we noted that they represent unity. They also correspond to each other regarding the mitzvah of tefillin itself and their portrayal of the concept of unity therein. In the first *parshah* we are told that the tefillin should be "for *you* as a *sign*." The Gemara[1] explains this to mean that not only are the hand tefillin to be a single *os* (sign) on the outside (i.e., in one box, which everyone can see is one), but they must also be "for *you* [the wearer] as a [single] sign." This means that all four *parshiyos* — which are within the box and known only to the wearer — should appear on one piece of parchment. In other words, the hand tefillin must be a single sign not only from without, but also from within.

There is a special lesson in this *parshah* in connection with the head tefillin as well. We are told they should be a זכרון, a single remembrance. This indicates that even though the head tefillin is to consist of four separate *batim* (compartments), these four *batim* must be made from *one* piece of skin.[2]

The third *parshah* also contains an allusion to the unity of the head tefillin. In this *parshah*, the word טטפת (a reference to the head tefillin) is spelled without the letter *vav*.[3] This alludes to the singular.[4] All these factors pointing to the unity of the tefillin

---

1. *Menachos* 34b and *Rashi* there.
2. *Menachos* 34b.
3. See *Minchas Shai* on Devarim 11:18.
4. *Menachos* 34b. In Hebrew, the feminine plural form is (almost) always indicated with a written and pronounced *vav tav* ending, pronounced "*os*." However, occasionally, the *vav* is not written, only pronounced. See also the discussion on the *lulav* on p. 189.

appear only in the first and third *parshiyos*, whereas in the second and fourth *parshiyos* they appear in the plural.[1]

Paralleling the Tetragrammaton

This phenomenon may be discerned vis-à-vis the four letters of the Tetragrammaton as well. We see that the first and third letters are written as unified wholes, in one stroke with no breaks or pieces. As we know, the *yud* represents Purpose. Since the *yud* is an unbroken unit, it thus represents the unity of Purpose. The *yud* also represents the world of *Atzilus*,[2] which is the realm of God's unity.[3]

The unity of the *vav* symbolises the unity of the Present. It Links Above with Below, as opposed to the *yud*, which denotes His unity Above. Similarly, the first and third *parshiyos* deal with the unity of *kedushah*, and with the fusing of the physical world with the One God respectively, and therefore correspond to the unified *yud* and *vav*. Thus the *yud* and the *vav* parallel the unity of the first and third *parshiyos*.

On the other hand, the second and fourth letters are both *hey*. The letter *hey* is made up of two pieces. This implies multiplicity and runs parallel to the second and fourth *parshiyos*. Furthermore, both the second and fourth *parshiyos* deal with the destruction and fragmentation of evil; hence they correspond to the two *hey*s, which are broken letters.

IN THE SEDER

The Seder also parallels the dichotomous pattern of unity versus multiplicity. The first and third sections of the Seder — *Kadeish* and the Meal (also symbolised by the *yud* and *vav*) — em-

---

1. See *Tefillin: The Inside Story*, pp. 231–235.
2. See n. 1 on p. 242.
3. *Nefesh HaChaim* 1:13.

body the concept of unifying, as *Kadeish* relates to the realm Above wherein all is one, and the Meal is the unifying of opposites in this world and Above with Below, as we have seen.[1] Conversely, *Maggid* and *Hallel* — the second and fourth stages of the Seder — embody the concept of multiplicity, as in both *Maggid* and the *Hallel* we see diverse reactions to diverse types, i.e., Israel versus the nations.

DIAGRAM 35

---

1. Pages 98–100.

Giving versus Receiving

We just saw that the tefillin display a division of unity versus multiplicity. There is another such dichotomy that appears in the grouping of four — that of giving and receiving. We will now examine this contrast in the tefillin, the Tetragrammaton, and the Seder.

IN THE FOUR *PARSHIYOS* AND THE TETRAGRAMMATON

The first and third *parshiyos* of the tefillin both deal with the concept of giving. In contrast, the second and fourth deal with receiving.

DIAGRAM 36

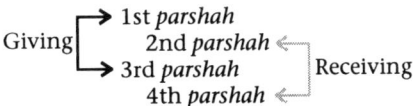

Similarly, just as we saw that the letters of the Tetragrammaton parallel the four sections of the tefillin and the Seder in terms of unity and multiplicity, they parallel them in the dichotomy of giving and receiving as well. Let us examine this in depth.

In Jewish thought, giving is the male element and receiving is the female element. The present work is not the forum to examine this idea in depth, and we will touch on it but briefly. The most obvious example of this concept is reflected on the physical level: the male gives (active) seed, and the female receives (passive) it, and thereby the egg is fertilized. However, this concept goes much deeper than this and appears in many facets and areas. Let us look at this relationship from the perspective of the four tefillin *parshiyos*.

The first and third *parshiyos* of the tefillin relate to God's kindness to us, the mitzvos He gave us, and the performance of our obligations toward Him — giving to God. This corresponds to the first and third letters of the Tetragrammaton — the *yud* and the *vav* — which are similar in appearance. The *yud* relates to the emitting of Divine influence, which takes place Above in the realm of Purpose, and the *vav* draws and Links the Divine influence of the *yud* down to this earth, into the realm of the Present. This all relates to the male element of giving.

Conversely, the second and fourth *parshiyos* deal with the Results of the Egyptians' and our deeds respectively. They are concerned with judgement — reward and punishment — which relates to the female realm: receiving. This corresponds to the second and fourth letters of the Tetragrammaton — the two *heys* — which represent this world of receiving, both in the Past and in the Future.[1]

At this point, the following picture of the tefillin and the Tetragrammaton emerges:

---

1. Interestingly, the second and the fourth *parshiyos* both begin with the same word, והיה, "and it shall be," and they deal with similar concepts of receiving.

DIAGRAM 37

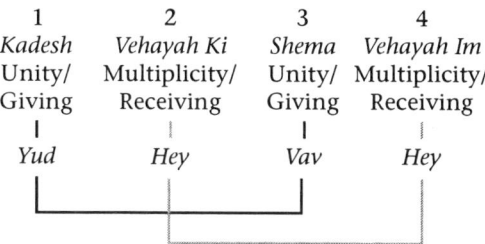

There is yet another similarity between the first and third *parshiyos* and the first and third letters of the Tetragrammaton. The first and third *parshiyos* are the only ones in which the name "Yisrael" is mentioned. This name was given to Yaakov when he rose to the level in which he overcame both an angel from Above and man Below, as it says, כי שרית עם אלקים ועם אנשים ותוכל, "...for you have contended with an angel and with men, and you have prevailed."[1] Therefore, the name "Yisrael" appears only in these two *parshiyos*, as they are the *parshiyos* of the *yud* and the *vav*, the letters which signify the realm of giving from Above and the lowering down of that which is being given to Below, respectively.[2]

The two *hey*s of the Tetragrammaton are each made of *two* parts. This represents the Past and Future of the second and fourth *parshiyos*, which both relate to *two* opposite Results: the evil that befalls the wicked, and the good that is received by those deserving it. We see that once again the first and third concepts parallel each other, and the second and fourth concepts parallel each other.

---

1. Bereishis 32:28.
2. Furthermore, both the dimensions of Purpose and Present — the realms of the first and third *parshiyos* and letters respectively — can be with us in the Present. Present and Purpose are thus revealed simultaneously, whereas Past and Future — the realms of two and four — are not with us; for the Past has already gone, and the Future is not yet known to us.

THE FOUR *PARSHIYOS* AND "*BARUCH HAMAKOM*"

Let us see how the contrast of giving and receiving we discovered in the tefillin *parshiyos* corresponds to the same pattern we saw in the four parts of "*Baruch HaMakom.*" The *parshah* of *Kadesh* deals with God's *imparting* His *kedushah* to the Jewish people, and our subsequent responsibility to take that *kedushah* and impart sanctity to the rest of the world. This corresponds to the concept of God being called "*Makom*" (ברוך המקום, "Blessed be the Master of place") in that He continuously gives of His *kedushah* to the *makom*, the world.

Vehayah Ki Yeviacha, the second *parshah*, deals with the concept of receiving. In it Pharaoh and the Egyptians *receive* their punishment. It deals with the side of the receiver in the physical world — the world of receiving, in which the Giver is hidden. This corresponds to ברוך הוא, "Blessed be He," where God is hidden.

The *parshah* of *Shema*, which deals with Torah being *given* daily, corresponds to ברוך שנתן תורה לעמו ישראל , "Blessed be the One Who *gave* the Torah," and thus also embodies the concept of giving.

Vehayah Im Shamoa deals with what is *received* when we adhere — or don't — to God's commandments. This corresponds to the second ברוך הוא, as this *parshah* speaks of our receiving in the material world, where God is *hidden*.

IN THE SEDER

The Seder also parallels the dichotomous pattern of giving and receiving. The first and third sections of the Seder — *Kadeish* and the Meal (also symbolised by the *yud* and *vav*) — embody the concept of giving. In *Kadeish* we mention the giving from Above to Below — God sanctifying us from Above. The Meal is our giving from Below to Above wherein we unify the spiritual with the physical from Below.

The second and fourth stages of the Seder (symbolised by the two *hey*s) are aspects of receiving, in that we mention in them what both the Jewish nation and their enemies receive from God. Therefore, *Hallel* appears in both sections, praising God for what was received in the Past, and for that which will be received in the Future.

DIAGRAM 38

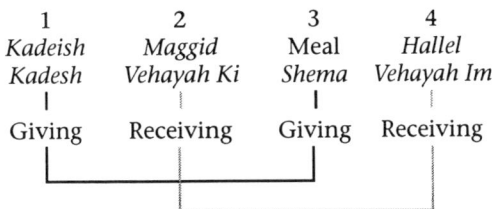

Let us take a moment to summarise what we have seen so far. The four parts of *Yotzer Ohr*, the Tetragrammaton, the four *parshiyos* of the tefillin, and the four stages of the Seder all correspond to one another. In all three, sections one and three represent the concepts of unity and giving, and sections two and four represent multiplicity and receiving. Indeed, in terms of the language used in the verse from Yirmeyahu, "darkness" and "evil" (the realms of two and four) exist only as a result of the positivity of light and peace of realms one and three, for the negative receives its existence from the positive, as we saw, for example, with the two sets of sons, where the *rasha* and *she'eino yodea lishol* were redeemed in the merit of others. We therefore have the following:

DIAGRAM 39

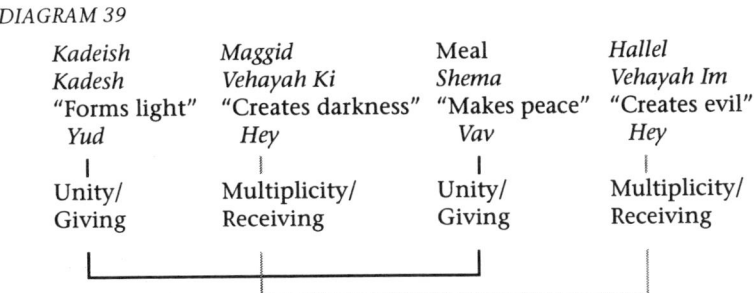

Dichotomy in the Sons and Species

UNITY VERSUS MULTIPLICITY

With the Four Sons

The dichotomy of unity versus multiplicity can be traced in connection with the four sons. The *chacham*, who belongs to the first realm, and the *tam*, who belongs to the third realm, both symbolise unity. When the *chacham* asks his question, he unifies himself with God and the rest of Israel. He says, "What is the meaning of the testimonies, and the statutes and laws, which Hashem our God has commanded you?"[1] He thus unifies himself with the One God and with the rest of the nation. Similarly, as we have seen before,[2] the *tam* is also unified with God and His Torah. Moreover, we have seen explicitly[3] that Yaakov the *tam* symbolises unity.

---

1. Devarim 6:20.
2. Page 152.
3. Pages 167–169.

The antithesis of the unity of Yaakov is Eisav the *rasha*. Eisav hated Yaakov and wished to kill him.[1] He also despised the service of God.[2] He therefore turned his back on the unity of God. In this way he parallels the *rasha*, who represents the realm of diversity, as he separates himself from God and Israel. The *she'eino yodea lishol*, who keeps what mitzvos he does only as a matter of tradition, also does not connect himself to the unity of God.

This dichotomy is also reflected in the language that the Torah uses in conjunction with the four sons. Concerning the *chacham* and *tam* it says, "When your son [singular] will ask."[3] However, concerning the *rasha* it says, "And it shall come to pass, when your *sons* [plural] will *say* [plural] to you..."[4] Similarly, we answer the *rasha* in kind; since he removes himself from the *klal*, the unity of Israel, we say to him, "Because of this did Hashem do for *me* when I left Egypt."[5] The Haggadah explains this to mean "to me and not to him," i.e., "Had he been there, he would not have been redeemed." In his question the *rasha* separated himself from the unity of God and Israel. We therefore answer him that had he been there, he would have been separated from the rest of the people, lost to the Jewish nation. The same verse used in answer to the *rasha* is used to initiate the discussion with the *she'eino yodea lishol*.

From all of the above we see that the *chacham* and *tam* belong to the unified realms, whereas the *rasha* and *she'eino yodea lishol* belong to the realms of diversity.

We therefore have the following pattern in the order that the four sons are mentioned:

---

1. See Bereishis 27:41.
2. Ibid. 25:34 and *Rashi* there.
3. Devarim 6:20; Shemos 13:14.
4. Shemos 12:26.
5. Ibid. 13:8.

DIAGRAM 40

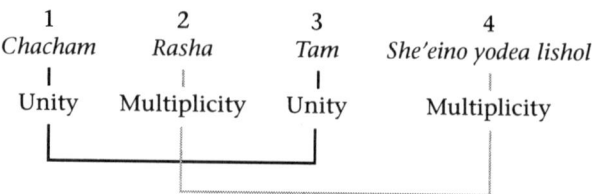

With the Four Species

The pattern of unity and multiplicity is apparent in the four species as well. We see that there is only *one esrog* and *one lulav*, whereas there are *two aravos* and *three haddasim*. Observing it from another angle, the *esrog* is *one* mass; the *lulav* must have its leaves together and bound so as to appear like *one* mass.[1] On the other hand, the branches and leaves of the *haddasim* and *aravos* are separate from one another and neither adhere nor are they fastened to one another. We see the following pattern:

---

1. See also *Rabbeinu Bachya*, Vayikra 23:40. Although both the *esrog* and the *lulav* represent unity, they reflect different *types* of unity, the *esrog* symbolising the absolute unity of Above, and the *lulav* representing the unity of Below. This can be seen in the fact that the *lulav* is only unified once it is bound, which represents the drawing down of unity into the world by unifying separate parts (see pp. 189–190). Additionally, we have seen before that the realm of the *lulav* is in effect an extension of the *esrog*. This parallels the fact that the *esrog* is the fruit of the tree itself, whereas the *lulav* only represents the fruit, but it itself is only leaves of a fruit-bearing tree. This represents the relationship of the *vav* to the *yud*. The *yud* resembles a dot of complete unity (*Nesivos Olam, Nesiv HaTorah*, ch. 1), whereas the *vav* is also one unified body, but it is stretched downwards. Moreover, this parallels the difference between the first and third *parshiyos* of tefillin: *Kadesh* is absolute unity, whereas *Shema* is the unifying of opposite sides — good and bad, and other extremes in this world.

DIAGRAM 41

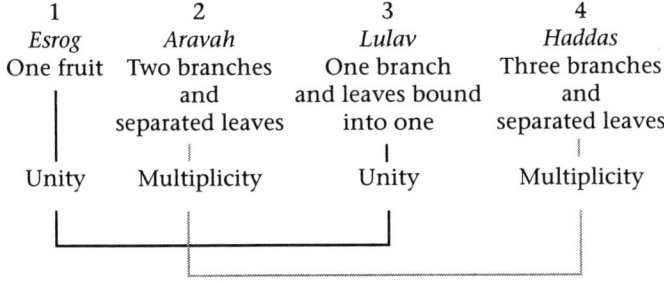

This pattern parallels that of the tefillin *parshiyos*:

DIAGRAM 42

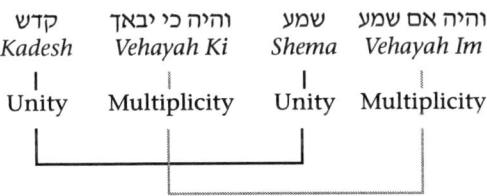

This pattern also follows that of the Tetragrammaton, in which the *yud* is *one* mass, followed by the *hey* with *two* parts to it, then the *vav* as *one* mass, and finally the second *hey* again with its *two* sections:

DIAGRAM 43

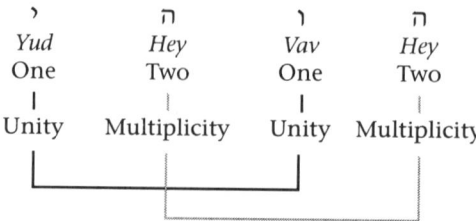

From the above discussion we see that the four sons, the four species, the four tefillin *parshiyos*, and the four letters of the Tetragrammaton all follow the same order and represent the same concepts.

GIVING VERSUS RECEIVING

With the Four Sons

The four sons also correspond to the pattern of givers and receivers that we mentioned previously. The first and third sons are givers, and the second and fourth are receivers. This can be explained as follows.

The first and third sons have the wisdom of Torah, in whose merit the Jewish people exist and were found worthy to be taken out of Egypt, for Torah was the cause of the Exodus.[1] These two sons are therefore givers, as they caused redemption for the others. The second and fourth sons, however, do not have Torah and exist only in the merit of the forefathers and the righteous that have Torah.[2] They are therefore receivers.

---

1. See *Rashi*, Shemos 3:12; *Ramban*, Shemos 13:9; *Ma'aseh Nissim* on "Baruch HaMakom."
2. See *Ma'aseh Nissim* loc cit.

With the Four Species

We saw earlier that the pattern of unity versus multiplicity is reflected in the four species. The four species reflect the dichotomy of giving and receiving as well. However, before being able to see this, we must note some other aspects of the four species.

Symbolising the Jewish People

We have seen that the four species are compared to the four types of people within the Jewish nation, which actually comprise the four sons of the Seder.[1] The *esrog*, which has taste and a pleasant fragrance, symbolises those who have Torah (taste) and mitzvos (fragrance). The *lulav*, which has a taste but no smell, represents those whose strong point is Torah learning rather than the fulfilment of mitzvos. The *haddas*, which has a smell but no taste, represents those whose strong point is the observance of mitzvos, but lack Torah study. The *aravah* has no taste or smell, symbolising those who lack both Torah learning and observance of mitzvos. God says let them all be taken together, and they will atone for one another.[2]

Looking at the pattern of the four species in this order, we see the following:

DIAGRAM 44

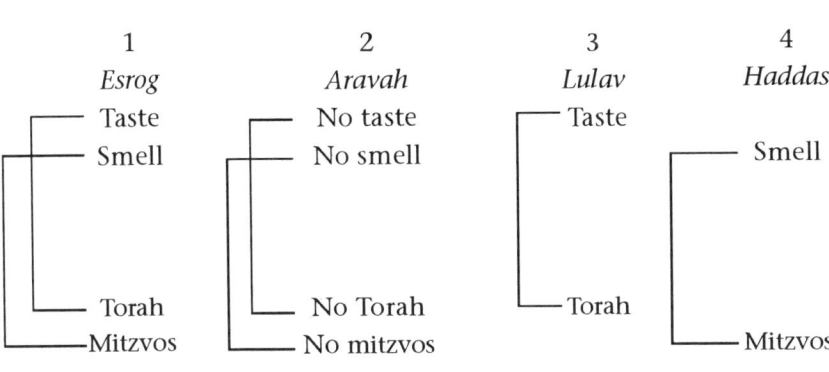

---

1. See pp. 151–154.
2. *Vayikra Rabbah* 30:12.

Let us also note the order of the four species. The Torah tells us: "And you shall take for yourselves on the first day the fruit of the beautiful citron [*esrog*] tree, and the date-palm branch [*lulav*], twigs of myrtle leaves [*haddas*], and willows of the brook [*aravah*]."[1] In this verse, the *esrog* is mentioned next to the *lulav*, and the *haddas* next to the *aravah*. However, as noted previously,[2] we actually hold them in the following order:[3]

DIAGRAM 45

1	2	3	4
Esrog	*Aravah*	*Lulav*	*Haddas*

There are two distinct patterns here: in the Torah the species are arranged such that the two species which come from trees that bear fruit are first mentioned together, followed by the two species which are from trees that are only leaf-bearing. However, we hold them in the order of fruit, leaves, fruit, leaves. This arrangement is very profound and follows the pattern of the letters of the Tetragrammaton, in which like letters are separated — the letters *yud* and *vav* are similar but separated from one another within the Tetragrammaton, and the two *heys* are separated from one another.

In addition to resembling the Tetragrammaton, the four species have a similarity to the four *parshiyos* of the tefillin. We have shown the four species from left to right in the way that they are held and that the four *parshiyos* follow the same order from the left to the right of the wearer. The *parshah* of *Kadesh* is worn on the left side; the others follow in order from left to right.[4] The *esrog* and the *parshah* of *Kadesh* therefore hold the same position.

---

1. Vayikra 23:40.
2. Page 153.
3. See also diagram 18, p. 151.
4. See diagram 20, p. 179.

Dichotomy in the Sons and Species

Furthermore, the *esrog* is not tied together with the other species, and it is held separately. Similarly, the *parshah* of *Kadesh* is on the side of the four-armed *shin* of the head tefillin, which represents the dimension of Above. It is thus considered higher and distinct from the other three *parshiyos*, which are represented by the three-armed *shin*, which represents our realm,[1] on our right side.[2]

Givers and Receivers

We will now discuss the four species in the context of giving and receiving. The *esrog* and *lulav* both have taste and are from fruit-bearing trees, the fruit being the essence of the tree in terms of humanity, whereas the *aravah* and *haddas* are leaves — things which are secondary in importance to humanity. The *esrog* and *lulav*, which relate to the fruit, the essence of the tree, represent those who learn the Torah, which is the "fruit," the essence of our existence. Those who lack Torah learning are represented by the leaves, the secondary part of the tree. The fruit, besides being the essence of the tree, is also considered in the category of giver, as it gives taste and nourishment to mankind, whereas the leaves are the receivers, as they recieve their existence in God's plan only because of the fruit, the essence of the tree.

Thus we have the following picture:

DIAGRAM 46

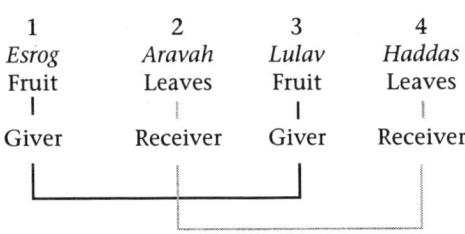

---

1. See diagram 20, p. 179.
2. See pp. 155 and 179.

Internal versus External

IN THE FOUR SPECIES

The four species bring to light yet another contrast between the groups of one and three and two and four — the concepts of internal and external. The fruit is the internal substance (which gives nourishment to humanity) within the peel. This parallels the realms of the *esrog* and the *lulav*, both from fruit-bearing trees. As leaves are external, the *haddas* and *aravah*, which have only leaves, represent the external.

The internal-external and giving-receiving aspects of the fruit and leaves of the four species allude to the following verses:

> Fortunate is the man who did not walk in the counsel of the wicked, and stood not in the path of sinners, and sat not in the company of scorners. But in Hashem's Torah is his desire, and in his Torah he meditates by day and by night. He will be like a tree planted on brooks of water that gives its *fruit* in its right time and whose *leaf* does not wither...
>
> (Tehillim 1:1–3)

The person whose whole desire is bent on understanding God's Torah will have his fruit come in its time, and his leaf will not wilt. This means that he will attain the essence — an expression of the internal (fruit) — of life, and he will also obtain the externals (leaf), i.e., material well-being, meaning that even the externals will be part of the overall Purpose, serving the fruit (the Purpose of life). This, of course, corresponds to the first and third of the four types of people — the ones who embody Torah. The converse is also true: persons two and four, who have no Torah, connect to the external aspects of existence. This relates also to the discussion of giving and receiving, as the external — material well-being (leaf) — receives its existence only because of the spiritual, internal Torah (fruit).

DIAGRAM 47

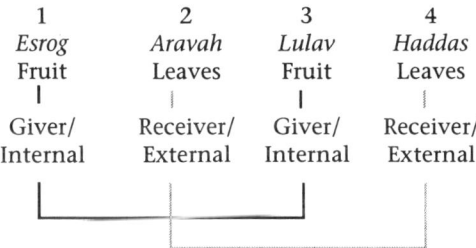

Corresponding to the Organs of the Body

The patterns of giving and receiving and of internal and external correspond perfectly with another interpretation of the symbolism of the four species. We have previously mentioned[1] the observation of the Midrash that the four species hint at four major organs of the body. The *esrog* is compared to the heart, the

---

1. Pages 219–220.

lulav to the spinal cord,[1] the *haddas* to the eyes, and the *aravah* to the lips.[2]

The heart and spinal cord are major parts of the body. They are also *givers*. The heart pumps blood, the life-giving force of the body. The spinal cord, together with the brain above it, constitute the central nervous system. The spinal cord conducts impulses between the brain and the rest of the body and is a centre for reflex activity.[3] Consequently, the *esrog* and the *lulav* represent the organs of the body that are *givers*. Furthermore, the heart and spinal cord are *internal* organs.

Moreover, *Midrash Tanchuma*,[4] in a slightly different vein, tells us: "Why [do we come before God on Sukkos] with the *esrog*, which is similar to the heart? To atone for the thoughts of the heart... And why with the *lulav*? To tell you that just as the *lulav* has only one *heart* [i.e., the letters *lamed* and *beis*, which spell the word *'lev,'* are contained in the word *'lulav'*], so Israel have only one *heart* toward their father in heaven." Thus, both the *esrog* and the *lulav* symbolise the heart, the *internal* organ that gives blood to the rest of the body. Yet again we see that these two species represent the concepts of *giving* of the *internal*. Indeed, only these two species, which represent fruit and taste and which symbolise Torah and those who learn it, are compared to the heart.

This is very significant in that the Torah itself concludes and begins with the letters *lamed* and *beis*, which spell the word *"lev"* (heart). The appearance of these two letters at the beginning and the end of the Torah indicates that Torah epitomises the concept of the *lev* — the *internal* life-*giving* force of the Jewish nation. The *esrog* and *lulav*, which symbolise aspects of the

---

1. See *Ramban*, Vayikra 23:40; *Shlah, masseches Sukkah, Amud HaShalom, Perek Torah Ohr; Rikanti, parshas Emor*.
2. See *Vayikra Rabbah* 30:14.
3. See also *Rabbeinu Bachya*, Vayikra 23:40 — "And the spine is a major part of the body..."
4. See *Kol Bo* in the name of *Tanchuma, Emor* 20.

heart, therefore hint at the Torah.

On the other hand, the *haddas* and *aravah* represent the eyes and lips respectively, which are *external* organs and are not vital in terms of giving life to the rest of the body. Rather, they *receive* their vitality from the internal heart and from the brain, where the spinal cord begins, and are dependent upon them.

Four Types of Jews Paralleling the Four Organs

We have just recalled two *midrashim* which characterise the four species in two different ways, comparing them to four different kinds of Jews and four different organs of the body respectively. We now have the following picture of the concepts of these two *midrashim* paralleling each other:

DIAGRAM 48

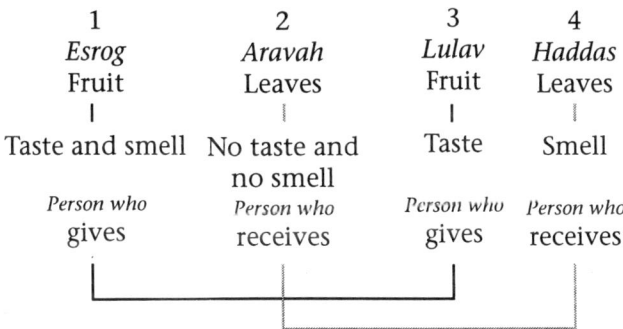

This parallels the *midrash* about the four organs:

DIAGRAM 49

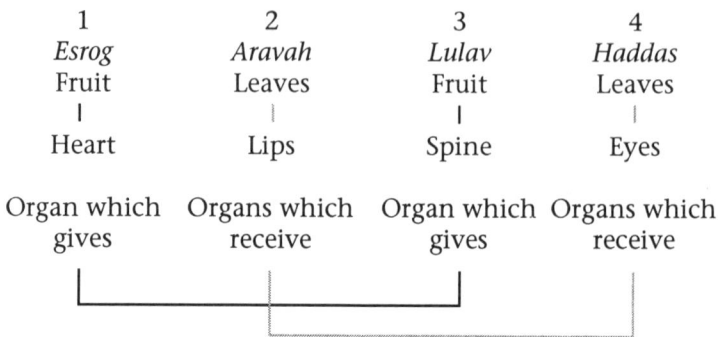

IN *YOTZER OHR*

Going back to the verse upon which the blessing of *Yotzer Ohr* is based, we see the same pattern of internal and external, as well as giving and receiving. The verse states: "...forms *light* and creates *darkness*, makes *peace* and creates *evil*." The first and third expressions of this verse, light and peace, are internal *essence*, as they are part of the Purpose and unity of creation. The second and fourth, darkness and evil, are *external*, as they gain their existence from, and are only the result of, light and peace. In this way we can also construe the first and third as *givers*, and the second and fourth as *receivers*.[1]

---

1. The expression, ובורא, "and creates," is used in connection with both darkness and evil, the second and fourth components of the verse. This follows the pattern of the second and fourth letters of the Tetragrammaton — which are also the same — which appears in the continuation of this verse: "I am *Y-h-v-h*, Who makes all these." This is because they both represent similar realms — the world of *receiving* — as the first *hey* represents the world of the Past, and the last *hey* represents the Future, perfected world, wherein both the righteous and the wicked received and will receive their just deserts.

IN "BARUCH HAMAKOM"

We noted earlier that the order of the four sons reflects the pattern of unity versus multiplicity and giving versus receiving. Similarly, the blessing of *"Baruch HaMakom,"* which parallels the four sons, contains the patterns of giving versus receiving and of internal versus external.

With the first and the third son (*chacham* and *tam*) we bless God as Master over place and as the One Who gives the Torah, respectively. The *chacham* and *tam* relate to these two concepts, connecting themselves to God the Creator — Master over place, and the Giver of Torah — thus *giving* of themselves by doing God's will as opposed to their own. They thereby relate to their Purpose, which is the internal, spiritual essence.

On the other hand, the *rasha* and the *she'eino yodea lishol* are the *receivers*, because they partake of God's bounty and do not have a proper connection to God. Therefore the blessing that relates to them is simply "Blessed be He," as God is hidden from them. They do not give appropriately to God, and God does not give to them directly and in a revealed way.[1] Again the first and third are connected to the Essence (God), the internal, whereas the second and fourth are not properly connected to Him and are left out — external.[2]

---

1. See *Ma'aseh Nissim*.
2. The double expression ובורא, "and creates," in the verse of *Yotzer Ohr* which denotes elementary creation (יש מאין, "something from nothing"), parallels the *rasha* and the *she'eino yodea lishol* (the second and fourth sons). This reflects the fact that they are the ones who are far from completion, and are receivers from whom God is hidden. It is also interesting to note that in reference to the questions of the *chacham* and the *tam* (the first and third sons) the Torah uses the term *"machar,"* tomorrow (Shemos 13:14; Devarim 6:20), for only they have a true "tomorrow," as they cleave to God and His Torah, which are eternal.

DIAGRAM 50

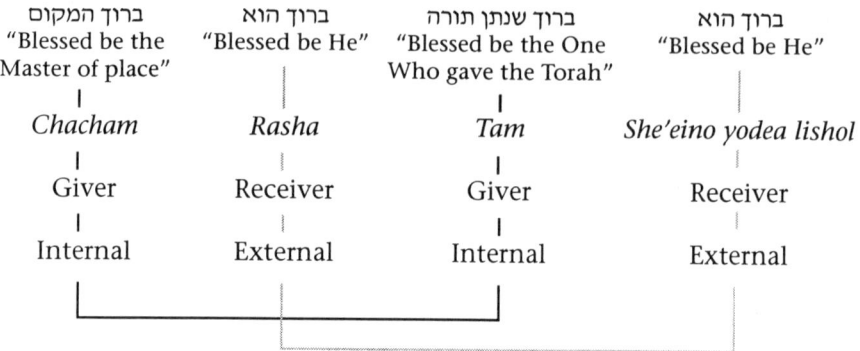

IN THE FOUR *PARSHIYOS*

The four *parshiyos* of the tefillin also reflect the dichotomy of internal and external in the first and third and second and fourth *parshiyos*. The first *parshah* speaks of Purpose, which can be defined as the internal reason for the external phenomena that take place. Specifically, it speaks of the Purpose of the Exodus — the reason for the going out of Egypt — which was to receive the Torah and to obtain *kedushah*.[1]

The second *parshah* speaks of the external factors of the Exodus — the historical background and that which physically happened to Pharaoh and Egypt. Here we see a more detailed account of the outer manifestation of the Exodus.

The third *parshah* speaks of total preoccupation in learning Torah, and in doing God's will with all one's heart, soul, and possessions — serving and *giving* of oneself totally to God. It mentions no *outward* results of *receiving* in this material, outer, and external world. Again the third parallels the first, in that both reflect the concept of internal.

---

1. See *Ramban*, Shemos 13:9.

The fourth *parshah* also deals with serving God with one's heart and soul, but no mention is made of serving Him with all one's *me'od*, i.e., being prepared to give up all one's possessions for God. This is so because the *parshah* speaks of those who are involved in the material world and not totally immersed in their learning and service of God and are thus still connected to the externals of physicality; they are not prepared to give them totally for the sake of God. Also, this *parshah* mentions the material advantages resulting from our deeds, in this physical, external world.[1]

DIAGRAM 51

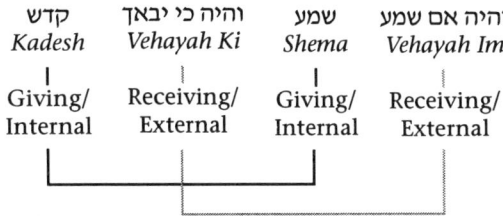

The Climax of the Four *Parshiyos*

Looking at the final verses in the four *parshiyos* of the tefillin, we see that they embody a most phenomenal synopsis of the themes of Purpose to Future, Above to Below, unity versus multiplicity, giving versus receiving, and internal versus external (spiritual versus physical) that we have been discussing. The last verse of the first tefillin *parshah* is "And you shall observe this statute in its correct time *miyamim yamimah*."[2] This refers to the realm of Above and Purpose, as explained before.[3]

The last verse of the second tefillin *parshah* reads: "And it shall be a sign on your arm and *totafos* between your eyes,

---

1. See *Tanchuma, parshas No'ach*, ch. 3.
2. Shemos 13:10.
3. Page 159.

because with a strong hand *Hashem* brought us out of Egypt."[1] This is a lower-level commandment than the *chukim* (statutes) of the previous verse, as a rational reason is given for putting on tefillin — because of the Past Exodus.

In the third tefillin *parshah* it says, "And you shall write them upon the doorposts of your house and upon your gates."[2] This commandment must be performed in the Present and is expressed in the Present without relating a reason associated with the Past or Future. At this level we Link the most High with our material houses down Below by means of the mezuzah.

In the fourth tefillin *parshah* it says, "In order to increase your days and the days of your children on the land that Hashem swore to your fathers to give to them as the days of the heaven on the earth."[3] This level descends still further than the previous one, and deals with the level where heaven touches earth and the dead Below the ground will be revived. This is also mentioned in the language of Results — do the mitzvos *"in order* to increase your days..."

Looking at these verses, we see that they follow the order of unity versus multiplicity, giving versus receiving, and internal versus external.

DIAGRAM 52

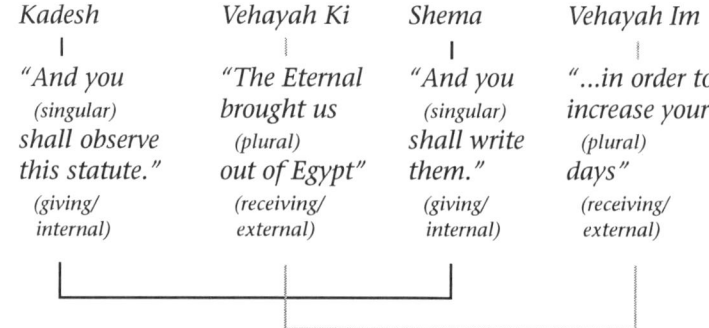

---

1. Shemos 13:16.
2. Devarim 6:9.
3. Ibid. 11:21.

IN THE FOUR MITZVOS OF THE SEDER NIGHT

The four main mitzvos of the Seder night — *pesach, sippur, matzah,* and *marror* — also correspond to the pattern of internal and external that we have seen in the four species of Sukkos and the four tefillin *parshiyos*.

We have seen that the *pesach* sacrifice and the *esrog* relate to *Kadesh* and Purpose. They represent the concept of *essence* as opposed to the external. The *esrog* is the fruit, and the *pesach* sacrifice has its sanctified meat eaten.

Sippur and the *aravah* relate to *Vehayah Ki Yeviacha*, the second *parshah* of the tefillin, and to the Past. Furthermore, the *aravos* are likened to the lips (external organs), and *Maggid* is performed with the lips (external organs).

Matzah and the *lulav* relate to the *parshah* of *Shema* and the Present. They represent the concept of the fruit — the *essence*. Matzah is manufactured from flour — the essence of the wheat plant. The *lulav* is taken from the date palm, which produces fruit.

Marror and the *haddas* relate to the *parshah* of *Vehayah Im Shamoa* and the Future, and both involve the concept of the external. Leaves of the various species of *marror* are eaten to fulfil the mitzvah of *marror* on the Seder night.[1] Likewise, the *haddas* is leafy. The *marror* and the *haddas* therefore represent the external.

We arrive at the following diagram:

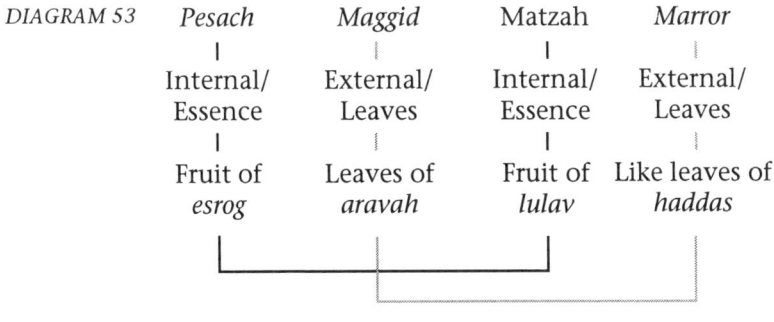

DIAGRAM 53

Pesach	Maggid	Matzah	Marror
Internal/ Essence	External/ Leaves	Internal/ Essence	External/ Leaves
Fruit of esrog	Leaves of aravah	Fruit of lulav	Like leaves of haddas

---

1. *Shulchan Aruch, Orach Chaim* 473:5.

We thus see how the mitzvos of *pesach*, tefillin, and Sukkos correspond to one another.

IN THE TETRAGRAMMATON

We saw earlier in the chapter how the letters of the Tetragrammaton correspond to the contrasting patterns of one and three, and two and four, in conjunction with the blessing of *Yotzer Ohr* and the four *parshiyos* of the tefillin, as well as other groups we have discussed. Let us examine the correspondence of the Tetragrammaton to some of these groups as reflected in the dichotomous pattern.

The Tetragrammaton and the Four Species

Before taking the four species on the festival of Sukkos we say the following prefatory invocation: "Through the fruit of the beautiful citron tree, and the date-palm branch, twigs of myrtle leaves, and willows of the brook, You [God] shall bring the letters of Your unified name close to one another." Thus we see that there is an explicit connection between the four species and the letters of the Tetragrammaton. As we have noted, the *esrog* and *lulav* — the first and third of the species — represent unity, giving, and internality, as do the *yud* and *vav*, the first and third letters of the Tetragrammaton. Similarly, the *aravah* and *haddas* — the second and fourth of the species — represent multiplicity, receiving, and externality, as do the two *hey*s, the second and fourth letters of the Tetragammaton.

The Tetragrammaton, *"Baruch HaMakom,"* and the Four Sons

In the first part of the four blessings of *"Baruch HaMakom,"* God is called *"Makom"* because Before He gave the Torah to the Jewish nation neither He nor His wisdom was known, for it was as something hidden in a concealed, spiritual *place* that could not be seen.[1] Thus, *"Baruch HaMakom"* alludes to the hidden wisdom of God. This parallels the letter *yud* of the Tetragrammaton, which is the smallest letter of the *alef-beis*, and therefore represents the realm of wisdom, as it says, "But wisdom — where will it be found?"[2] meaning that wisdom is not something material (external) and therefore cannot be found in any material *place*.[3] Since *Chochmah* corresponds to the *yud* of the Tetragrammaton, the *chacham*, who has attained this *Chochmah*, also pertains to this realm.

The repeated expression of ברוך הוא, "Blessed be He," corresponds to the repeated *hey* of the Tetragammaton. We have seen that "Blessed be He" is the dimension where God is hidden from the *rasha* and *she'eino yodea lishol*. This parallels the two *heys*, which deal with the external, physical world, which incorporates evil and thus veils the clear revelation of the Divine.

The blessing of ברוך שנתן תורה לעמו ישראל, "Blessed be the One Who *gave* Torah," is an extension of ברוך המקום. They both relate to Torah (the internal essence) — the hidden Torah of God and the Torah He gave us. These levels of Torah parallel the *yud* and the *vav* of the Tetragrammaton. As we have noted before, the *yud* is the only letter that does not extend to the bottom line, demonstrating God's hidden wisdom, which does not reach our world. This corresponds to the expression ברוך המקום, which hints at God's hidden wisdom, and also to the *chacham*, who has a higher form of wisdom. The *vav*, which reaches the bottom line, is an extension of the letter *yud*, representing God's wisdom extending and reaching this world. This parallels ברוך שנתן תורה לעמו ישראל. This is the level in which God gives of His wisdom to His people, Israel, and matches the *tam*, whose wisdom comes through the

---

1. *Ritva.*
2. *Iyov 28:12.*
3. *Metzudas David.*

Torah.[1] The *yud* and *vav*, which relate to *giving* and the internal, thus correspond to the *chacham* and *tam*, who are the givers, as explained previously.

On the other hand, the two *hey*s represent those who receive but do not have their own merit — the *rasha* and *she'eino yodea lishol* receive redemption only in the merit of others and are thus considered external.

The Tetragrammaton and Tefillin

We mentioned earlier in this discussion that the four *parshiyos* of the tefillin correspond to the Tetragrammaton in the realm of unity versus multiplicity, and in the realms of giving and receiving. We also saw that the four *parshiyos* parallel the dichotomy of internal versus external. They correspond to the Tetragrammaton in this respect as well, as both the first and third *parshiyos*, and the *yud* and the *vav*, represent the internal and essence. Similarly, the second and fourth *parshiyos* relate to the externals of this physical world, and therefore correspond to the first and last *hey* of the Tetragrammaton, which represent this world.

Looking at the pattern of *Yotzer Ohr*, the four letters of the Tetragrammaton, the four species, the four sons, the four expressions of blessing, which correspond to the four sons, the four stages of the Seder, the four mitzvos of the Seder, and the four *parshiyos*, we see that they all follow the pattern of first and third representing the concepts of unity, giving, and internality, and the second and fourth representing multiplicity, receiving, and externality. When looking collectively at the above-mentioned factors of the chapter, we arrive at the following picture:[2]

---

1. See *Ma'aseh Nissim*.
2. For more on these concepts, specifically regarding stages one and three, see Appendix III.

TABLE 26

YOTZER OHR	"Forms light"	"Creates darkness"	"Makes peace"	"Creates all"
TETRAGRAMMATON	Yud	Hey	Vav	Hey
SPECIE	Esrog	Aravah	Lulav	Haddas
Tree Type	Fruit	Leaves	Fruit	Leaves
Organ	Heart (one)	Lips (two)	Spine (one)	Eyes (two)
Type	Taste and smell (Torah and mitzvos)	No taste, no smell (no Torah, no mitzvos)	Taste (Torah)	Smell (mitzvos)
SON	Chacham	Rasha	Tam	She'eino yodea lishol
BLESSING	"Baruch HaMakom"	"Baruch Hu"	"Baruch shenasan Torah"	"Baruch Hu"
SEDER	Kadeish	Maggid	Meal	Hallel
MITZVAH	Pesach	Maggid	Matzah	Marror
TEFILLIN	Kadesh	Vehayah Ki	Shema	Vehayah Im

Unity   Multiplicity   Unity   Multiplicity
Giving   Receiving   Giving   Receiving
Internal   External   Internal   External

Further Connections

The Special Pattern in Creation

Until this point we have discussed the fourfold pattern of history — Purpose, Past, Present, and Future — as it relates to the order of the Seder and the tefillin, and how it may be discerned in various other groups of four as well. In fact, this order of four preceded all of these things which represent it, and was actually encoded into the universe from the time of creation itself.

The pattern of creation was as follows: Light was created on the first day. Water and air space were created on the second day. On the third day dry land was created and filled with vegetation. The luminaries were created on the fourth day. On the fifth day, fish and birds were created. Animals and man were created on the sixth day. On the seventh day rest was created.

Our rabbis[1] tell us that the creations of the first three respective days are associated with the creations of the next three re-

---

1. See *Bereishis Rabbah* 11:8, 12:5; Rabbi S. R. Hirsch, Bereishis 1:20.

spective days. The light created on the first day received bearers on the fourth day (the luminaries). The water and air space of the second day received their occupants on the fifth day (fish and birds). The dry land, which was created and filled with vegetation on the third day, received its living inhabitants on the sixth day (animals and man). This, of course, left the seventh day as an entity unto itself, with no other day in creation to be its associate. However, we are told that the Jewish nation was destined to become its partner.

Accordingly, the seven days of creation may be divided into the following *four*-part breakdown:

1. Day 1 / Day 4
2. Day 2 / Day 5
3. Day 3 / Day 6
4. Day 7

These four groupings parallel the concepts embodied by the four stages of the Seder and *parshiyos* of the tefillin:

TABLE 27

DAYS	Day 1 / Day 4	Day 2 / Day 5	Day 3 / Day 6	Day 7
STAGE	Purpose	Past	Present	Future
DIMENSION	Above	Higher	Link	Lowest
SEDER	*Kadeish*	*Maggid*	Meal	*Hallel*
TEFILLIN	*Kadesh*	*Vehayah Ki*	*Shema*	*Vehayah Im*

Let us now delve into the relationship between these groupings — both the pairs themselves and their individual components — and their respective stages.

DAY ONE AND DAY FOUR

The account of the first day of creation begins with the words *"Because of reishis* [the Torah and Israel], God created the heaven and the earth."[1] As we discussed previously, this expresses the Purpose of creation. We also saw that Bereishis is associated with the concept of *kedushah*.[2] This therefore relates to the first stage of the Seder, *Kadeish*, and the first *parshah* of the tefillin, *Kadesh*.

The primordial light created on the first day was a special elevated light of *kedushah*, which alluded to the Divine light of the Beis HaMikdash.[3] The luminaries created on the fourth day are an extension of the light of the first day. This is because the big light and the small light mentioned on the fourth day[4] allude to the first and second Temples respectively.[5] The sanctity of the Beis HaMikdash, associated with both the first and fourth days of creation, corresponds to the first stage of the Seder and the first *parshah* of the tefillin.

Light, the aspect of creation that is shared by days one and four, is associated with the element of fire, which is considered the highest element.[6] It therefore corresponds to *Kadeish*, the highest realm.

Finally, the account of the first day of creation concludes with the words "And there was evening and there was morning, one day."[7] As we have noted previously,[8] by using the expression "one day," as opposed to "first day," the verse is conveying that on the first day, there was no other besides God. It was יוֹם אֶחָד,

---

1. Bereishis 1:1.
2. Pages 134–141.
3. See pp. 137–138.
4. Bereishis 1:16.
5. *Ramban*, Bereishis 2:3.
6. See above, p. 221, in the name of *Rabbeinu Bachya* on Bereishis 1:2.
7. Bereishis 1:5.
8. Page 139.

the day of "one" — the One and Only God. This parallels the *yud* of the Tetragrammaton, which is a unified mass.[1] Thus we have a connection between the first day of creation and the world of Above, which is represented by the *yud* of the Tetragrammaton.[2]

DAY TWO AND DAY FIVE

On the second day,[3] the elements of air and water were put into place. They are a level Lower than the element of fire.[4] A key aspect of the second day was the creation of divisions and barriers, as we read: "And God said, 'Let there be a firmament in the midst of the waters, and it should divide between the waters and the waters.' And God made the firmament, and divided between the waters which were under the firmament and between the waters which were above the firmament; and it was so."[5] This division parallels the letter *hey* of the Tetragrammaton, which is comprised of two parts, and so is divided.

Division and barriers are an expression of *gevurah* (strength) being used to separate, distinguish, or protect two sides — in this case, the two waters — from one another. The Midrash[6] relates that the words *"ki tov* — and it was good" are not mentioned on the second day, as they are on all the other days of creation, because on the second day division was created. It was thus the beginning of all controversy and dispute.[7]

Furthermore, our rabbis explain[8] that the division between the waters hints at the separation that took place between the

---

1. See page 288, n. 1.
2. See *Nesivos Olam, Nesiv HaTorah,* ch. 1.
3. Bereishis 1:6–8.
4. As noted above, p. 221, in the name of *Rabbeinu Bachya* on Bereishis 1:2.
5. Bereishis 1:6–7.
6. *Bereishis Rabbah* 4:6.
7. *Rabbeinu Bachya,* Bereishis 1:4.
8. See *Ramban,* Bereishis 2:3.

The Special Pattern in Creation

righteous No'ach and his sons on the one side, and the wicked people who were punished by the Flood waters on the other.[1] The second day thus relates to the Past, as the wicked were relegated to the Past through the waters of the Flood. Indeed, this is another reason why *"ki tov"* is not mentioned on the second day, as it would not be correct to mention "it was good" in relation to that which alludes to the destruction of the world.[2]

Finally, Gehinnom, where the wicked receive their just deserts, was created on the second day. The second day thus relates to the concept of *din* (judgement). This is yet another reason why *"ki tov"* is not mentioned on this day.[3]

All these aspects of the second day relate to the second stage of the Seder and the second *parshah* of the tefillin, which are both concerned with the separation of the Jews from the Egyptians and the revelation of God's strength in punishing the Egyptians for their treatment of the Jews. Furthermore, in the second stage of the Seder we mention the drowning of the Jewish children in water and the resultant punishment of the Egyptians in water. The separation between the Jews and the wicked Egyptians parallels the separation between No'ach and the wicked people of his generation by the waters of the Flood. Moreover, the second stage of the Seder involves using salt water, which corresponds to days two and five, on which God worked with water.

The fifth day also alludes to negativity, and so, besides being an extension of the second day — they both deal with water — they parallel each other in this aspect as well. The creatures that swarmed the seas and the birds that flew above the earth on the fifth day hint at the fifth millennium in which the nations (who are compared to these creatures) would exile Israel.[4]

---

1. See *Bereishis* 7:11–24.
2. *Rabbeinu Bachya*, Bereishis 2:3.
3. *Bereishis Rabbah* 4:6.
4. See *Ramban* and *Rabbeinu Bachya*, Bereishis 2:3; see also *Avodah Zarah* 9a, which says that the history of this world consists of six millenia.

DAY THREE AND DAY SIX

On the third day it says: "Let the waters under the heaven be gathered together to *one* place."[1] This parallels the *Shema*, which emphasises our obligation to unify everything to the One and only God.[2]

Concerning the third day, the words *"ki tov"* are repeated,[3] because only when there is unity is it genuinely good.

Of the third day it says: "And God called the dry land earth; and the gathering of the waters He called seas; and God saw that it was good... And God said let the earth sprout forth herbage, each herb yielding seed, fruit tree yielding fruit after its kind... And the earth brought forth grass and herb...and tree yielding fruit...and God saw that it was good."[4]

These verses, concerning the *third* day, allude to the *third* millennium of creation.[5] The sprouting forth of the vegetation and the flourishing of the trees and fruit hints at the sprouting forth of Torah in the world. This began with the righteous Avraham, who began disseminating Torah to the world in the third millennium, and culminated with the receiving of the Torah on Mt. Sinai and the building of the Temple, which housed the To-

---

1. Bereishis 1:9.
2. On the first day of creation it also says the word אחד, but as a reference to God (*Rashi*, Bereishis 1:5) — the absolute *Echad*. The relationship between the *echad* of the first and third days parallels the relationship between the first and third letters of the Tetragrammaton — the *yud* and the *vav* — which both symbolise unity: the *yud* representing the unity of Above, and the *vav* symbolising the unity of the extremes of Above and Below, Past and Future, and bad and good. Likewise, the *echad* of the first day represents the unity of God Above, whereas the *echad* of the third day represents the unity of the diverse factors within creation. This parallels the difference between the unity of the *esrog* and that of the *lulav* (see p. 288, n. 1).
3. Bereishis 1:10, 12.
4. Ibid., 10–12.
5. *Ramban* and *Rabbeinu Bachya*, Bereishis 2:3.

rah, which also took place in the third millennium. We see, therefore, that the third day of creation and the third millenium are intimately connected to the Torah. This corresponds to the Present, for, as we have noted previously, the Torah is being continuously given in the Present. Additionally, the word תדשא (let sprout forth) has the same letters as the words אש דת, which hint at the Torah, which is called *"eish das"* (a fiery law).[1] This alludes to the fruition of Torah.[2] Again, Torah is hinted at on the third day. The repeated *"ki tov"* also alludes to the Torah, which was given in the third millennium,[3] as Torah is called *"tov."*[4] *"Ki tov"* is repeated in these verses, as Torah is the ultimate *tov*.

The sixth day, which is the extension of the third day, also corresponds to the Present. We read, "And God saw everything that He had made, and behold, it was very good. And there was evening and there was morning, the sixth day."[5] This is the only day preceded by the definite article, "the." Which day is *"the* sixth day"? It is the sixth of Sivan, the day we accepted the Torah.[6] Therefore, the sixth day of creation also represents the continuous giving of the Torah in the Present. Additionally, the sixth day parallels the *parshah* of *Shema*, which itself is connected to the number six, as we have seen,[7] and which also symbolises the continuous giving of the Torah in the Present.[8]

Concerning the creation of man, which took place on the sixth day, it says, "And God said, 'Let us make man in our image, after our likeness; and let them have dominion over the fish of the sea, and over the birds of the heaven, and over the cattle, and

---

1. Devarim 33:2.
2. Rabbeinu Shimshon.
3. *Rabbeinu Bachya*, Bereishis 2:3.
4. Tehillim 119:72.
5. Bereishis 1:31.
6. See *Rashi* loc. cit.
7. See above, pp. 256 and 267.
8. See above, pp. 132–133, 197–198.

over all the earth, and over every creeping thing that creeps upon the earth.' "[1] Man, who has a soul from Above and a body from Below, is the Link between heaven and earth.[2] It was God's plan that man should have complete dominion over all that is in heaven and earth and thereby unify the entire creation to God.[3] This unity which is to be achieved by man also parallels the *parshah* of *Shema*, in which we unify everything to God.

Furthermore, the Midrash[4] explains the words "and behold, it was *very* good"[5] of the sixth day as referring to the good inclination and its rival, the evil inclination, and life and its antithesis, death, teaching us that even the bad ultimately serves to facilitate good.

These factors are included in the third *parshah* of the tefillin in the verse "And you shall love Hashem your God with all your heart and with all your soul and with all your possessions."[6] "With all your heart" means with *both* your good inclination and your evil inclination. "With all your soul" means even if one must give up one's soul and die.[7] "With all your possessions" means that whatever measure He metes out to you, be it the measure of good or the measure of misfortune, you shall thank Him.[8]

This unification of the good and evil inclinations, life and death, and *"me'od"* of the third *parshah* parallels the unification of the self-same factors referred to as *"tov me'od"* (*very* good), of the sixth day of creation. Again we see that the third and the sixth levels parallel one another in the unifying of diverse factors.

---

1. Bereishis 1:26.
2. See *Rashi*, Bereishis 2:7.
3. See *Malbim*, Bereishis 1:26, and Tehillim, ch. 8.
4. *Yalkut Shimoni* 16.
5. Bereishis 1:31.
6. Devarim 6:5.
7. *Berachos* 54a.
8. See *Ramban*, Devarim 6:5.

In the third stage of the Seder we use and become united with the creations of the third and sixth day. On the third day of creation the herbs and fruits were created "to be eaten." In the third stage of the Haggadah we are commanded in the Torah to eat from the herbs of the third day. On the sixth day of creation the animals were created, and in the corresponding third stage of the Seder we eat the *pesach* offering, which is a lamb or goat, created on the sixth day. Man, who was also created on the sixth day, becomes unified with all these factors within the third stage of the Seder. This therefore corresponds to the third *parshah* of the tefillin, which is the unity of individual parts into a greater whole, as opposed to the absolute unity of God represented by the first stage.

Finally, the unity seen in the third and sixth days of creation corresponds to the letter *vav* of the Tetragrammaton — the letter of unity that bridges Above to Below and Past to Future.

DAY SEVEN

The seventh day of creation was the completion of heaven and earth, as we read, "And the heavens and the earth were finished, and all their hosts."[1] It thus represents the Future, the "day which will be entirely Shabbos and rest, for everlasting life," when the world will reach the goal that God intended from the very beginning.[2]

The words "And the heavens and the earth were finished" parallel the words "as the days of heaven on earth," of the fourth tefillin *parshah*. The World to Come will be a life of heaven on earth, and this in itself will be the final completion of God's plan in creation.

Concerning the seventh day of creation, it says, "And God

---

1. Bereishis 2:1.
2. *Ramban*, Bereishis 2:3.

blessed the seventh day and sanctified it; because on it He had rested from all His work, which God created to make."[1] The words "which God created to make" incorporate all the events that were to transpire in the Future.[2] This also corresponds to the fourth *parshah*, the *parshah* of the Future. Indeed, our rabbis explain[3] that the word לעשות, "to make," means, "Even though it says God rested from all His work, this means that He rested only from the work of His world. However, He did not rest from the work of the wicked and the work of the righteous, for He still intended to work with these and with those in the Future..." God did not cease to work after creation, for He let the world be led according to the deeds of people.[4] God let the deeds of people have an influence on how He runs the world. Thus, the fourth *parshah* of the tefillin, which deals with what transpires in the world as a result of the deeds of the righteous and the wicked, parallels this day of creation.

The Tetragrammaton is hinted at in the following words: יום הששי ויכלו השמים, "...the sixth day. And the heavens were completed."[5] The first two letters of the Tetragrammaton are hinted at in the words יום הששי mentioned in connection with the sixth day of creation. However, the last two letters are hinted at in the first words of the next verse, which is concerned with the seventh day of creation — ויכלו השמים.[6] Thus the Tetragrammaton is only complete on the seventh day. As we noted previously, the Tetragrammaton is deficient at Present, as a result of Amalek's attacking Israel shortly after the Exodus from Egypt.[7] The *vav* and *hey* will be returned only in the Future, when the

---

1. Bereishis 2:3.
2. *Ramban* loc. cit.
3. *Bereishis Rabbah* 11:10 and *Yefeh To'ar* there.
4. *Maharzu*.
5. Bereishis 1:31, 2:1.
6. See *Ba'al HaTurim*, Bereishis 1:31.
7. See above, p. 66.

hand of God will once again be seen clearly. We see, therefore, that both creation and the Tetragrammaton were completed simultaneously on Shabbos, which alludes to the Future perfection of the world and the completion of God's name, at the time when even the Lowest world will reach perfection. This also corresponds to *Hallel*, the fourth part of the Seder, which deals with the Future perfection of the world.

God's Day

Our rabbis tell us[1] that "God's day" is divided into twelve hours. In the first three hours He occupies Himself with the study of Torah. In the next three hours He judges the world. In the following three hours, He provides sustenance for the world. In the last three hours of the day He delights in the *livyasan*, as it says, "You created the *livyasan* to sport with."[2] We shall see that the pattern of God's day parallels the stages of the Seder and the four *parshiyos* of the tefillin.

THE FIRST QUARTER

The first quarter of the day, in which God occupies Himself with the Torah, is the dimension of Purpose, for the world was created for Torah. God occupies Himself with Torah — which existed Before the world and which was the blueprint of creation[3]

---

1. *Avodah Zarah* 3b.
2. *Tehillim* 104:26; see also *Bava Basra* 75a; *Yalkut Shimoni* on *Tehillim* 104, which says that the *livyasan* is a giant fish that will be used for the righteous in the Future.
3. *Bereishis Rabbah* 1:1.

— Before He busies Himself with the affairs of this world. Furthermore, God busies Himself with Torah, which is the instrument whereby He created the world, in order to continue the renewal of creation.[1] Thus, in this first part of the day, God busies Himself with the instrument that existed Before creation so as to renew creation. The first period of God's day therefore represents the dimension of Purpose and Before, which effects continuous creation and renewal. It therefore parallels the first stage of the Seder and the first *parshah* of the tefillin.

THE SECOND QUARTER

The judgement that takes place in the second quarter of the day parallels the judgement and retribution of the Egyptians in the second stage of the Seder and the second *parshah* of the tefillin. In both cases the wicked — the forces of the Past — were reduced to the Past.

THE THIRD QUARTER

God's feeding the world in the third quarter of the day corresponds to our partaking of the meal of the third stage of the Seder, which corresponds to the Present, and to the third *parshah* of tefillin, which also deals with the Present.

THE FOURTH QUARTER

God's delighting in the *livyasan* in the fourth quarter of the day parallels the Future, as the delight in the *livyasan* by the righteous will take place in the Future.[2] Furthermore, the fourth quarter of the day is the time when the accumulated good deeds of the day are stored away for the Future.[3]

---

1. *Asarah Ma'amaros, Ma'amar Chikur Din* 1:2.
2. *Yalkut* on Tehillim 104:26.
3. *Asarah Ma'amaros, Ma'amar Chikur Din* 1:2.

TABLE 28

HOURS OF DAY	First quarter	Second quarter	Third quarter	Fourth quarter
OCCUPATION	Learns Torah	Sits in judgement	Feeds the world	Delights in the *livyasan*
STAGE	Purpose	Past	Present	Future
SEDER	*Kadeish*	*Maggid*	Meal	*Hallel*
TEFILLIN	*Kadesh*	*Vehayah Ki*	*Shema*	*Vehayah Im*

Israel and the Silkworm

Our rabbis compare the Jewish nation to the silkworm.[1] This is because the Jewish people have no strength with which to overcome their adversaries other than with the power of their mouths; only the power of their prayer can defeat their enemies. A worm's power, too, lies only in its mouth, with which it wears through everything. Therefore, the prophet Yeshayahu addresses the Jewish people, saying, "Fear not, O worm of Yaakov, the people of Israel;[2] 'I have helped you,' says Hashem and your Redeemer, the Holy One of Israel."[3] They further explain[4] the words "Fear not, O worm of Yaakov" to mean that the history of the Jewish nation is compared to the miraculous development of the silkworm.

This amazing creature hatches from an egg and matures on the leaves of the mulberry tree. It feeds and grows until it reaches a certain size, at which point it begins enwrapping itself in a co-

---

1. *Zohar, VaYishlach* 177b–178a.
2. See *Abarbanel*, which says that the words *"mesei Yisrael"* hint at the dead of Israel, that they shall not be afraid.
3. Yeshayahu 41:14.
4. *Zohar, VaYishlach* 177b–178a.

coon that it spins from a single interwoven strand of silk[1] wrapped layer by layer around its body. When the worm finishes spinning its cocoon it dies, leaving a "seed," or chrysalis, within the cocoon. After about two weeks' time, the chrysalis breaks through the cocoon, transformed into a living, winged moth. The *Zohar* concludes by noting that the Jewish people are the same: even though they die, they will return to life as before, at the resurrection of the dead.[2]

The stages of development of this worm can be delineated as follows: (a) the egg stage, (b) the worm stage, (c) the cocoon stage, and (d) the moth stage. These four stages parallel the four stages of history.

The egg stage, the time Before the worm comes into existence, represents the realm of Before.

Next is the worm stage, which represents the Past. The Midrash[3] says that the Jewish people crying in prayer in Egypt — the stage of the Past — is compared to the power of the mouth of the worm. The Midrash further states that the power the Jewish people have with their mouth against their adversaries is symbolised by the power that the worm of this stage has with its mouth. Thus, the emphasis here is the fight between the Jewish people and the other nations, this being the realm of the second stage of the Seder and the second *parshah* of the tefillin, which stress the difference and separation between the Jewish people and other nations.[4] Furthermore, the Egyptians were destroyed as a result of the power (*gevurah*) of the Jewish people's prayer to the Almighty. This relates to the second stage of the Seder and of the tefillin, wherein the Egyptians were overcome and destroyed — a manifestation of *gevurah* — and were left in the Past.

---

1. Approximately nine hundred feet long.
2. See *Yad Yehudah* on *Asarah Ma'amaros, Ma'amar Chikur Din*, par. 30.
3. *Tanchuma, Beshalach* 9.
4. See p. 132.

This stage of the silkworm is also related to the second level of the time line in that at this stage the silkworm just *takes* from the world. It is thus the realm of receiving, which epitomises the second stage in the Seder and the tefillin.

In the third stage, the silkworm is active and spins a cocoon, creating a *unified* mass, *giving* to mankind of its treasured silk. This is also the transitionary stage between the worm of the Past and the moth of the Future, and thus represents the intermediate stage of the time line — the Present.

Finally, the fourth stage — the emergence of the winged moth — represents the Future resurrection of the dead, paralleling the fourth stage of the Seder and of the tefillin.

The Thirteen Principles of Faith

The four stages of the Seder are also reflected in the order of the thirteen principles of faith.[1] Consequently the Seder corresponds to the most basic tenets of our faith.

The thirteen principles, generally found in the siddur at the end of *shacharis,* are as follows:

1. I believe with complete faith that the Creator...creates and influences all living things, and that He alone made, makes, and will make all things.
2. I believe with complete faith that the Creator...is One, and there is no unity like His in any way, and that He alone is our God, and that He was, He is, and always shall be.
3. I believe with complete faith that the Creator...is noncorporeal and is not affected by physicality, and there is nothing like Him at all.
4. I believe with complete faith that the Creator...is the first and last.

---

1. These thirteen principles are based on Maimonides' commentary to the Mishnah, *Sanhedrin* 10:1.

5. I believe with complete faith that the Creator...is the only One to whom it is proper to address prayers, and it is not right to pray to anything else.
6. I believe with complete faith that all the words of the prophets are true.
7. I believe with complete faith that the prophecy of Moshe our teacher...was true, and that he was the father of the prophets, those before and after him.
8. I believe with complete faith that the entire Torah which we now possess is that which was given to Moshe our teacher...
9. I believe with complete faith that this Torah will not be changed, and there will never be another Torah from the Creator...
10. I believe with complete faith that the Creator...knows all the actions and thoughts of people, as it says, "He creates their hearts together; He understands all they do."[1]
11. I believe with complete faith that the Creator...rewards with good those who observe His mitzvos and punishes those who violate them.
12. I believe with complete faith in the coming of the Messiah, and even though he may delay, even so I await his arrival every day.
13. I believe with complete faith that there will be a revival of the dead at a time that pleases the Creator...

These thirteen principles are also summarised in the *Yigdal* prayer that precedes the morning service:

1. Exalted be the living God and praised; He exists and His existence is not limited by time.
2. He is one, and there is no unity like His unity; hidden and infinite is His unity.
3. He has no form of body nor has He a body; nothing can be

---

1. Tehillim 33:15.

likened to His holiness.

4. He existed before anything that was created; He was first, and there was no commencement to His beginning.
5. He is Master of the universe to all that are created; He shows His greatness and kingship.
6. The abundance of His prophecy He granted to his special and glorious people.
7. There never arose anyone in Israel like Moshe, a prophet whose vision of God was so clear.
8. He gave a Torah of truth to His people, through the hand of His prophet, the faithful one of His house.
9. God will never change or exchange His law for anything else forever.
10. He sees and knows our secrets; He sees the end of a matter at its beginning.
11. He rewards man with kindness according to his action; He metes out evil to the wicked according to his wickedness.
12. He will send our Messiah in the end of days to redeem those awaiting the final time of His salvation.
13. God will revive the dead in His abundance of kindness; blessed be His praised name forever.

Each of these principles can be explained in relation to the Seder.

BEFORE AND ABOVE

The first five principles correspond to the first stage, *Kadeish*. In *Yigdal*, principle 1 says that God "is not limited by time." This parallels *Kadeish*, which is the dimension Above and is outside of time and relates to creation.

Principle 2 mentions that "there is no unity like His unity; hidden and infinite is His unity." This also fits with *Kadeish*, which deals with the realm of Hashem Himself, with that which is the ultimate unity, Above and hidden from us.[1]

Principle 3 declares that God "has no form of body nor has He a body; nothing can be likened to His holiness." Whereas even angels have a form of a spiritual nature, God has no body or form whatsoever. In this sense God is *kadosh*, Above all creatures. Therefore "nothing can be likened to His *holiness*." This holiness again corresponds to *Kadeish*.

In principle 4 we are told that "He existed *Before* anything that was created; He was *first*..." This all parallels *Kadeish*, which is the realm of Before creation.

Regarding principle 5, the Rambam[2] states, "The Holy One, blessed be He, is the only one to whom it is appropriate to worship, exalt, praise, and obey. One should not do this to any of His subordinates, whether it be an angel or luminary... One must be cautious to worship Him alone and no other, lest he be guilty of idolatry." God is Master over creation and *Above* it. Hence we must serve Him alone and not any lower creations, such as angels.

This fifth principle, which states that it is proper to serve only God and nothing else, fits very well with what we have seen elsewhere,[3] that *Kadeish*, the first part of the Seder, corresponds to the offering of the *pesach* sacrifice, which is an *avodah* (service) to God, negating the idolatry of Egypt. We also saw[4] that *Kadeish*, the first stage of the Seder, is the opposite of עבודה זרה, "idolatry," and therefore parallels the fifth principle.

This principle also parallels the first *parshah* of tefillin, in which we are told to serve God with the *pesach* offering in order to negate the idolatry of Egypt.[5]

---

1. This also corresponds to the first letter of the Tetragrammaton, the *yud*, which is the most unified letter of the *alef-beis*, since it resembles a dot (*Nesivos Olam, Nesiv HaTorah*, ch. 1).
2. Commentary to Mishnah, *Sanhedrin* 10:1.
3. Pages 181–184.
4. Pages 205–206.
5. See p. 205 and *Tefillin: The Inside Story*, pp. 38–39.

PAST AND LOWER

The next two principles deal with the next level down. This is the human dimension, in which enlightened people receive prophecy from God.[1] A prophet can perceive things that an ordinary person cannot, be it past events, present revelations, or future occurrences. However, while it is a very high level, it is still a lower one than that of God himself.

Regarding principle 6 the Rambam explains[2] that prophecy is given only to one who possesses great wisdom and is already on a high spiritual level, someone who continually conquers his *yetzer hara* and who is not drawn after the material world. Because prophets have exceptional traits and have attained a high degree of perfection in their characters, their human intellect clings to the Creator, and they receive elevated emanation from Him. A prophet's success in attaining this state is consistent with the second stage of the Seder, which deals with the breaking of the forces of evil and materialism (the Egyptians), whereby Israel were able to cling to the spiritual.

Prophecy relates to the Past in that it preceded the giving of the Torah.[3] The period of the prophets also ended during the Second Temple era.

We have seen that the second stage of the Seder deals with receiving — the hardships and the exile that the Jewish nation went through, the subsequent redemption, and the punishments the Egyptians received. The power of prophecy is also something

---

1. So whereas the first set of principles deals with the realm of Above, from where everything emanates (represented by the *yud* of the Tetragrammaton), the second set of principles deals with receiving prophecy from the Most High. This receiving is hinted at by the second letter of the Tetragrammaton — the *hey*.
2. *Mishneh Torah, Hilchos Yesodei HaTorah* 7:1.
3. As the Rambam's seventh principle, concerning Moshe Rabbeinu's prophecy, states, "He was the father of the prophets, those *before* and after him." See also *Sefer HaIkarim*, toward the end of 3:12.

received from God.

Additionally, the word נבואה (prophecy) stems from the word ניב (speech) as it says, "Who creates the utterance [ניב] of the lips."[1] Consequently, this also corresponds to the second part of the Seder, *Maggid*, which involves speech.

We have also seen that of the four species of Sukkos, the *aravah* corresponds to *Maggid*, since the *aravah* is compared to the lips, with which we tell of the Exodus. This in turn corresponds to prophecy, which is uttered with lips.

The seventh principle speaks of Moshe Rabbeinu as a prophet. The Rambam, in his commentary to the Mishnah, says that the level of prophecy attained by Moshe Rabbeinu was the Highest one that a human can reach, *and that no prophet will ever attain this level of prophecy again*. Therefore, Moshe's prophecy, the topic of the seventh principle, is related to the realm of the Past.

PRESENT AND LINK

The next three principles deal with the Present and correspond to the third section of the Seder. In principle 8 we confirm the validity of the Torah we have in the Present.

The Rambam says that the mitzvos we observe *today*, such as sukkah, *lulav*, shofar, *tzitzis*, matzah, and tefillin, are in exactly the same form as those which God revealed to Moshe. This is fundamental to our faith and is harmonious with the third section of the Seder, in which we experience the Past in the Present.

The third set of principles relates to a level that is lower that that of the first two levels. Whereas the first set of principles dealt with God Himself, and the second set dealt with the prophets, the first principle of the third set deals with everybody, distinguished or lowly: "I believe with complete faith that the entire

---

1. Yeshayahu 57:19.

Torah which *we* now possess is that which was given to Moshe…" — "which *we* now possess," all of us, the entire nation, small and great alike. This idea is also reflected in the phrasing of the eighth principle that appears in the *Yigdal* prayer: "He gave a Torah of truth to His *people*" — to the entire Jewish nation. Hashem Above becomes Linked to the whole nation through the Torah. This corresponds to the Meal of the Seder, for, as we have mentioned previously, through the meal and the blessings after the meal, we fuse Above and Below, Linking them together.[1]

Whereas the eighth principle shows that the Torah of the Present is the same as the Torah of the Past, as it says: "I believe with complete faith that the entire Torah which we *now* possess is that which *was given* to Moshe," the ninth principle shows that there will be no alteration of the Torah in the Future: "This Torah will not be changed, and there will never be another Torah from the Creator…" As phrased in *Yigdal*: "God will never change or exchange His law for anything else forever." The Torah of the Present will remain as it is, in the Future.

Together, principles 8 and 9 show that Torah constitutes the Link between the Past and the Future and retains the same form in the Past, Present, and Future.

The tenth principle also evokes the third level, for it deals with all the members of the Jewish nation, similar to the eighth principle. This principle is concerned with God's providence, which "joins" Him to this world. Thus, principle 10 also demonstrates the Link between the upper, spiritual world and the lower, physical one.

The phrasing of the tenth principle, where the Creator "*sees* and *knows* our secrets" and where "the Creator *knows* all the actions and thoughts of people," is expressed in the Present tense, since God's awareness and providence is constant at all times.

---

1. Again, this corresponds to the third letter of the Tetragrammaton, *vav*, which represents Link.

Similarly, by God "knowing the *end* of a matter at the *beginning*," the Past and Future become Linked. This is the concept of Present. This principle therefore corresponds to the third section of the Seder, which is the demonstration of our freedom in the Present, and which provides a living illustration of Divine Providence through the very fact of our continued existence.[1] In this stage of the Seder we also acknowledge that God is the One Who feeds us and looks after us in the Present.

RESULT, FUTURE, AND LOWEST

We now come to the last three principles, which deal with Result and the Future — concepts related to the fourth part of the Seder. Principle 11 talks of God's system of reward and punishment, the consequences of man's actions. The twelfth principle declares our faith in Mashiach's imminent arrival. The thirteenth and last principle is about the revival of the dead of the future.[2]

These self-same factors appear in the fourth section of the Seder, which begins with "*Shefoch chamascha...* — "Pour out Your wrath upon the nations...for they have devoured Yaakov and destroyed his habitation." This is repayment to the nations for all they have done to Israel. The fourth stage then continues with *Hallel*, which is replete with verses portraying reward and punishment, the redemption, and revival of the dead, which will take place in the Future, exactly paralleling the order of the last three of the thirteen principles.[3]

---

1. Indeed, this is the greatest miracle of all time. See *Siddur Beis Yaakov*, introductory essay.
2. The last three principles pertain to receiving from God down here on earth. Additionally, the resurrection of the dead takes place from the earth. This level therefore corresponds to the last *hey* of the Tetragrammaton.
3. Repayment, redemption, and revival of the dead will be the rectification of the bloodshed in the Future. Therefore, we say in the final stage of the Seder, "*Pour out* Your wrath upon the nations" because they poured out Jewish blood (see p. 24). See also above, p. 208, where we explained that the fourth stage of the Seder is the reparation of the sin of murder (שפיכות דמים).

The Rambam concludes his thirteen principles with the following words: "When a person believes in all these principles and his faith in them is clear, he is considered a member of the Jewish nation and it is a mitzvah to love him... Then, even if he transgresses a sin out of weakness...he still receives a portion in the World to Come."

We see, therefore, that belief in these principles causes a person to be considered a true Jew and brings him into the World to Come. The Seder, which is the celebration of our freedom and of our becoming a nation, embodies these all-important principles and attaches us to them.

In summary:

TABLE 29

PRINCIPLE	1–5	6–7	8–10	11–13
STAGE	Before	Past	Present	Future
DIMENSION	Above	Higher	Link	Lowest
SEDER	*Kadeish*	*Maggid*	Meal	*Hallel*

Conclusion

We have shown in this work that a clear, systematic pattern encompasses every facet of creation and history. This pattern emanates from Hashem Himself. It extends to the angels[1] and then down to the earthly elements in this world Below. There is a consistent pattern and unity of this theme in all respects.

This pattern is intertwined and interlocked within many themes of Judaism, which in turn relate to and influence creation and the universe. We are thereby led to a deep appreciation of the unity that exists in the Jewish religion as a whole, and the realisation that there is a unifying principle generated by a unifying Force — God Himself. This unity is manifest in the combination of many complex, diverse topics, and the inescapable conclusion can only be "Hear, O Israel, Hashem our God, Hashem is *One!*"

On the Seder night — the night of our freedom — the Jewish nation became attached to this profound order for the first time at the Exodus. On this night each year we become attached yet again to this same pattern and to the truly free One, Who is un-

---

1. See pp. 82–83; see also *Tefillin: The Inside Story*, pp. 456–457.

encumbered by all the restrictions of this diverse and non-unified world. We become attached to Him and His unity, and achieve freedom, by performing the mitzvos of this great night.

We can only become truly aware of God's unity and of the unity, harmony, and freedom within Judaism through the study of Torah, which reveals the inner homogeneity, harmony, and synthesis of our wonderful religion. We now understand in a deeper sense what our rabbis say: "There is no freer man than he who engages in the study of Torah."[1] The study of Torah frees one from the limited perspective of this world, releasing us to probe into the profound depths and unity of the mitzvos in particular and of our existence in general.

May we merit to experience and uncover the depth of the patterns manifest within Torah more and more, even beyond the scope of the limited illustration of the unity of Torah provided by this book, thereby achieving greater and greater heights of freedom!

---

1. *Avos* 6:2.

Appendix I
Hallel and Future

The commentaries[1] explain that in the latter section of *Hallel* (which we say in the fourth section of the Seder), King David is expressing the sentiments that the entire Jewish nation will give voice to after the coming of the *Mashiach*: their reflections on their Past troubles and their subsequent deliverance from them.

This section of the *Hallel* begins with the words "Not to us, O Hashem, not to us, but to Your name give glory, for the sake of Your kindness and for your truth."[2] This is said in reference to the epoch of the *Mashiach* and the Future battle of Gog and Magog.[3]

We then read:

> Why should the nations say, "Where now is their God?" But our God is in the heavens; He does

---

1. Our main source of commentaries on *Hallel* is the *Haggadas Ba'alei HaTosafos*, an amazing compilation of the early commentaries on the Haggadah.
2. Tehillim 115:1.
3. *Pesachim* 118a.

whatever He pleases. Their idols are silver and gold, the work of men's hands. They have mouths, but they do not speak; they have eyes, but they do not see. They have ears, but they do not hear; they have noses, but they do not smell. Their hands do not feel, they have feet but do not walk, and no speech comes through their throat. Those who make them should become like them — everyone who trusts in them! O Israel, trust in Hashem; He is their help and their shield. O House of Aharon, trust in Hashem; He is their help and their shield. You who fear Hashem, trust in Hashem; He is their help and their shield. Hashem has remembered us, He will bless; He will bless the House of Israel; He will bless the House of Aharon. He will bless those who fear Hashem, both small and great. May Hashem increase you, you and your children. May you be blessed by Hashem, the Maker of heaven and earth. The heavens are the heavens of Hashem, but he has given the earth to the children of man. The dead do not praise the Lord, nor do those who go down into silence. But we will bless the Lord from this time forth *and forevermore. Halleluyah!*

(Tehillim 115:2–18)

We will praise God for all eternity, for the Jewish nation is everlasting. Therefore, even after we have left this world, we are considered living.[1]

We then proceed to the next chapter of *Hallel*. Let us study these verses in detail.

> I love Hashem, because He hears my voice and my supplications. Because He has inclined his ear to me,

---

1. See *Tanchuma, VeZos HaBerachah* 7.

therefore I will call upon Him all my days.
>> (Ibid. 116:1–2)

These verses speak of the Future, when the Jewish people will express their love for God because He listened to their voice in the exile and delivered them.[1]

The next verse reads:

> The ropes of death surrounded me, and the confines of the grave seized me; I found trouble and sorrow.
>> (Ibid., 3)

The words "death," "confines of the grave," "trouble," and "sorrow," hint at the nations Persia, Macedonia, Kasdim, and Seir, who caused death, trouble, and sorrow for the Jewish nation while they were in exile.[2]

The words "I found trouble and sorrow," in this verse, and the words "O Hashem, save my soul," in the next verse, are the words of the Jewish people in the Future expressing what happened in *galus*, and that they prayed and He delivered them.[3]

The Jewish people go on to relate what transpired in exile:

> Then I called upon the name of Hashem; O Hashem, save my soul. Gracious is Hashem, and righteous; our God is compassionate. Hashem guards the simple; I was brought low, and He saved me.
>> (Ibid., 4–6)

They then say:

> Return to your rest, O my soul, for Hashem has dealt kindly with you. For you have saved my soul from death, my eyes from tears, and my feet from

---

1. *Machzor Vitri* and *Ra'avan*.
2. *Roke'ach*.
3. Ibid.

> stumbling. I will walk before Hashem in the land of the living.
>
> (Ibid., 7–9)

This means: "You extricated my soul from the exile and redeemed me. I will walk before You in the land of the living, i.e., in the Land of Israel, which is called the 'land of the living' because its dead will be the first to be revived in the Future."[1]

We then read:

> I trusted, even when I said, "I am greatly afflicted." I said in my haste, "All men are false."
>
> (Ibid., 10–11)

After the redemption, the Jewish people reflect and say, "I was afflicted greatly in the exile, and it was thought that the prophets had prophesied falsely when they said I would be redeemed.[2] They continue by expressing their sentiments of gratitude for the redemption wrought for them:

> How shall I repay Hashem for all His kindness toward me? I will raise the cup of salvation and call upon the name of Hashem. I will pay my vows to Hashem in the presence of all His people. Precious in the eyes of Hashem is the death of his pious ones. O Hashem, for I am Your servant; I am Your servant, the son of your maidservant; you have opened my bonds. I will offer to you thanksgiving offerings and will call upon the name of Hashem. I will pay my vows to Hashem in the presence of all His people, in

---

1. Ibid; see also *Pesachim* 118a and *Yalkut Shimoni* on Tehillim 116, which state that this verse refers to the revival of the dead. This runs parallel with the fourth *parshah* of the tefillin, which hints at the revival of the dead (*Rashi* on Devarim 11:21).
2. *Machzor Vitri* and *Ra'avan*.

the courts of Hashem's house, in your midst, O Jerusalem. *Halleluyah*!

(Ibid., 12–19)

The next chapter also refers to the Future:

> Praise Hashem, all the nations; laud Him, all the peoples. For His kindness was mighty upon us, and the truth of Hashem endures forever. *Halleluyah*!
>
> (Ibid. 117:1–2)

This means that in the end of days the nations will be called upon to praise God, Who redeemed us in His great kindness. This redemption revealed that the words which He spoke to the prophets were eternally true, and therefore "you, nations, upon seeing this, *Halleluyah* [praise God]."[1]

We then read verses that further refer to the Future of the Jewish nation:

> Give thanks to Hashem, for He is good; His kindness endures forever. Let Israel now say, "His kindness endures forever." Let the house of Aharon now say, "His kindness endures forever." Let now those who fear Hashem say, "His kindness endures forever."
>
> (Ibid. 118:1–4)

It then says:

---

1. *Machzor Vitri* and *Ra'avan*.

> From the restricted confines I called upon the Lord; He answered me with the breadth of freedom. Hashem is for me; I will not fear — what can man do to me? Hashem is with me through those who help me; therefore I shall gaze upon my enemies. It is better to take refuge in Hashem than to trust in man. It is better to take refuge in Hashem than to trust in princes.
>
> (Ibid., 5–9)

The *Machzor Vitri* and *Ra'avan* explain the sequence of these verses in the following way:

> "From the restricted confines," i.e., in my exile, I called Him, and He answered me and took me out into "the wide expanse of freedom." I will therefore not be afraid of any person, for what can he do to me? And since He is "with me through those who help me," I am sure that "I will witness the downfall of my enemies." It is therefore "good to rely on Hashem."

We further read:

> All nations surround me, but in the name of Hashem I cut them off. They surround me, indeed, they surround me; in the name of Hashem I cut them off.
>
> (Ibid., 10–11)

These verses refer to the War of Gog and Magog, in which all the nations will take part.[1] The next verse also refers to this battle.[2] That verse and the verses which follow go on to speak of our deliverance from exile and the thanks expressed for our deliverance. They also reflect on the past hardships the Jewish nation

---

1. *Machzor Vitri*.
2. Ibid.

experienced in the exiles that transpired before the final redemption:

> They surround me like bees; they are extinguished like a thorn fire; in the name of Hashem I cut them off. You pushed me many times that I might fall, but Hashem helped me. The Lord is my strength and song, and this was my salvation. The voice of rejoicing and salvation is in the tents of the righteous; the right hand of Hashem does valiantly. The right hand of Hashem is exalted; the right hand of Hashem does valiantly. I shall not die, but I shall live and tell the deeds of the Lord. The Lord has surely chastised me, but He has not given me over to death.
>
> (Ibid., 12–18)

The next verse reads:

> Open to me the gates of righteousness; I will enter them and thank the Lord.
>
> (Ibid., 19)

The gates spoken of in this verse are the gates of the Future Temple, destined to be rebuilt after the salvation.[1] The Temple gates will be reopened to those who ascend to the Sanctuary for the festivals.

The forthcoming verses also refer to the Holy Temple and to the sacrifices that will be offered there:

> This is the gate of Hashem, into which the righteous shall enter. I thank You, for You have answered me, and You have become my deliverance. The stone which the builders rejected has become the cornerstone. This is Hashem's doing; it is wondrous in our

---

1. *Rashi.*

> eyes. This day Hashem has made; we will be glad and rejoice in Him.
>
> (Ibid., 20–24)

We then say:

> O Hashem, save us! O Hashem, make us successful!
>
> (Ibid., 25)

This verse is a prayer expressing the wish that the Future redemption should be an everlasting and triumphant one.[1]

We then say:

> Blessed is he who comes in the name of Hashem; we bless you from the house of Hashem. The Mighty One is Hashem; He lit up for us; bind the festival sacrifice with cords to the corners of the altar. You are my God, and I will give thanks to You; my God, I will exalt You. Give thanks to Hashem, for He is good; His kindness endures forever.
>
> (Ibid. 26–29)

In the last verse we are called upon to praise God for all that He has done for us, for through the final redemption we see that His kindness to the Jewish nation endures all the way to the Future.[2]

The above four verses also refer to the time in the Future when the Holy Temple will be rebuilt and the sacrifices will be offered there. This is alluded to in the words "Bind the festival sacrifice with cords to the corners of the altar."[3]

---

1. *Ra'avan.*
2. *Machzor Vitri* and *Ra'avan*. The words "His kindness endures forever" mean that God's kindness is eternal, even enduring until the Future World to Come (*Roke'ach*).
3. *Roke'ach.*

Appendix II
The Time Line and the Seder Night in the Torah

In *parshas Re'eh* we read the following about the Seder night:

> Keep the month of Aviv, and make the *pesach* for Hashem your God; for in the month of Aviv Hashem your God took you out of Egypt at night. You shall sacrifice the *pesach* to Hashem your God, of the flock and the herd, in the place which Hashem shall choose to rest His name there. You shall eat nothing leavened with it; seven days you shall eat unleavened bread with it, the bread of affliction; for you came out of the land of Egypt in haste, that you may remember the day when you came out of the land of Egypt all the days of your life. And there shall be no leaven seen with you in all your borders seven days; neither shall there remain from the meat, which you slaughter in the evening of the first day until

morning. You may not slaughter the *pesach* in any of your gates, which Hashem your God gives you. But at the place which Hashem your God shall choose to rest His name, there you shall slaughter the *pesach* in the evening, at sunset, the time when you went out of Egypt. And you shall roast and eat it in the place which Hashem your God shall choose; and you shall turn in the morning and go to your tents. Six days you shall eat unleavened bread; and on the seventh day a holding back to Hashem your God; you shall do no work.

(Devarim 16:1-8)

Verse 3, "You shall eat nothing leavened with it...that you may remember the day when you came out of the land of Egypt all the days of your life," shows that on the Seder night we traverse the dimension of Before right through to the Future.

We are told that when we have the *pesach* sacrifice, which represents the dimension of Before, we must avoid *chametz*, which is in the dimension of the time zone, part of the Past, and eat *matzos,* which have not been affected by the time continuum because we went out of Egypt בחפזון, "in a hurry," i.e., in no time — above the restrictions of time.[1]

The verse tells us that the reason for this commandment is in order "that you may remember the day when you came out of the land of Egypt all the days of your life." Our rabbis explain:[2] "If the verse only stated, 'the days of your life,' it would refer solely to this world; however, since it actually says '*all* the days of your life,' it includes the Future time of the *Mashiach*."

Thus, we become attached to the dimension of Before and Above time, in order to remember "the day when you came out" of the Past, during "the days of your life" of the Present, and also

---

1. See *Rashi*, Shemos 19:4; see also above, pp. 80–81.
2. *Berachos* 1:5 and the Haggadah.

"*all* the days of your life," in the Future.

In effect we are being told that by being attached to the dimension of Before and Above time on the Seder night, we will thereby remember the Past, in both the Present and the Future. This, of course, fits in with the name given to the evening's proceedings — the Seder — because it follows a special *order* that traces the development of history, from Purpose, through Past, Present, and Future.

Appendix III
Stages One and Three: A Deeper Look

DIAGRAM 54
```
Pesach      Matzah
  |           |
Esrog       Lulav
```

PESACH AND MATZAH

The *pesach* sacrifice is prepared on the fourteenth day of Nissan, *Before* the night of the fifteenth,[1] as it represents the Purpose that existed Before this world: *kedushah*. Matzah — although mentioned in *parshas Kadesh*, which therefore associates it with the dimension of Before and timelessness — relates principally to the dimension of the Present. This is because matzah is not governed by time (as it may not be left to rise), and thus it remains in the Present. Therefore matzah is included in the dimension of Before, and at the same time it represents the Present. We find

---

1. See p. 183.

the same with the Torah, which preceded and came Before the world, and yet it is also part of the Present. Even though it is mentioned in the first *parshah* of the tefillin, the realm of Before, it also parallels the Present, because it is continuously being given in the Present.[1] Matzah has to be eaten on the night of the fifteenth of Nissan, and there is no Torah obligation to prepare it beforehand, as it mainly represents the Almighty giving to us in the Present. It therefore corresponds to the continuous giving of the Torah, as opposed to the *pesach* sacrifice, which had to be prepared Before and thus entirely represents the dimension of Before.

There is yet another interesting distinction between the *pesach* sacrifice and matzah, in that the *pesach* sacrifice is intrinsically *kadosh*, whereas matzah, even though it ties us to *kedushah*,[2] is itself mundane and not intrinsically *kadosh*.[3]

Thus, the *pesach* sacrifice represents the realm of Above, and matzah represents the Link to the *kedushah* of Above — the realm where the spiritual and the physical meet.

We thus have:

DIAGRAM 55

Before/ Above	Present/ Link
|	|
Pesach	Matzah

ESROG AND *LULAV*

The same phenomenon exists in relation to the *esrog* and *lulav*, which are both fruit-bearing species and thereby represent Torah learning, which is considered the fruit. However, there is a crucial difference between them: the *esrog* is the actual fruit,

---

1. See pp. 132–133.
2. See p. 187.
3. *Tosafos, Pesachim* 28b.

whereas the *lulav* leaves are only a representation of the fruit-bearing date palm. Thus, the *esrog*, the actual fruit, hints at a higher level of Torah, the Torah of Above, whereas the *lulav* represents the Torah given to us, the category of ברוך שנתן **תורה** לעמו ישראל — the Torah of Link.

Furthermore, since the *esrog* represents the dimension of Before, which is removed from the physical dimension of time, it is separated from the rest of the species and not bound with them. The *lulav*, however, represents the Torah being given in the Present and is therefore bound with the other species.

The *esrog*, representing Before and Above, is thus the companion of the *pesach* sacrifice, whereas the *lulav*, which represents the Present and Link, is the companion of matzah. We therefore have the following picture:

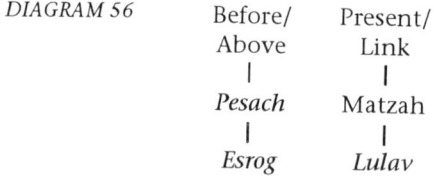

DIAGRAM 56

Before/Above — Pesach — Esrog

Present/Link — Matzah — Lulav

YUD AND VAV

The *esrog* is a small fruit[1] and resembles the letter *yud*, which is Above the bottom line and the smallest letter in the Hebrew alphabet. Conversely, the *lulav* is the longest of the species[2] and resembles the *vav*, which is drawn down to the bottom of the line. It therefore represents the Link between Above and Below. This parallels the fact that the *esrog* represents the Torah of Above, whereas the *lulav* symbolises the Torah which was given to us from Above to Below.

---

1. Indeed, it is the shortest of the four species — all the others have to be a few *tefachim* long in order to be halachically valid, while the *esrog* has no such requirement.
2. See *Sukkah* 37b.

Stages One and Three: A Deeper Look

As we noted, both the *yud* and the *vav* are written as unified wholes written in one stroke, with no breaks or pieces. However, the *yud* represents the unity which is Above this world, and the *vav* is the unity of God brought down and joined to this world. This leads us to the following: we noted previously that the *esrog* represents the *lev*, the heart. We also saw that the *lulav* derives its name from its comparison to the *lev*, as the word לולב is made up of the words לו לב, literally, "[there is] to him a heart," i.e., "he has a heart." The question arises, Why are there two species that represent the heart? Furthermore, we saw earlier[1] that the *lulav* symbolises the spine. How can we then say that it represents the heart?

The answer to these questions will reveal yet another connection of the *esrog* and *lulav* to the levels of Above and Link. We noted earlier that the *esrog* is the fruit itself — the essence — whereas the *lulav*, which the Midrash says is a fruit, is not the actual fruit but represents the date palm — a fruit-bearing tree. The *esrog* thus represents the hidden, concealed, inner heart, whereas the *lulav* symbolises that "he has a heart" — it is apparent from the outside that this person has a heart, meaning that he has a Link to the Almighty. This parallels the symbolism of the spine, which shows that the person is upright and striving to rise upwards to his Maker.

Again we have a parallel to the *vav* drawing down the hidden spirituality and *kedushah* of the *yud* and Linking it to us.

The relationship between the *esrog* and *lulav* parallels the relationship between the *pesach* offering and the matzah, in that the *pesach* offering is called "*gavohah*" (high), as it is holy[2] and is therefore Above. This is similar to the *yud* and the *esrog*. Conversely, matzah is not *kodashim*, and symbolises the *vav* and the

---

1. Pages 188 and 207.
2. *Kodashim* (holy sacrifices) are called *gavohah* — belonging to the Most High, Who is Above.

lulav, which are the Link between the Upper and the Lower.

Similarly, just as we have the Torah, which existed Before and Above, down here in the Present, so too, the *vav* of the Present and Link embodies the *yud*, which is Above and Before. *Kedushah* relates to the realms of Above and Link simultaneously, and therefore Torah is part of both realms. In a like manner, the matzah is associated with the *pesach* sacrifice in the first *parshah* of *Kadesh*, but is then extended downwards to be part of this world and the Present. This can be seen in that matzah is the only food that we are obligated from the Torah to eat in the Present.[1]

We therefore have the following:

DIAGRAM 57

---

1. As mentioned on p. 185.